BLOODY GROUND

Black Rifles in Korea

By

COL John B. Holway (Ret.)

Library of Congress Cataloging-in-Publication Data

Holway, John B., Bloody Ground: Black Rifles in Korea, oral history of African-American troops in the Korean War

Summary: Korea was also our last segregated war, and one of our bloodiest. And no regiment in Korea suffered more deaths than the all-black 24th Infantry Regiment. These unsung black warriors of an unsung war were teen-age kids, who had enlisted in peace-time, because it was the best job they could find. Award-winning oral historian John Holway, who served with an integrated platoon six months after the black 24th was disbanded, interviewed these men for the most intimate portrait of a combat unit ever written about any comparable unit in any country in any war.

ISBN: 978-1-939282-28-6

Published by Miniver Press, LLC, McLean Virginia
Copyright 2014 John B. Holway

First edition June 2014

Cover: Captain Charles Bussey. Design by Andrew Baah-Ptabitey

To all the men and women
who fought in all America's wars.
Gratefully.

To General Carroll LeTellier
A brave man and a
great help in
writing this book.

[signature]

The way you paved has led us to today, where black GIs are again serving their nation in combat, this time side by side with their buddies of every hue and color, race and creed, from every town and city in America. This time all are equal. From the top GI to the bottom, we are all measured only by our competence and our character.
And that's the way it should be.
General Colin Powell

TABLE OF CONTENTS

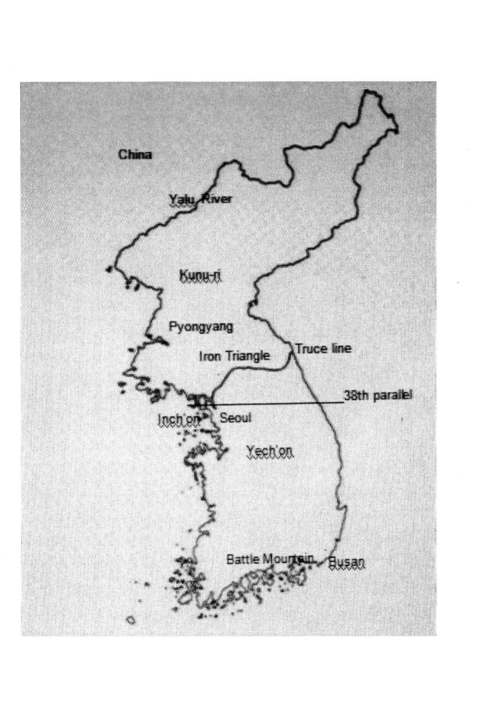

ARMY CHAIN OF COMMAND

Far East Command General MacArthur, Ridgway
 X Corps   Lt Gen Almond
 Marines
 3rd Division
 7th Division
 ROK Divisions
 8th Army   Lt Gen Walker, Ridgway
 ROK Divisions
 1st Cavalry Division
 2nd Division
 24th Division
 25th Division 18,000 men Maj Gen Kean, Bradley
 27th Inf Regiment 3,000
 35th Inf Regiment
 24th Inf Regiment COL White, Champeny, Corley, Britt
 1st Battalion 1,000 Lt Col Miller
        Company A 200
        Company B
        Company C
Company D (Weapons Company)
heavy machine gun,
heavy mortar,
.57 recoilless rifle)
2d Battalion Lt Col Clayton
        Company E
        Company F
Company G
Company H (Weapons)
3rd Battalion Lt Col Pierce, Blair, Mouchet
Company I
Company K
Company L
Company M (Weapons)
Attached:
77th Engineer Company

159th Artillery Battalion (105 mm howitzers)
Battery A
Battery B
Battery C

Companies and batteries are commanded by a captain or 1st lieutenant.
Each rifle company has
 three infantry platoons, 30 men each, commanded by a lieutenant or sergeant
 one weapons platoon (light machine gun, light mortar, bazooka)
Each rifle platoon has
 three infantry squads of 12 men each (11 riflemen plus a BAR - automatic rifle)
 a weapons squad (light machine gun, light mortar, bazooka)

"For what is history but a myth agreed upon?
Napoleon

The Untold Story

They were the last of America's segregated fighting men. For 60 years they, like all black units before them, have been tarred with one damning charge, that they "bugged out" - ran before the enemy. Even the Army's official history repeats it. However, the Army's official records contradict its own history. When the unit was disbanded, the black 24th Regiment lost considerably more blood than either of the 25th Division's two white regiments – about 50% more:

Casualties
24th Infantry 4,887 44%
27th Infantry 3,179 29%
35th Infantry 2,978 27%
Source: 25th Division Command Report, September 30 1951

If the "Deuce-4" had been bugging out, they either weren't running fast enough or they were running in the wrong direction.

They are the forgotten men of a "Forgotten War," one of the most savage and deadliest wars America has ever fought. If all the names of the killed and missing in Korea were engraved on a memorial wall in Washington, it would be larger than the Vietnam Memorial. And Korea lasted only three years; Vietnam, ten.

As one back veteran of both wars, Sergeant Floyd Williams, put it: "Vietnam was a Sunday school picnic compared to Korea."

This is not to belittle the sacrifices of the men who fought in Vietnam. It is intended only to put into perspective the sacrifices of the men who left their blood in Korea.

For over half a century the history of the Korean War (as of all American wars) has been written by whites. It has either been unflattering to the thousands of black troops who fought and died, or it didn't mention them.

In Korea there were actually two wars - and two Deuce-4s. One was recorded in ink by whites; the other was written in blood by blacks. The black war has never been adequately told before.

This is especially true of the Army's official histories. In both Roy Appleman's *From the Naktong to the Yalu (1968)* and the Army's *Black Soldiers, White Army* (hereafter, *BSWA*) (2001). White writers leaned heavily on accounts of white veterans to report the black record. In the segregated Army of 1950, the 24th Infantry Regiment was all-black in the enlisted ranks and almost all-white in the officer corps. Many of the officers were Southerners, and all, North and South, shared similar cultural perceptions of Negroes. Most of the officers didn't want to be in the regiment. Those with the best efficiency reports got assignments with white regiments. The others were sent to the 24th.

Some white troops broke and ran; so did some blacks. So did some white officers. If a white lieutenant of the 24th got knocked off a hill, he had a ready excuse. "It wasn't my fault, my troops bugged out." Whether true or not, the lieutenant could be assured of a sympathetic pat from his captain or colonel: "I understand, son, I know what you're up against." He would also be given a sympathetic nod from white historians.

John French (77th Engineer Company):
General Custer said he'd never serve with "brunettes" - he was talking about the black Ninth and Tenth Cavalry. Can you imagine what they would have said if he'd led them into the Little Big Horn? It would have been all the troops' fault.

Yet Korea was not only among the darkest hours of American military history. It was the midnight of segregation, the darkest hours before a new dawn.

When the war erupted in 1950 none of the American regiments in Japan, black or white, was ready for combat. They were enjoying soft occupation duty, more familiar with *geisha* houses than rifle ranges. For most, it was the first taste of combat, against a savage foe. Just about everyone was scared to death.

Six months later, in one of the most humiliating chapters in U.S. military history, the entire American Army in Korea broke and ran for hundreds of miles, pell-mell, before the Chinese army. As a black captain who was there, Charles Bussey, commented drily, "That's when I discovered that whites could run as fast as blacks."

The Army preaches that a commander is responsible for "everything his unit does or fails to do." Without intending to, the white Army historians penned a damning indictment of the leadership of the 24th Infantry.

Good leaders had troops who fought well. Bad leaders had troops who bugged out.

Bussey writes [*Firefight at Yechon*]:

In my unit, I saw all types of soldiers and large amounts of heroism, sacrifice, and leadership. This contrast between what I experienced and what was written has bugged me until today.

The authors of BSWA chose not to interview Bussey.

A white officer who also was pointedly not interviewed was Lyle Ryshell, author of Wit*h a Black Platoon in Combat:*

My troops were as good as, if not better than, any troops at any time. .There was never a time when [*they*] left a position without an order to withdraw.

A black GI, Robert Fletcher, put it in more earthy language:

I never saw a GI run. Shit, no! If he ran, we'd shoot him ourselves. If you ran out of ammunition, you threw grenades. If you ran out of grenades, everybody was coming out.

In the desperate stand at the Pusan Perimeter, the black regiment guarded the shortest road to Pusan, the vital supply base for the Allies. If it fell, all South Korea would fall. Unlike the other divisions, U.S. and Korean, the 25th Division and its black regiment did not have a river to its front to help hold off the enemy. The GI's held on by their fingertips. But they held.

By far, the most dangerous job in the military was the infantryman. They suffered 80% of the casualties but made up only 4% of all military personnel. And the infantrymen who were in most danger were black.

White kids, like former Vice-President Dick Cheney, escaped the draft by going to grad school. Others, like former President George W Bush, got plush state-side slots in the National Guard, which they left as soon as the danger was over. Others got married. Some joined the Navy or Air Force, which, except for pilots, by 1950 were pretty safe jobs. Of those who did get drafted, many got soft rear-area duties as chaplains' assistants or company clerks.

I went to college, took ROTC, and didn't arrive in Korea until 1952, the worst of the war was over.

The men in these pages had none of these options. Most of them needed the money. They fought one of the most hellish wars in American history. They, and thousands of others like them, both black and white, fought a war that most Americans their age missed.

Korea was America's last "good" war. Vietnam, Iraq, and Afghanistan were and still are debated. But Korea had to be fought. At least the first phase of it did. We had to push the North Korean invaders out of the South to protect Japan. However, the second phase, when China pushed us out of the North, is more problematic and tragic. It could have, and should have, been avoided, at a saving of many thousands of lives. It needlessly made an enemy of China. It was the fear of China that mistakenly propelled us into Vietnam.

Korea was also America's last segregated war. It was the midnight of the old America, just before the dawn of the new.

America in 1950

The men of the Deuce-4 were also the kids of the Forgotten Depression. When most of them were starting first grade in 1934, the unemployment rate was 34%, compared to about 8%

in the recession of 2012. Although things were better in 1950, they grew up and joined the Army because that was still the best job they could find.

Racism was still taken for granted in the Army and in America in general. When I went to the University of Iowa in the late '40s, there wasn't a single black basketball player - in the entire Big Ten! And nobody thought it was strange.

Both Northerners and Southerners generally shared the same perceptions of blacks. Except for Jesse Owens, Joe Louis, and several singers and band leaders, they simply were not considered to be on a par with whites. Our movies reflected the same white world. Only occasionally did blacks appear, and then as comic characters, singers, or servants. School libraries carried a popular children's book, *Little Black Sambo*. In class we sang "Carry Me Back to Ol' Virginie," etc.

There was not much mingling of races to dispel the stereotypes. I grew up in New Jersey, but there were no blacks in my school or my neighborhood. I might as well as have lived in Alabama.

The Army's Histories

That was the world of Roy Appleman, who wrote the Army's first official history of the Korean War, *South to the Nakong, North to the Yalu*. It reflected and repeated the stereotypes of the rest of the culture. The worst of these, which he passed on, was that black troops "bugged out" - threw down their guns and ran. One black vet, Floyd Williams, picked up a copy in his base library, read a few pages, and almost threw it out the window in anger.

Bussey:

Appleman strikes me as unfair and not representing what I saw personally. Mr Appleman was never in the combat zone... (He) interviewed only one black officer and no black enlisted men. He never talked to me. In his reports of the behavior of

Negro troops, he quotes only the white officers. In some cases these officers may have provided self-serving accounts, seeking to blame the troops for their own leadership failures.

I was there. The historians were not.

Following his and other complaints, the Army's Office of Military History tried again. It issued *BSWA,* which was not much different from Appleman's. Major General Carroll Le Tellier, a white South Carolinian, was a lieutenant in Bussey's company and later the CO:

The first book [*Appleman*] was unfair, and I don't think it was particularly correct. If the first was unkind, the second was tragic. The implication was that segregated Caucasian units had never, in that fluid situation, abandoned a position. But everyone was doing it. Actually, the 24th spent more time on line than any other regiment.

I begged them, if they honestly felt that that [*second book*] was the result of their further investigation, they shouldn't publish it.

In 1948 President Harry S Truman had ordered the Armed Forces to desegregate. The Marines already had 18,000 blacks in uniform, although no black officers. The Air Force also fell in step fairly quickly, thanks in part to the reputation left by the famous Tuskegee Airmen, the "Red Tail" fighter pilots of World War II.

But the Army and Navy dragged their feet. When the Korean War broke out in 1950, the Army was still rigidly segregated. Blacks served in separate units, usually under white officers, as they had since the Civil War. Often they were assigned to labor units and other non-combat tasks.

When I reported to the Infantry School at Fort Benning as a second lieutenant in 1951, the bars had begun to come down a bit, and there were two black officers in my basic platoon leaders' class. A year later, when I joined the Seventh Division in Korea, my platoon was pepper-and-salt. I don't recall any black officers in my regiment. The Army had disbanded its last all-black regiment, the 24th "Blockhouse Busters," who had fought on the Western Plains and with Teddy Roosevelt at San Juan Hill.

Charlie Bussey

I became interested in the story after interviewing Colonel Bussey for my book, *Red Tails, Black Wings.* Bussey, a pilot in that unit, wound up in the ground forces in Korea. He told an amazing story of mowing down 258 attacking North Koreans with three men and two machine guns on a hill. If he did what he says he did - and there is compelling evidence that he did and no hard evidence that he didn't - it would be the greatest feat of arms in the annals of the American Army.

America's most decorated soldier, Audie Murphy of World War II, was credited with killing "about 50" enemy. Private Jose Lopez received the Medal of Honor for killing "about 100" Germans with a machine gun at the Bulge. Sergeant Alvin York in World War I killed or captured 133 Germans single-handedly.

According to Bussey, the 25th Division commander, Major General William Kean, promised him "the Big Medal." But his regimental commander downgraded it, because, he said frankly, Bussey was black.

Historical precedents were all against Bussey. If he had been awarded the Medal, it would have been the first for a black since the Spanish-American War, the first ever for a black officer, and the first for anyone in the Korean War.

In July 1950 the Army desperately needed heroes - white ones.

I began interviewing comrades who might shed light on the controversy. I found that, contrary to the John Wayne movies, one out of every three soldiers on the early western frontier was black. These "Buffalo Soldiers" fought Geronimo and helped capture Billy the Kid. When a wagon train was endangered by hostiles, it was often black troopers who galloped to the rescue.

I visited the Army's Center for Military History to talk to the authors of *BSWA* and found that eyewitness testimony and photographic evidence had been swept under the rug.

One is a photo of the mass grave, where Bussey's victims were buried. The photographer, Sergeant Alfonzo Spencer, gave an affidavit that he went back to the scene with Bussey and a bulldozer and dug the grave, then photographed the bodies in it.

Private LaVaughn Fields swore that he saw Bussey firing from the next hill..

BSWA buried the citations in a brief footnote, but did not tell the reader what they said.

The Army historians claimed the photo was of another mass grave, which appeared in the official history of another regiment. But after pulling out all the regimental histories on their shelves and flipping through them, they shrugged that they couldn't find it. They also declared that the hills in the background were not the same as those at Yech'on. In 2009 I visited Yech'on, climbed "Bussey's Hill" and photographed it. Off to the east the low hills were not unlike those in Spencer's photo.

As I left, I rubbed shoulders with their boss, the Chief of Military History, Brigadier General John S Brown. I sketched my interest and asked for an opportunity to talk to him. He pointedly turned his back. I followed up with a letter asking for an interview, signing it with my reserve rank of colonel. He never wrote back. I began to suspect a cover-up.

And if the Army's methodology was open to questions in a case I knew something about, could its research into other matters also be open to question?

Following the Trail

The quest led to more research. I found that the Army has a long record of bias in conferring Medals of Honor.

	Total		Blacks		Pct	
Civil War	1196		19		1.6%	
Indian wars		428		13		3.0
Spanish-American	30		6	20.0		
World War I		99		0*		0.0
World War II	301		0*		0.0	
Korean War		86		2		2.3
Vietnam	156		20	12.8		

Total	2,296	50	2.2%

*Decades later Presidents George HW Bush and Bill Clinton bestowed one Medal to a World War I vet and seven to heroes of World War II.

Blacks made up 30% of the troops on the western frontier. Perhaps half in Korea.

There was a clear pattern of discrimination lasting 60 years between the Spanish-American war and Vietnam.

I began attending reunions of the 24th to gather more accounts. They revealed a much different version of events than the Army has acknowledged. I found stories of endurance and bravery that have been systematically suppressed.

Of course black troops bugged out sometimes. So did whites, especially in the first weeks of the war. Then the whole American Army bugged out of North Korea one jump ahead of the Chinese. Along with the Bataan surrender in 1942, it was the worst humiliation in U.S. military annals. In world history it ranks with Hitler's and Napoleon's headlong retreats from Moscow. Comments Bussey: "That's when I discovered that whites could run as fast as blacks."

The Grunts' Tales

There were two wars in Korea. One was reported by white writers. The other war was lived by the black GIs, slogging and bleeding up hills and down, through burning summer and numbing winter, through mud and blood.

They describe a new hidden war that had never been documented before. Nothing has ever been done for a unit of similar size in any war at any time. If we had had tape recorders in., in the Revolution, we may well have heard similar stories.

Today the dashing Red Tail fighter pilots have caught the public's imagination. However, they risked their lives in the clouds, where the mortality rate was much lower than that of the grunts in the mud.

But the Deuce-4 veterans are still virtually unknown

9

The white press simply did not report the black war. Jimmie Hicks of the Baltimore *African-American* did an excellent job of covering the Deuce-4, crawling into foxholes with the grunts and getting their stories.

But I know of no white reporter who visited the 24th regiment's area.

Jim Thompson:

We stayed 186 days - six months - on the line, but I never - never - saw a white reporter. No reporters wanted to be with the 24th. They wanted to be with the 27th or the 1st Cavalry. They would stop at Division headquarters and write down what the people there told them. When you pinned them down later, they'd say, "Well, this is what we heard."

The darling of the press was right next door to the 24th - John "Mike" Michaelis, the charismatic commander of the 27th Wolfhound regiment, who had jumped in Holland, then served on Eisenhower's staff before Korea. Reporters hung on his every word. They dubbed him "Iron Mike" and made him the best known army colonel in Korea and his Wolfhounds the most celebrated regiment.

Much of Michaelis' fame came in dispatches from the New York *Herald-Tribune's* cute, tousle-haired reporter, Marguerite Higgins, who wrote colorful stories about his exploits. The two were a couple made in Hollywood. The joke that made the rounds of the foxholes was, "Maggie Higgins made Colonel Michaelis, and Colonel Michaelis made Maggie Higgins."

Even in the U.S. Archives, photos of the Division's two white regiments out-number those of the 24th about 10-1.

Also many correspondents confused the 24th Infantry Regiment with the 24th Division. The latter had been rushed to Korea first and was almost destroyed by the Communists. When the 24th Division lost a hill, some reporters mistakenly said it was the 24th Infantry.

The stories below reveal tales of agony and courage, among the most exciting told by warriors in any war. The reader is invited to read them and *BSWA* and other white histories side-by-side and come to his own conclusion.

I.

Black Rifles

The Revolution

Some 5,000 blacks served in the War of Independence - 10,000 counting irregulars, says historian Alan Gropman.

Crispus Attucks was the first man to die, in the Boston Massacre.

Peter Salem, a slave, and **Salem Poor**, a freedman, fought on Bunker Hill. Poor shot and killed the British commander after he saw "the whites of his eyes."

Lemuel Haynes fought at Fort Ticonderoga.

Although George Washington tried to get all blacks out of the Army, his slave, **William Lee**, crossed the Delaware with him. So did **Prince Whipple**, the son of an African king. **Oliver Cromwell** also crossed the Delaware and fought at Valley Forge and Yorktown.

When Washington relented, **Agrippa Hill** fought at Saratoga, **Edward Hector** at Brandywine, and **Austen Dabney** at Cowpens South Carolina.

James Forten, 15, was thrown into a prison ship but gave up his chance to escape to let a younger white take his place.

The governor of Rhode Island bought freedom for a black battalion to stop the British invasion. The British governor of Virginia also offered freedom to slaves who joined his "Ethiopian Regiment."

According to Gropman, one of every four American seamen was black. One, **Deborah Gannett**, was a woman. Another, **Henri Chistophe**, was a future emperor of Haiti.

Poet John Greenleaf Whittier called them "America's black Founding Fathers." But after victory, they were all mustered out. Some received pensions, even in the South. Others died penniless.

War of 1812

Again both sides competed for Negro troops. The British recruited ex-slaves in Maryland and Virginia. Other blacks were called into federal uniform over the objections of President James Madison of Virginia.

They sailed with Commodore Perry and "met the enemy" on Lake Erie. "They seemed absolutely insensible to danger," Perry said.

Some 600 Negroes fought with General Andrew Jackson at New Orleans. After the victory, Jackson told them, "I expected much of you ... but you surpassed my hopes."

However, once more, after victory the black troops were dismissed. Most who had expected freedom were returned to their masters instead. In 1819, Jackson led the Army into Spanish Florida to recapture slaves who had fled to the Seminole Indian nation.

Negroes also died at the Alamo and helped win Texas' independence at San Jacinto.

The Civil War

Many Northerners, such as Lincoln, opposed both slave labor and free black labor in western territories; they were both considered threats to white working men.

Shields Green died at Harpers Ferry with John Brown.

After the Union's Fort Sumter fell in 1861, over 100 students from Wilberforce College tried to volunteer but were told, "This is a white man's war." Lincoln didn't want to lose the four pro-slavery border states that had remained loyal.

Then once more, when the war news grew desperate, the country turned to African Americans.

Men of Color, to Arms! posters proclaimed. Frederick Douglass declared, "Let the black man ... get an eagle on his buttons, a musket on his shoulder, and bullets in his pocket, and there is no power on earth that can deny that he has a right to citizenship."

One out of every eight Yankee soldiers and one of every four seamen was black, though they served for less pay than their white comrades. More than 180,000 African Americans served, and more than 30,000 died. The black casualty rate was higher and the desertion rate lower than those of the rest of the Army.

Ex-slave **Harriet Tubman** (left), a heroine of the Underground Railway, volunteered at the head of a contingent of men to raid behind Southern lines.

Robert Smalls (right) commandeered a Confederate ship and sailed it through a Southern blockade at Charleston. He later became a U.S. Congressman.

Opothleyohola, a black-Creek chief, and **Six Killer**, a black-Cherokee, fought as irregulars in Kansas and Missouri.

Martin Delaney, a graduate of Harvard Medical School, rose to the rank of major.

Sergeant William Carney fought with the 54th Massachusetts, which was made famous in the movie "Glory," in the assault on Fort Wagner South Carolina. He seized the flag and carried it alone to the gates of the fort, where he was shot in the scalp. But, he boasted, "The flag never touched the ground, boys."

Carney was the first black to win the Congressional Medal of Honor.

Lincoln declared that "Negroes have demonstrated with their blood their right to citizenship."

After the war, William Tecumseh Sherman, the nation's top general, recommended integrating the Army, but the idea was rejected. The Navy did likewise.

Medal of Honor Winners

Powhattan Christian James Thomas
Beaty Fleetwood Harris Hawkins

James Murray Alexander John Henry
Garner Holland Kelly Lawson

Robert Pinn Andrew Jackson Smith

Others:

Aaron Anderson, Bruce Anderson, Robert Blake, James Brown , William Brown, Wilson Brown, Decatur Dorsey, Alfred Hilton, Miles James, James Miflin, Joachim Pease, Edward Ratcliffe

The West

In 1805, when Lewis and Clark, made their epic journey to the Pacific, they received critical help from a native-American woman, Sacajawea, and a strapping black man known as "**York**."

Jim Beckwourth (left) helped blaze the trail to California that the Forty-niners followed in the great Gold Rush.

Nat Love (center) known as "Deadwood Dick," was a gunslinger and cattle puncher

Bill Pickett (right) invented the rodeo sport of bulldogging. His trick - bite the bull in the nose. His white buddies, Will Rogers and Tom Mix, went on to Hollywood stardom, but Pickett was nixed (though he got on a postage stamp before Mix).

It is estimated that one-fifth of all cowboys were black, though they are not seen in most modern movies and television shows.

One of every three cavalry troopers was African American. The Indians called them "buffalo soldiers," perhaps because of their woolly hair, perhaps because they fought like wounded buffalo. The blacks were segregated and fought under white officers. They guarded stagecoaches, bumping along on top, not inside. One even died with Custer.

Hollywood, which loves to depict the cavalry galloping to the rescue, carefully depicts only white cavalry. However, artist

Frederick Remington captured the truth in canvases such as "Ninth Cavalry to the Rescue." He gave the black troopers high marks for doing the toughest jobs without complaining. They were given the worst posts and the worst nags in the Army, but the blacks' alcoholism rate was lower than whites' and their desertion rate was one-tenth as high. Young John Pershing commanded a black company, earning the nickname "Black Jack" or "Nigger Jack."

William Cathy served two years in the ranks before anyone discovered that he was actually **Cathy Williams**, a woman.

The black-Indian **Seminole Scouts** were possibly the most decorated unit in the Army.

In Texas rioters attacked a black sergeant, so the troopers strode into a saloon and fired into the crowd of cowboys and gamblers, killing two. Police arrested two soldiers, and when their comrades staged a shoot-out at the jail, each side lost one man killed.

Buffalo Soldiers won 13 more Medals of Honor, though this was only three percent of the total.

Emanuel Stance, who stood only five feet tall, won the first. He was cited for rescuing two captured children at Kickapoo Springs Texas.

George Johnson won another for leading 25 troopers against 100 Native Americans.

Moses Williams stood by his white lieutenant under fire and saved the lives of at least three comrades.

When white lieutenant John Bullis lost his horse in an attack by 30 Comanches, Sergeant **John Ward,** bugler **Isaac Ward,** and Private **Pompey Factor** galloped back, guns blazing. Bullis leaped up behind the sergeant, who "just saved my hair." All four won Medals of Honor.

One winner was later shot-gunned in the back by a sheriff.

Medal of Honor Winners

John Denny Pompei Factor Henry Johnson

George Johnson **Isaiah Mays** William McBryar

Joshua Pease Thomas Shaw Brent Woods

Bloody Ground

Robert Blake

Others: Aaron Anderson, Eugene Ashley, Thomas Boyne, **Benjamin Brown**, William Brown, Wilson Brown, William Bryant, Rodney Davis, Decatur Dorsey, Clinton Greaves, James Miflin, Adam Paine, Isaac Payne, manuel Stance,Augutus Walley, John Ward, Moses Williams, William Wilson

Mays and Brown were members of 24th Infantry .

West Point

In the 1870s two black plebes were forced out of the Naval Academy.

From 1870-89, 12 black cadets entered West Point **Johnson Whitaker** was found tied to his bunk and beaten unconscious, with his ear slit. An official inquiry concluded that he had done it to himself.

Henry O Flipper was the first to graduate, in 1881. He was later court-martialed for embezzling funds, a case that remains a mystery. Flipper claimed he was railroaded because he had gone riding with a white lieutenant's fiancee. However, another study suggests that his Mexican mistress had stolen the funds. We may never know.

He became a civilian mining engineer In the Southwest and Venezuela. Meanwhile, he never stopped fighting to clear his name, and 45 years after his death in 1941, the Army reversed the decision and changed his dishonorable discharge to honorable.

John H. Alexander graduated in 1887 but died seven years later, leaving little record.

Charles Young

Born in a Kentucky log cabin in 1864, he was the son of a free black soldier in the Union Army. He entered West Point in 1884, enduring what the Washington *Post* would call "a lonely cadet life" in "a silent environment." One classmate, later Major General Charles Rhodes, wrote that "we esteem him highly for his patient perseverance."

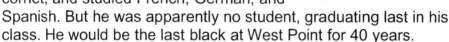

A white cadet from South Carolina came to Young's defense after a Yankee classmate made a remark "that reflected on the chastity of the Negro's female forebears." They met in a bare knuckles duel behind the barracks at four o'clock one morning.

Young wrote poems and composed songs, played the piano, harp, and cornet, and studied French, German, and Spanish. But he was apparently no student, graduating last in his class. He would be the last black at West Point for 40 years.

Young served with the cavalry in Nebraska and Utah and was the only black officer in the Army.

When the Spanish-American War broke out in 1898, Young hoped for a combat command. But that would have meant a promotion to colonel, a move the Army forestalled by giving him command of a volunteer black regiment in the States.

He was also sent as military attache to Liberia, where he was wounded while rescuing an embassy officer from a tribe of "man-eating folk."

In 1916, by then a lieutenant colonel, he rode with Pershing in Mexico, pursuing the bandit Pancho Villa.

Spanish-American War

Twenty-two black sailors died in the sinking of the battleship *Maine* in Havana harbor, the incident which ignited the war. One of them earned the Medal of Honor.

The Army accepted 200,000 black volunteers. Some received reserve commissions. Eight states, including Alabama, formed Negro regiments.

When the 10th Cavalry left for Cuba from its base at Missoula Montana, townsfolk postponed church to wish them farewell. But in Florida, the reception was different. They were herded into the holds of segregated troop ships, where they were kept for a week in burning heat with only candles for light while white troops occupied the breezier upper decks.

About 9,000 blacks saw service in Cuba under former Confederate General Joe Wheeler. All four of the Army's regular black regiments fought in Cuba, brigaded to Teddy Roosevelt's Rough Riders.

With John J Pershing at their head, the 10th Cavalry charged up San Juan Hill. When Roosevelt arrived, the 10th was already on top, and its band broke out with "A Hot Time in the Old Town Tonight." Seventeen blacks died getting there, and they won six Medals of Honor. Pershing said he could have "taken our black heroes in our arms."

TR also praised his black comrades: "I could wish for none better... They can drink out of our canteens."

Frank Knox, Roosevelt's deputy and Secretary of the Navy in World War II, declared, "I never saw braver men."

In the Philippines, which were acquired from Spain, black infantry regiments helped put down an insurrection. It was "the white man's burden," as poet Langston Hughes wrote, but blacks helped bear it.

Philippines governor (and later President) William Howard Taft wrote that prejudice was "almost universal throughout the country. It is a fact, however, as shown by our records, that the colored troops are quite as well disciplined and behaved as the average other troops" and showed less "intemperance." Communities that were at first hostile later "entirely changed their view and commended their good behavior to the War Department."

Medal of Honor Winners

Edward Baker Dennis Bell Robert Penn

Others: Fitz Lee, William Tompkins, George Wanton

The Brownsville Incident

In Brownsville Texas, across the border from Mexico, violence followed the pistol-whipping of a Negro National Guardsman by a local policeman. One civilian was killed and a policeman wounded, and cartridges that were found the next morning implicated the soldiers. All denied guilt, and no court martial was ever held. Nevertheless, President Roosevelt ordered three companies of the 25th discharged *en masse* without honors. Later a Senate investigation concluded that the cartridges could not have come from Army weapons and suggested that townspeople planted the evidence.

Seventy years later President Richard Nixon exonerated the men, including the last living survivor, who was allowed to enter a Veterans' Administration hospital. But Brownsville left a strong impact among African-American troops for years to come.

Meantime blacks were again eased out of the military. By 1917, only three percent of the army was black.

Benjamin Davis Sr.

One African American commissioned in the Cuba crisis was Ben Davis, son of a middle-class Washington family. When he was turned down by West Point, he enlisted with a view to winning a commission through the ranks. Riding with the cavalry in the Utah desert, Davis met Young, who coached him on the coming exam. Davis finished third among 23 candidates.

There were only a few career paths open to a black officer. He could serve as a lieutenant in a black regiment until he was promoted above white officers in the same unit. Then he had to be assigned either as a military attache to a black nation or as an ROTC instructor in a black college. At that time there were only two independent black nations, Haiti and Liberia, and only two black colleges that offered ROTC, Wilberforce in Cleveland, and Tuskegee in Alabama. For the next two decades, Young and Davis rotated from one of these assignments to the next.

Blacks also fought in the Philippine Insurrection and with Pershing chasing Pancho Villa out of the United States.

World War I

Southern officers had recovered from the Civil War and moved into leadership positions in the Army.

Both Young and Davis hoped for battlefield commands at the head of black regiments, something unprecedented in U.S. history.

Pershing, the commander of U.S. troops in France, nominated Young to the rank of full colonel. However, a lieutenant from Mississippi protested to his senator that this would put Young in command of whites, and President Woodrow Wilson, a Virginian, agreed that this could produce "trouble of a serious nature." Doctors flunked Young on his promotion physical, though he rode a horse from Ohio to

Washington, DC, to dramatize his good health. He was forced to retire and died in 1922 in Nigeria.

As for Davis, the Army sent him on a tour of China and Japan.

However, 300,000 colored soldiers did join the colors, 30,000 of them in combat. A black Officers Candidate School was established and turned out 700 second lieutenants.

The Houston Riot

Meanwhile, another race riot erupted. In Houston a 24th Infantry soldier was clubbed and jailed for trying to stop a policeman from beating a black woman. Some 150 troops marched on the city, battling civilians and police. Sixteen townspeople and four soldiers were left dead.

A quick and secret court martial was held. The all-white tribunal sentenced 19 soldiers to death, and they were summarily and secretly hanged before a judicial review could be held.

President Wilson rallied the country to a war "to make the world safe for democracy." "Why not make *America* safe for democracy?" asked the NAACP. However, its founder, W.E.B is, urged African Americans to "close ranks"; the country first, then rights, he declared. A. Phillip Randolph, head of the Pullman Porters Union, asked dryly what rights blacks had ever won by their war-time sacrifices?

The Army's four regular black regiments were all kept home. When men of an Illinois regiment refused to sit in the back of a streetcar in Virginia, the Army tried to disband the unit.

Two black divisions, did serve in France.

92nd Division

The 92nd had been parceled out to seven sites for training to allay public fears of 19,000 black men with guns in one place. As a result, it never developed an *esprit*. Most of its recruits were illiterate, and its general, a white man, was a racist.

But Pershing welcomed them: "They are American citizens, and I cannot discriminate against them."

At the battle of Meuse-Argonne, the division was severely criticized for its performance, although Pershing didn't join the criticism. "The only regret expressed by colored troops," he said, "is that they are not given more dangerous work to do."

No men of the 92nd, serving under the U.S. flag, received Medals of Honor, although their white officers did.

Henry Lincoln Johnson (right) repulsed an attack by 20 Germans, fighting them with grenades, rifle, rifle butt, and a bolo knife (*machete*).

William Butler rescued five comrades, killing eight enemies in the fight. The Germans reported they had been attacked by "overwhelming numbers."

Freddie Stowers, the grandson of a slave, was assaulting a hill when heavy machine gun fire wiped out half his company, including all the officers and sergeants. Stowers took command and crawled toward the first enemy trench, calling his men to follow. They stormed the trench and knocked out the guns, then charged the second trench-line. He was hit but continued forward before collapsing from loss of blood, and his men drove the Germans off the hill.

Stowers was put in for the Medal of Honor, but the Army later said the request was mis-placed. Seventy-three years later, in 1991, President George HW Bush presented it retroactively.

93rd Division

Meanwhile, in the States, the 93rd Division bandmaster was beaten for not doffing his cap in town, whereupon members of the unit marched on the town and shot it up. The division was hastily shipped to France. Pershing (right), a Missourian, gave them to the French army but cautioned the French to observe American customs toward the black troops. The French ignored him. General Goybet declared that they showed "complete contempt for danger." They were awarded 171 *Croix de Guerre*

Blacks in the U.S. Army fought in the Meuse-Argonne campaign, losing 2,500 men in hand-to-hand fighting. The 371st regiment lost half its men. The 369th New York Infantry, "the Men of Bronze," spent more than six straight months on the line, more than any other American regiments, and boasted that it never lost a trench or a prisoner and returned to a ticker-tape parade down Fifth Avenue.

Eugene Jacques Bullard

As a boy, Bullard had run away from home in Georgia to escape the Ku Klux Klan, stowed away on a ship to France, and worked as a stevedore, boxer, and carnival hand.

When war broke out he joined the famous Foreign Legion serving in an African regiment nicknamed "the Swallows" - the Germans called them "the Black Swallows of Death." They arrived at a town called Verdun, which was to become probably the bloodiest battlefield in history. They knew they were in hell, he wrote in his journal, when they found "men and beasts hanging from the branches of trees, where they'd been blown to pieces."

I was in charge of a machine gun. We were taking shelter in what was left of a farmhouse. I pulled a mattress over myself to protect me from fragments of shrapnel.

Ten minutes later those parts of hell that had been late getting there arrived. They exploded on what remained of the roof of the farmhouse, killing four of us and wounding 11. A very close friend by the name of Poireau was cut in half.

I had all of my top front teeth and all but four of my bottom teeth knocked out. The only thing that saved me was God and the mattress.

Knowing where Commander Nouvious' post of command was, I made lightning dashes in the direction of it, throwing myself to the ground between thunderous shell bursts, which came every 20 feet or less. Blood was flowing from my mouth.

Just as I arrived at full speed at the entrance, I heard the whistling of one special shell that sounded as if it was saying my name, 'Gene... eene ... eene." I dove for the entrance. At that split second the shell exploded and blew me flying over a table, where two officers were sitting by a candle stuck in a bottle. As the explosion blew everything out of the way, there was no light. They didn't even see me pass over the table.

I heard the Commander say, "That was not far off," as he scratched a match.

"*Non, mon Commandant*," I said, talking as best I could without my choppers.

Every man got one wore hole than he was born with, or, if he was lucky, he ducked into a series of shell holes, as I did. Even then he was not safe. A lost pigeon, which fluttered into one, in which I was about to duck, proved that. The bird seemed to explode into loose feathers and blood. We were damn near wiped out dodging from shell hole to shell hole under fire.

My machine gun had grown too hot and was jammed with dirt, but I still had my carbine. During the confusion I had scrambled into a deep shell hole. Seconds after I slid to the bottom, I had one of the greatest shocks of my life: I looked up, and there, above me, sliding into my hole was a huge, tall soldier. His uniform was not French.

I pulled the trigger. Thanks be to God, I pulled it in time. The big *Boche* [*German*] rolled the rest of the way into the hole.

31

Believe me, if anyone had seen me run out of that shell hole, he would not have recognized me, because I was white.

In ten months at Verdun, 250,000 men were killed. A mountain of skulls remains as a memorial to their agony.

Bullard tried to join the U.S. Air Corps but was turned down for flat feet and bad tonsils. "I'm not going to march across France or sing grand opera," he protested. So Gene joined the French Air Service. Another volunteer, James Norman Hall, co-author of *Mutiny on the Bounty,* described the new cadet:

Suddenly the door opened to admit a vision of military splendor... His jolly black face shone with a grin of greeting and justifiable vanity. He wore tan aviator's boots, which gleamed with mirror-like luster.

He also wore a *fouragere* [*shoulder cord*] of the Foreign Legion, plus "an enormous pair of wings." While the other pilots gasped, Hall "repressed a strong instinct to stand at attention."

With his mascot, Jimmy the monkey, dressed in a tiny uniform and tucked inside Bullard's own jacket, Gene flew his bi-winged Spad fighter on patrol over Verdun at speeds up to 125 miles an hour. He called it a *cage au poule*, "a chicken coop" held together with wire and glue. On the side he painted his motto, "All blood runs red." He described his first mission:

In the distance we spotted four big German bomber planes with 16 German fighter planes to protect them.... As the *Boches* kept coming, we got the signal from the Commandant to divide into sevens and maneuver into fighting position. Then the attack was on.

An air battle generally lasts from one to three minutes - very rarely as long as three. In this one everything happened so fast that I didn't have time to get frightened.

All I could see were burning planes earthbound and a long trail of smoke coming from one of the German bombers which ... exploded in the air....

I started shooting at every damn enemy plane that I even thought might be heading in my direction. It was all very confusing with planes roaring by and the smoke-filled air resounding with the *tat-tat-tat* of machine guns.

On the ground he and Jimmy counted seven holes in their own plane.

After the war Bullard opened a Paris night club, played jazz drums, spied for the French, married a countess, and escaped from Paris one jump ahead of the Nazis. He got his head smashed while working on the New York waterfront, then marched in protests with singer Paul Robeson and got it smashed again, by police.

President de Gaulle, on a visit to America, personally decorated him with the *Croix de Guerre*.

Between the Wars

White sailors refused to eat or bunk with black shipmates, who were restricted to mess stewards. In 1919 the Navy cut off all new black enlistments.

That year bloody race riots erupted in several cities. In Chicago 38 persons were left dead and 500 injured. Lynchings spread across both North and South - 77 were reported in all; some blacks died merely for wearing their old uniforms. Thousands of hooded Ku Klux Klan paraded down Washington's Pennsylvania Avenue.

The low point came in 1925. The Army chief of staff, Tasker Bliss of Missouri, commissioned a War College study, which concluded that the cranial cavity of the Negro "is smaller than a white man's and therefore he is inferior in intelligence, unless he happens to have 'a heavy strain of white blood.'" It added that a black is superstitious and "a rank coward in the dark." In addition, he is prone to "petty thievery, lying, promiscuity, and... atrocities connected with white women."

Socially, the War College said, the Negro could not associate with "any except the lowest class of whites," although it conceded that "Negro concubines" did sometimes attract white men. As for the Negro officer, the War College said, he shared "all the faults and weaknesses of character inherent in the Negro race, exaggerated by the fact that he wore an officer's uniform." Even Negroes didn't want to serve under Negro officers, it said.

This became Army policy for the next 15 years, even after Pearl Harbor. Army recruitment policies reflected this attitude. In the 1930s African Americans made up less than 2% of the men in the Army as scarce Depression openings went to whites.

Benjamin Davis was then a colonel and, aside from three chaplains, the only black officer on active duty.

Alonzo Parham was admitted to West Point in 1929 but flunked out in his first year.

West Point was about to get another black cadet.

Benjamin O Davis Jr

Called B.O., he was born in 1912 while his father was serving on the Mexican border. When the boy was 12, he sat with his father, mother, and sister on the porch of their Tuskegee home one summer night with the porch light defiantly lit, grimly watching torch-waving Ku Klux Klansmen march past.

The youth attended Western Reserve University and the University of Chicago before a West Point appointment appeared.

Davis:

The roof kind of caved in on the third night when I went to attend a meeting and was told I was not supposed to be there. The purpose of the meeting was to instruct my classmates to make me withdraw from the Academy.

For four years I was "silenced." I became an invisible man. My classmates treated Filipino, Nicaraguan, and Thai cadets better than they treated me.

Not another cadet spoke to him. Davis roomed alone, sat alone on the bus going to football games, and when he attended mandatory dance classes, he also danced alone. Although he was assigned a table at the mess hall, Sunday breakfast was "open seating," and he was forced to go from table to table, mess tray in hands: "Request permission to join your table."

"Permission denied."

Davis:

West Point is supposed to train leaders, but there was no damn leadership at all. The first captain of cadets was William Westmoreland [*later commander of U.S. forces in Vietnam*]. If he'd been a true leader, he would have stopped that crap.

It was designed to make me buckle, but. I refused to buckle. They didn't understand that I was going to stay there, and I was going to graduate.

Felix Kirkpatrick, 17, joined Davis in 1935:

You have to know something about the West Point tradition: The southern boys at that time were bitterly against blacks. I had a room built for four, but I lived in it by myself. Going to church, I was in a pew by myself.

They'd tell someone, "Go over there and gig Mr. K.".... "Mr. K., straighten your hat." I'd put my hand up, and my hat was already straight, but when you saw the gig sheet, it said, "Hat on head crooked."

I was always walking the yard on punishment tours. The main idea was to keep you away from your studies, but I was in the upper third of my class.

Kirkpatrick was forced to leave after one year for too many "gigs." He later became a Tuskegee Airmen.

Davis survived and graduated in 1936, ranking 35th in a class of 276. Pershing presented lieutenant's bars to the cadets. When Davis stepped up, his classmates dropped their silent treatment and gave him a cheer.

He had only two choices, infantry or cavalry. Assigned to the Infantry School in Fort Benning Georgia, Davis was assigned to the black 24th Infantry regiment.

I was the training officer for young black recruits. What happened to them after they were trained? They were given duties as servants in officers' quarters. The 24th had no combat mission.

Spain

When General Francisco Franco led an army revolt to overthrow the democratic government, Hitler and Mussolini backed him with planes and armor. Though the U.S. government was neutral, American idealists - Communists, labor leaders, poets, students - rallied to the Spanish government side. Known as the Abraham Lincoln Brigade, almost none of them had ever fired a weapon. One of the few who had was a former corporal in the 24th Infantry, Oliver Law.

The first 1,000 were given three bullets each to fire for practice, then they charged headlong into their first attack outside Madrid. One in three never returned.

The American "commissar," or political officer, Steve Nelson, called Law "calm under fire, dignified, respectful of his men, and always given to thoughtful consideration of military missions." At the next battle, Brunete, Law was named commander, the first time an American black had ever commanded whites. He jumped into the lead and ran to the top of the hill, waving his men on, before machine gun fire cut him down. (There was a report that he was shot why his own men, but this is not confirmed.)

Jim Peck

Overhead, Peck, a jazz drummer from Pittsburgh, was flying a snub-nosed Russian fighter. He is credited with five victories, which would make him history's only black "ace." However, he himself claimed only three. He described his first combat in a book, *Armies With Wings*:

> We open with a solid wall of fire... I line up on one of the enemy, slightly below and to my right.
>
> A tiny streamer flies from the pilot's helmet. Only the squadron commander wears that ribbon! I had to choose the best pilot for an enemy!
>
> Suddenly it happens - my ship is hit. A long burst of slugs chews its way into my lower wing with a succession of thudding impacts.
>
> As his biplane flashes by close beneath, I pull up into the tightest wing-over turn that I can execute.
>
> But the commander has out-witted me by making a left turn. He executes an Immelmann [*a climbing turn*], the ship rolling right side up at the top - then, before I realize it, his guns are spewing more of those slugs into my tail. This guy is clever.
>
> I whip into a tight vertical turn. He sticks behind me as if I were towing him on an invisible rope. Our ships wind up chasing each other around in a circle, nearly opposite each other. Perhaps if I take the initiative I may gain a momentary advantage. But whoever breaks the circle leaves himself wide open for an interval.
>
> I roll over on my back upside down. The pull-up slows down one's forward speed and the other plane gains during this interval. I stop the biplane's roll, and the commander's plane is directly opposite, and he is just waking up. But he is too late. From my inverted position I clearly see the glass and metal frames of his goggles, the gray, set face, that streaming ribbon. I fire all four guns.

Tracers and a crazy line of bullet holes stitch along the bottom of his cockpit and creep back along the fuselage. That ugly, black cross on the plane's rudder seems to disappear in a shower of flying tracers, metal and fabric. Then the ship is gone. A cloud swallows him up, like some eerie thing devouring a victim.

Victory in my first combat.

World War II

The nation's top soldier, George C Marshall, a graduate of Virginia Military Institute, reiterated the Army's long-standing policy:

Experiments within the Army in the solution of social problems are fraught with danger to efficiency, discipline, and morale. The Army is not a social laboratory.

However, with the 1940 election coming up, President Roosevelt nominated Ben Davis for a star. But he was not welcome in the officers' mess, so he brought a brown bag and ate at his desk.

Negro nurses, one percent of the nurse corps, didn't have many black casualties to attend to, so they were sent to care for German POWs. Some 4,000 African-American women joined the WACs; while white WACs typed, black WACs worked in the laundries and mess halls.

When Japanese planes struck Pearl Harbor, the armed services were still rigidly segregated. In the Navy, for example, blacks were used almost entirely as mess stewards. But **Dorie Miller**, a cook, rushed on deck, seized a gun, which he had never fired before, and began blasting away. He also pulled a wounded officer to safety. He was killed two years later when another ship was sunk by Japanese guns.

When an ammunition ship exploded at Port Chicago California, 300 dock workers were killed, most of them African Americans. Survivors who refused to return to the job were court-martialed for mutiny and were defended by Thurgood Marshall, later a Justice of the Supreme Court.

24th Infantry Regiment

The Deuce-4 arrived in the Pacific trained as infantrymen, but they were assigned as laborers, although one battalion later saw action as jungle fighters at Bougainville. The regiment was next sent to Saipan to mop up after the Marines, digging Japanese out of caves and jungles.

Emlen Tunnell

Coast Guardsman Emlen Tunnell was unloading explosives in New Guinea when a Japanese torpedo opened a gaping hole in the ship's side. An explosion ignited the gasoline, and Tunnell, one of only five blacks on the ship, saw a flaming figure running toward him. "The horrible figure was unrecognizable, he was covered with fire." Tunnell chased him, beat the flames out with his hands, and carried him to safety.

The man recalled that Tunnell "ran after me across that deck. He was burned too, but he didn't want to make a big deal out of it."

Two years later, off the coast of Canada, Tunnel jumped into freezing water to rescue another shipmate, though Em himself could barely swim. "You could have drowned," the man told him.

Tunnel shrugged: "I had to take the

chance."

He was nominated for a medal, which was awarded post-humously. In earlier days men received the Medal of Honor for the same thing.

Tunnell went on to star in football at Iowa, where I saw him, and then on the New York Giants and Green Bay Packers, becoming the first black man in the football Hall of Fame. No one knew of his war-time deeds. That's because he never mentioned it.

The Red Tails

The most celebrated black unit, of course, was the Air Corps' 332d Fighter Group, the "Red Tails," led by Lieutenant Colonel B.O. Davis Jr.

Black college students rushed to sign up. The cadets were segregated, but all agreed that the instructors, black and white, were top flight. The flyers themselves gave generous credit to a white ex-cavalry officer, Colonel Noel Parrish, the base commander, who gave up his own chance to make general in order to insure that the experiment would succeed.

After graduation, the pilots were kept out of combat for months, because no overseas commander wanted them. When the 99th Fighter Squadron finally arrived in North Africa, they were given P-40 Warhawks, 100 miles an hour slower than the German Messerschmitts. Their commander gave them ground strafing duties, while his white pilots (and he) flew off to shoot down Germans. He wrote that they had no enemy planes shot down, compared to his other squadrons, and the War Department prepared to disband the unit.

Transferred to a new superior, the 99th was finally unleashed over Anzio beachhead in Italy. In two days they destroyed 13 German planes and lost only one of their own. Exulted *Time* Magazine: "The Air Force considers the experiment proven and will take all the Negro pilots it can get."

Even as the news broke, three more squadrons, the 332d Fighter Group, were already on the high seas, bound for Italy. One of them was Charlie Bussey (right).

General Ira Eaker, chief of the US Air Force in the Mediterranean, promised to give the 332d the new long-range P-51 Mustangs, the best fighter planes in the world. Their mission: to escort the bombers over Germany, eastern Europe, and France.

Eaker stressed that he didn't want aces, he wanted pilots who would *stay with the bombers* and protect them. However, Eaker either didn't give his white the same lecture, or they ignored him. The Red Tails bitched. But they obeyed. As a result, they had the lowest record of enemy fighters shot down, but also the lowest number of friendly bombers lost. They painted their tails bright red so that both the bombers and the Germans would know who they were.

Four of their kills came against the Germans' new supersonic jets.

Clarence "Lucky" Lester

Several pilots shot down three planes in one day. One was Clarence "Lucky" Lester.

The fourth man in our flight drifted off six o-700 feet, and suddenly he was attacked from above. The other three of us made a turn around to head into them.

I dove in behind one plane and started  shooting, and the airplane started coming apart on him, smoke poured out of him, and he exploded. I was going so fast, I was sure I would hit some of the debris.

As I dodged pieces of aircraft, I saw this other plane to my right and turned onto his tail, going like a bat out of heck. I closed to about 200 feet and started over-running him and began firing.

His aircraft started to smoke and almost stopped. I was going so fast I skidded my airplane to the side, because I thought I was going to run right up his tail. I saw him climb out on the wing and bail out. I can still see him today with his blond hair, standing on the wing, just as plain as then. It was an amazing sight.

Then I saw a third airplane below me, and I took off after him. I picked him up going pretty fast. He started to dive, trying to out-dive my P-51. Well, there's no way he'd be able to do that.! When he got to about 1,000 feet, he leveled but I was still peppering him. He was desperate, because I'd scored so many hits, so he decided to roll over and pull the airplane down so he was going back the other way. He never made it and went straight into the ground.

Back home, one more war lay ahead. The Red Tails had to "mutiny" to win the right to use the white officers' clubs. One hundred were court-martialed, though all but three were acquitted, and years later those three had their convictions set aside too.

The 92nd Division

Black Buffaloes

On the ground the Army trained two black infantry divisions, the 92nd and 93rd. The latter included the old Indian-fighting 24th and 25th Infantry Regiments. It was sent to the Pacific, but was broken up and assigned to white units as laborers, security guards, and truck drivers.

The 92nd, the "Black Buffaloes," under General Ned Almond, trained in Fort Huachuca in the Arizona desert, possibly the worst hell-hole of all the Army's posts. Under Major General Ned Almond, a Virginian, the unit developed severe morale and training problem. In contrast to the black fliers, who had all black officers, the 92d officer corps was entirely white above the level of captain.

In Italy the Division was assigned the extreme left flank of the Allied line, facing a rugged mountain barrier, and went on the offensive in October. General Mark Clark would brand it the worst division in Europe.

One GI, **Herb Sheppard**, offered this first-hand summary of the Division's men and their record:

The field grade officers were white, and many of the company grade officers were white. Later they began to move blacks up into captains' positions.

A lot of the NCOs had pretty high IQs. The guys who had been trained on mortars weren't mathematicians, but they were accurate. But usually seasoned troops show the new guys all the things to watch out for; we didn't get any assistance.

Most of the enlisted men had a pretty high illiteracy rate; that was one of the major problems. Most of these fellows were from the deep South and had no schooling. Also, we didn't have many trained infantry replacements. A lot of them came from the stockades; the Army threw them right overseas as replacements. They used antiaircraft troops, quartermaster troops, truck drivers. That was another morale buster.

When I think of all the guys who didn't have that basic infantry, I appreciated that I did. You can show a guy how to field strip an M-1 rifle, but squad tactics, or coordinating with other units, you need a team that's been trained together. To get an anti-aircraft outfit and throw them into the line immediately, it was pretty rough.

The Division quickly got a reputation for "bugging out."

Sheppard:

We did take an awful lot of criticism, and we never got credit for doing things that were positive. Many good guys were wiped out and never got any credit. You'll find one or two in any division that might, after an artillery barrage, get nervous and fade out. But the way they tell it, whole units would just take off. Although it's true that some people didn't hold up their end of it, it wasn't an overall truth.

We weren't the only ones who lost ground when the Germans were looking down your throat from the high observation posts. Every division takes ground one day, loses it, and goes back the next day. But in our case they made a special issue of it.

James (Joe) Greene was Satchel Paige's catcher on the Kansas City Monarchs when he was drafted in 1942:

I was in a 57-mm anti-tank company on the front line eight months and had two battle stars. Company L was attacking, and they were going to take a pillbox. I got my binoculars and could see shells falling all around the  pillox on the top of the hill. Two Germans came out with machine guns. They probably would have wiped out that whole company. So I called the OP [*Observation Post*]. He said, "Are you sure they're Germans?"

I said, "Yes, I can tell by their uniforms. I can see 'em good."

He said, "We got men right up there under them."

I said, "I know it, but they can't see 'em. I can."

"Well, if you're sure they're Germans, you fire."

I told the guy, "Give me two rounds of H.E. [*high explosive*]." I reached for my binoculars. The first round hit right between them. Both of them went up in the air. By the time they came back down, the other round hit, and they went back in the air.

The guy said, "You get 'em?"

"Yeah, I got both of them. One shot was enough."

I went on special missions over there. One was a church, an O.P. [*observation post*] for the Germans. There was one squad, about eight of us, and we worked all night long, digging in that gun. Next morning, sure enough, those German shells started falling in there. We'd get in our holes, but they hit all around, busted both tires on the gun, knocked the shield off, and cut a hole through it.

I had another shell come in our hole and hit right on me, six or seven feet from me. I came off the ground from the concussion.

In all I had three guns tore up.

I got another close call when we were dug in and they found out where we were. We had a tarp to keep the water off us, and I wanted to get a stick outside to hold up one corner. I was crawling on my stomach and *brrrt* - just a line out of a burp gun about six inches in front of where my hands were stretched out. I don't know how I turned around, but they say I came sliding back on my stomach!

We drove from Leghorn clear up to Milan. I had a chance to see Columbus' home. And I got a chance to see [*the dictator*] Mussolini and his girl friend. The partisans got them. They had them hanging up, but we had to take them down.

Sheppard:

Captain Bundy, heavy weapons company, was up on a little cliff. He told his men to stand by, and he just went in there and attacked it himself. They really blew him away.

On the day after Christmas 1944, when his unit was forced to

withdraw from a village, **John Fox** volunteered to stay behind. From a second-floor window he called in artillery fire as the Germans swarmed closer and closer around him. Finally he called for fire on his own position, The stunned radio operator protested, "If we feel fire it, you'll be killed."

Fox replied, "Fire it!"

It turned the tide. When the Americans counter-attacked, they found his body surrounded by about 100 German soldiers. The town, Somacolonia, erected a memorial to him, and in 1997 he was awarded the Medal of Honor retroactively.

Vernon Baker was orphaned at four and grew up in Father Flanagan's Boys Town orphanage in Omaha. He tried to enlist before Pearl Harbor but was told, "We don't have any quotas for you people." But he persisted and was finally accepted. He won the Medal of Honor in Italy for leading an attack that destroyed three machine gun nests.

Sheppard:

They were trying to do us in, instead of using us the way everyone else was using their troops. It looked at times that they were trying to get us wiped out. Most commanders would send a company to take an objective; we'd send a squad or a platoon. They were whittling down our squads. We lost a lot of good guys. Morale sank to nothing. When they made all the remarks about the division, I was ashamed to say I was a part of it, until after I saw other divisions lose ground too.

General Mark Clark sent the 34th and the Texas 36th Divisions across the Rapido River, and they were drowned - they caught hell. It wasn't until years later that the Army acknowledged those mistakes.

Clark placed all the blame on our junior officers and enlisted men. The statement is unfair and untrue.

Whatever shortcomings the 92nd had rested entirely on the shoulders of General Almond. His entire staff was incompetent, excepting General Coburn, the artillery commander.

Later the best men in the 92nd were formed into one regiment and teamed with the famous *Nisei* "Go for Broke" 442nd Regimental Combat Team. Shepard called it one of the best divisions in Europe. The Nisei, by the way, were awarded 21 Medals of Honor; their black comrades received none until years later.

Almond would go on to serve on General MacArthur's staff in the Korean War. He won praise for his brilliant planning of the Inch'on landing that liberated South Korea, but he received much of the blame for the headlong retreat after the surprise Chinese invasion across the Yalu.

The Black Panthers

In Europe the 761st tank battalion, Jackie Robinson's old outfit, fought with General Patton, relieved the 101st Airborne at Bastogne, helped breach Germany's Siegfried Line, and linked up with the Russians in Austria.

Sergeant **Rubin Rivers**, who was half-Cherokee, suffered a bad leg wound but jumped into another tank and kept on fighting. When that one was knocked out, he commandeered a third tank and continued firing until a third enemy shell killed him. (It took over 50 years, but he finally got his Medal of Honor, along with Fox and Baker.)

One tanker was wounded and evacuated to a hospital. When a colonel came through the ward, handing out Purple Hearts, he stopped at the tanker's bed. "What are you in for," he asked, "the clap?"

John B. Holway

The Bulge

On December 8 General Eisenhower's European Theater already faced a shortage of 23,000 infantrymen. The next day Hitler struck in the Bulge - unleashing the costliest battle in U.S. history. Ike needed fighting men bad. The first place to look was the pool of black ground troops driving supply trucks on the "Red Ball Express" or in other rear-echelon tasks. Ike declared that it was: happy to offer to a limited number of Negro privates the privilege of joining our veteran units at the front NCOs may accept reduction [*in rank*] in order to take advantage of this opportunity.

The latter language was added to insure that white privates would not have to take orders from black sergeants.

One battalion (1,000 men) would be formed and could be expanded to a regiment (5,000 men) if needed.

Ike's chief of staff, General Walter Bedell Smith, was alarmed: It was "the most dangerous thing that I have ever seen in regards to Negro relations."

But by February 4,500 volunteers began infantry training. They were formed into platoons of 30 men under white lieutenants and sergeants. By March 1 the first 2,000 men were ready to join white divisions.

One platoon sewed on 78th "Lightning" Division patches just in time to make the first Rhine river crossing at Remagen. The Division's report:

Morale: Excellent. Manner of performance: Superior. Men are very eager to close with the enemy and destroy him. Their strict attention to duty, aggressiveness, common sense and judgment under fire have won the admiration of all the men in the company When given a mission, they accept it with enthusiasm. The officers and men of Company F all agree that the colored platoon has a calibre of men equal to any veteran platoon. Several decorations for bravery are in the process of being awarded.

Pfc Jack Thomas led his squad to knock out an enemy tank. He hurled two grenades, wounding several Germans, and when two of his men were wounded, he manned their rocket launcher, then carried one man to safety under fire. He was awarded the DSC, one cut below the Medal of Honor.

In the First Division ("The Big Red One"), its black platoon lost more than half its men killed and wounded, so the survivors formed squads and joined white platoons. Whites said they liked to fight beside them, "because they laid down a large volume of fire on the enemy." When their white lieutenant was downed, a black took over "in a superior manner." Their colonel reported: "They can most certainly be considered a battle success."

The 99th Division also said its black platoon was "particularly good in town fighting and was often used as the assault [lead] platoon." It killed or captured 600 Germans at a loss of 18 of its own men. One regiment's official history showed a photo captioned, "the Colored Platoon of Easy Company – one of the best platoons in the regiment."

Another platoon, facing heavy machine gun fire from a town, broke into a run with all rifles firing, charged 300 yards under a hail of fire, and quickly took the town. Their colonel called them brave, dependable, and proud.

They possess a fierce desire to kill the enemy, which I have never seen in white troops.

Edward Allen Carter

Born in Calcutta, the son of a black missionary and an East Indian mother, he grew up in Shanghai and ran away from home to join the Chinese Nationalist Army fighting the Japanese. He was commissioned a lieutenant until they found out he was only 15 and sent him home. The boy enrolled in a military school and studied German to add to his English, Hindi, and Mandarin. He also met a mystic, who told him he would become a great soldier.

Carter sailed to Spain to join the Abraham Lincoln Brigade of American Communists and idealists fighting the Hitler-backed army there. When they were disbanded, he sailed to the States and joined the American army shortly before Pearl Harbor. Officers kept a close eye on him, for signs of Communist sympathies, even after the United States became an ally of Russia. (He was labeled a "PAF" - "premature anti-Fascist.")

Carter was a sergeant with service troops when Eisenhower called for volunteers.

Eleven days later he was leading a tank platoon, racing to take a strategic river town when his tank was blown up under him. He led three men across 150 yards of open field to a bombed out warehouse. The others were killed or wounded. Carter was also hit by three machine gun slugs in the arm but wiped out the gun crew with a grenade. He inched along a ridge, firing as he went. Two more grenades blew up a mortar squad.

As he stopped to swallow a "wound pill," eight Germans advanced, and another bullet hit him, but he killed six of the attackers and captured the other two. Using them as a shield, he dashed for the warehouse. A German shell sent splinters into his leg, knocking him to the ground which more enemy advanced. "I was too busy to count them," he said, but the official report said there were "about 50," the same phrase used in the citation for Audie Murphy's Medal of Honor. Carter blew them away.

"He was a one-man army," said his commanding officer, who put him in for the Medal of Honor, though it was down-graded to a DSC.

Yet when Carter tried to re-enlist after the war, he was turned down because of his service with Communists in Spain.

He died before President Clinton could put the Medal of Honor around his neck.

When it was time to go home, the whites, who had been in combat longer, got on the boats while the blacks returned to their service units. They asked why they couldn't go home with the men they had fought beside, to show the world that they were more than truck drivers.

Post War

Would the post-war armed forces be segregated or integrated? In February 1946, the Army convoked a special committee to study how best to employ black troops in the future.

Witnesses included Ned Almond of the 92d Division, plus Benjamin Davis, his son, B.O. Davis of the famous Red tails, and General Noel Parrish, who had trained the Airmen.

The War Department named a panel of generals to study the

question. General Almond testified. So did Generals Iraq Eaker and Touey Spaatz of the Air Force. Eaker said he believed that both whites and blacks would do their best work when segregated. Spaatz also said he didn't think Negroes "could stand the pace" when integrated.

General Noel Parrish, who had trained the Red Tails, declared simply:

Whether we dislike or like the Negro, they are citizens under the Constitution with the same rights as all citizens.

The chief Army historian, Walter L White, told the committee:

My ultimate hope is that in the long run it will be possible to assign individual Negro soldiers and officers to any unit in the Army where they are qualified as individuals to serve efficiently.

The decision of the panel: Segregation was still desirable and the same separation that existed before the war would continue after it.

Then, in 1948, history was made. President Harry S Truman faced a seemingly impossible uphill fight in the election. The South had walked out of his party, and he needed every vote he could get. He issued a historic order:

It is hereby declared to be the policy of the President that there shall be equality of treatment and opportunity for all persons in the armed services without regard to race, color, religion, or national origin. This policy shall be put into effect as rapidly as possible.

The Air Force integrated without too much problem. Not the Army, however.

B.O. Davis:

The Army Chief of Staff, Omar Bradley, told Truman bluntly that the Army was not going to have anything to do with social reform. And it didn't do a damn thing about that Executive Order.

II.

Prelude To Korea

Boys of the Depression

The men of the Deuce-4 were about ten years younger than the illustrious Red Tails, now famous in books and movies.

The black GIs have a right to complain, "What about *us*?" One difference is that the Red Tails were mostly middle-class and college-educated. They were handsome and daring in their well-tailored uniforms and polished boots. The Deuce-4s were mostly from economically depressed homes. Their boots were muddy, their uniforms dirty from months on line without baths or de-lousing. Their life-expectancy in combat was a fraction of that of the more glamorous fliers.

The Red Tails were officers and gentlemen and demanded that they be treated as such. They risked prison, even death for mutiny, demanding the right to attend the officers' club.

For the men of the Deuce-4, this was the least worry on their minds. They faced much more serious problems, such as how to get rid of the damn lice, how to keep from freezing, and how to stay alive.

Yet there was not that much difference between the grungy grunts on the ground and their dashing older brothers in the air. Both battled mean-spirited prejudice and overcame it. Both were articulate and told their stories clearly and dramatically. Both sent their children to college and were proud of their achievements.

It's time to take a closer look at these black men who fought America's ground wars. The tales below reveal the heroism of the men of Korea. If we had similar first-person testimony by their fathers and grandfathers, going back to the War of 1812, we might discover stories equally courageous.

Ernest Collier (G Company):
I was an army brat. My grandfather was in the Civil War, the 64th Regiment. I found

his name on the Civil War wall in Washington.

My dad [*left*] got a commission and went to France in the 92nd Division. After that he was in the cavalry in the Philippines.

That's were I was born, in 1922. I grew up in Fort Huachuca Arizona - my father used to let me ride his horse - and I went to high school and junior college in San Diego, taking engineering. I ran the half-mile and was good for two minutes - that was a good time back then.

After World War II broke out, I wanted to be in my dad's regiment, and they sent me to the Ninth Cavalry, Second Cavalry Division, which was the old Ninth and Tenth Cavalry regiments.

Then the Army decided they weren't going to use horse cavalry, so they sent us to Africa - Casablanca and Algeria - as a port battalion. I was a buck sergeant then. We made two runs to Anzio to dump off supplies for the Italian invasion - get in there and get out fast.

The German planes were only 69 miles away in Rome, and they were bombing Naples at the time. Ten o'clock - here they come. They had everybody penned in.

I never understood why the Americans picked that spot for an invasion. It was rocky country, mountains all the way down to the ocean. The first couple times the LST [*Landing Ship, Tank*] could go right in. The last two times we had to unload off-shore.

They brought in the black 92nd Division to Italy, and after they had their first casualties, they asked for volunteers. Not too many guys did, but I did. My dad was in the 92nd, but I was stuck in the training command until the A-bomb ended my European tour.

I went to Japan in '47. I did two tours, then returned to the States. But 28 hours later the Korean War broke out. They woke everybody up and rounded up anyone who could walk or crawl - cooks and bakers and everyone else. We were going to Korea.

Bloody Ground

Robert Yancey (C Company):

I was born in 1925 in Sharon Hill Pennsylvania, and I was drafted in 1943. I was 18, a young buck, and went to the Navy. Didn't go to boot camp, went straight aboard a training ship. They were really hard up for men at that time, and.

Then I got sent to the Pacific, and we patrolled for submarines on the outside of convoys.

Everyone had a battle station. In the China Sea in 1944 on the way to the invasion of the Philippines, my station was all the way down in the bottom of the bilge, passing up ammunition. This guy said, "Hey, Yancey, you don't want to be down in that hole. If we get hit, they're going to dog that hatch down to save the ship from sinking, whether you're down in there or not."

So I told the skipper I" didn't want to be down there. "

"Well, where do you want to be?"

I said, "On an anti-aircraft gun."

He says, "You don't know anything about a gun."

I said, "I'm not stupid, I can learn just like anyone else."

"We're going to have target practice in a couple days. If you hit the target, you can have a gun."

I said, "Fair enough."

Lo and behold, a Piper Cub was pulling a target on a 30-foot cable. When the plane gets mid-ship, the order is "Commence firing." That plane was doing some fancy maneuvers, trying to get out of range of my firing. When they hollered, "Cease fire!" I didn't hear 'em.

They finally got me stopped. The skipper says, "You know, Yancey, you didn't hit the target, but you tried so doggone hard, I'm going to give you the gun, so you can shoot down *Japanese* planes."

One day, when I was up there working with the gun, I heard this plane. The Japanese used to come in through the rays of the sun, and I saw this red ball on the side of the plane, so I threw in a magazine and commenced firing. They heard me firing and sounded general quarters just in time to see the plane blow up. Well, I was king for three or four days. I could have slapped the hell out of the skipper. Then someone else got a plane, and I lost all my fame.

I went from the invasion of Leyte to Luzon, Manila, and Okinawa, which was the last invasion of World War II.

A typhoon hit with winds 150 miles an hour. You had waves so big they'd take the ship 60-70 feet in the air. You were tied to a life-line so you wouldn't go over. The storm was so bad, it carried an LST [*Landing Ship, Tank*] about five miles inland. You know how big an LST is!

Two destroyers were flipped over. All these troops in the water. You'd look down, and they looked like specks, that's how big the swells were. Our ship couldn't get anyone out. It was horrible. So many guys lost their lives.

I got out of the Navy in '47 and went into the reserve. In 1950, when Korea hit, they sent me a letter that the next notice I would receive would be a 24-hour recall. I didn't want to go back to the Navy - in In the Navy you could be only a cook or steward. So I enlisted in the Army.

Richard Sanders (M Company):
I was born in 1927 in Lake Alfred Florida, a little town near Orlando. My father worked in a phosphorous mine, my mother was a domestic. They had 15 children, eight boys and seven girls. I was the oldest.

I was drafted in 1945 when I was 18, but I got out of the service with the intention of going to college. This was during the old "civil war" days, and I thought I would be a teacher or a preacher - what else could I be? Not very much. So I reenlisted in 1948 and went to Japan.

Ellis Dean (D Company):
My great grandfather was born in Westmoreland County Virginia, the home of George Washington and Robert E Lee, and served in the Civil War with the Confederates. My father was in World War I, a stevedore, but the French were losing a lot of soldiers, so he fought with the French.

Bloody Ground

I was born in 1927 in Ambler Pennsylvania, near Philadelphia, and they still celebrate my birthday every year - October 12, Columbus Day. We had a lot of Quakers there, and if there was prejudice, I never saw it. I had no problems.

When I was 14 I was playing baseball with the older guys. We played soccer in the street, so we were tough - blacks, Italians, Polish kids.

In high school I was a C student but I was many-talented in sports. Football. I was little and skinny, a sub. I was a defensive back, I was good at jumping to intercept. I was so skinny I had to hide my legs, so I didn't play basketball. The high jump was my specialty. I was second in the state championship. A guy beat me by 1/4" with 6'1".

I was drafted, but they deferred me until I finished high school. I went to the Navy recruitment office. I wanted to be a petty officer on a ship, because I saw movies about sailors, but I was told politely the only position for Negroes was mess steward.

So in January 1947 I went into the Army and took basic training at Fort Jackson South Carolina. That's when I first found out there was segregation. On the train, after you pass Baltimore, the blacks had to sit in a car up behind the smoke stack with a curtain drawn. When I got to Fort Jackson, it was back of the bus, all that.

After that I was sent to Fort Riley Kansas. My first sergeant was getting paid to let me go to Kansas City for the weekend to play baseball against the Kansas City Monarchs and other Negro League teams like the Birmingham Black Barons and Cincinnati Clowns. I played against Satchel Paige. Satchel doctored the ball up. Man, that ball was hopping everywhere. How could you hit it? I got a walk, a fly, and was out on a ground ball to him. That was it.

My older brother, Jimmy, pitched in the Negro Leagues with the Philadelphia Stars. Buck O'Neil, the manager of the Monarchs, sent a bouquet to his funeral.

Donald Womack (77th Engineers):

I was born in 1927 in New Haven. I lived with my mother in a house called a "siding house" - the wind would blow, and the house would shake. As a kid I wasn't allowed to go into the country club, but I was allowed to be a caddy. And I worked in a chicken market; I cleaned chickens and threw the gizzards and feet away.

I played basketball with the community center team. We were state champions four years in a row. I played center. There was no such thing as dunking the ball back then. Our team was black, and we played both black and white teams from different cities. Several times we won games, and they wouldn't even let us get our things out of the lockers. We had to fight our way out.

I also played high school soccer and football. I caught passes.

Sonny Walker from New Haven was a short guy like Napoleon. Him and I got into it - teen-age stuff. He pulled his .22 and stuck it in my stomach. I'm looking to feel the pain, but it went click; the gun mis-fired. I took it away from him and shot it up in the air. Bam! Bam! It fired. Then I was angry for real!

It wasn't my day to go.

I drank, and I went to Alcoholics Anonymous. You had to stand up in front of the group and say your name, and say, "I'm an alcoholic." I cried. I don't know anybody who didn't cry.

In North Haven they had CAP [*Civil Air Patrol*], flying Piper Cubs. I could land with an instructor, but I quit before I soloed. I went to trade school to study aeronautics. I scored high and I wanted to get into the Tuskegee Airmen - I went to school with three of them - but I didn't have the education. My mother, my grandmother, and my aunt didn't have that kind of money to send me to college.

The only thing left was the Army. I was about 17, and they sent me to Fort Dix New Jersey. I couldn't go on the main post; I couldn't even catch a bus in the post bus terminal. But they promised they'd send me to airborne training at Ft Bragg. Then they sent me to Sam Houston Texas to be a combat medic.

In 1945 they shipped me to Okinawa. I've got pictures of the surrender, the Japanese handing over their swords.

Next they sent us to Kobe Japan. Korean workers rioted in 1948, and we broke that up, and we worked on the docks as stevedores. Then they sent us up to Gifu Japan in '48.

LaVaughn Fields of the 77th Engineers was also born in New Haven, in 1930. He went to high school with Womack, played football in high school, and in 1948 found himself competing for jobs with World War II vets. "My best shot was the Army," he says. He went to jump school, joined the 82nd Airborne, then shipped to Japan to the 24th Infantry.

Lloyd Collins:
My father was a Pullman porter, ran a crack train out of New Orleans to New York, the Crescent Limited. My mother died when I was nine months old, and my father kept the four of us together. In '48 I volunteered from Louisiana. It was out of economics - I couldn't get a job.

George Bussey (F Company):
I was born in Lincolnton Georgia, January 10, 1928, one of nine kids. We were sharecroppers, grew anything, like corn and watermelons. I finished high school when I was 17, joined the Army when I was 19, and was sworn in Christmas Eve, 1947.

Curtis Bolton (C Company) was born in Memphis in 1929, the son of a share-cropper and one of nine kids.

Albert Kimber (I Company):
I was born 1930 in a little place, Booneville North Carolina, in the country. I walked five miles one-way to school. All in a one-room schoolhouse, 25-30 kids in one room, one teacher taught all grades, the same teacher who taught my mother. All the books were hand-me-downs from white schools, but we were grateful to get them, because that's all we had.

We were sharecroppers. As I got older I realized there was something better than this. That's the reason I decided to go into the Army. I enlisted in November '46 - just a little fib.

John B. Holway

Floyd Williams (A Company):
I was born in 1930 in Carlisle Kentucky, a small town, maybe 2,000 population. There were 13 kids, I was the oldest. That was no place for me unless I wanted to work on a farm or clean someone's house. We weren't expected to do anything but work with our hands. So I joined the Army in 1948 and was off to the military when I turned 18.

Nathaniel Nicholson (B Battery, 159th Field Artillery):
I was born in Enid Oklahoma in 1931 and was reared in the Church of God in Christ. My father was the pastor of our church in Montclair New Jersey and died when I was nine. My mother was a praying woman and lived to be 84. She had two girls and four boys. I was the youngest. My parents provided us with lots of love and care.

Once in a church service in Honey Grove Texas, people were shouting and praising God until the service was interrupted by members of the Ku Klux Klan, who demanded that we keep our voices down. A man raised his hands and refused to stop, and the Klan simply left.

Another time, in Parsons Kansas, we lived in a rented house, but we were forced by the white landlord to move. That's when I realized that white folks had strength to do as they pleased with black folks.

We moved to New Jersey, sharing a neighborhood with Italians and Jews, I never experienced any more racial issues until I joined the Army. But I had a rough time in high school. All the teacher taught was Julius Caesar, Julius Caesar, Julius Caesar. I finished three years, but it was a waste of my time.

We went to church every Sunday, sat there all day. The church made too much noise - that's what I thought, that was my excuse.

But I witnessed miracles among many of the Saints. The Holy Spirit was nudging me, but although they meant well, the members pursued my salvation past what I could endure. On seeing a church while riding a bus, I would duck down in my seat.

So in 1948 I joined the Army to get away from the church. I asked my mother to let me go. "Take care of yourself," she said. Those were her parting words. Somehow I knew she was praying for me. I could feel it. Never underestimate the power of a praying mother.

I took medical training, and I was supposed to be a medical technician, but I couldn't even go in the hospital, because I was black.

After Christmas leave I missed a connecting flight, and it was assumed I had gone AWOL, so I was given orders to go to Japan. Unbeknownst to me, Japan was where black soldiers were sent who were considered unruly. But at the age of 18 I wanted to go somewhere else and experience something different.

In 30 days at sea, I was bored and played bingo. But God seemed to disapprove - I never won a single game. But I was the only passenger who didn't get sea-sick, and I knew it was the Lord who kept me healthy.

They sent me to the artillery, keeping the radios maintained, even though I had no artillery training whatsoever.

Ralph (Mother) Hubbard (M Company):

I was born December 30 1931 in Brooklyn and grew up in Bed-Stuy – Bedford-Stuyvesant. My grandfather was Welsh – Hubbard's a Welsh name, that's where that came from.

Five boys and two girls. I was smack dab in the middle. My mom spoiled us. It was us kids first. She was so busy, when I came back from Korea was the first time in my life I had private time with my mom. When we were of dating age, she wouldn't sleep until everyone was in that house. I said, "When do you sleep? I've never gone to bed after you or gotten up before you." She just looked at me and smiled.

She died young. She only met two of my children. She would have spoiled the hell out of them.

John B. Holway

My father used to play the Sousaphone, French horn, and cornet. Taught me to play. I knew everything Sousa ever wrote.

My brother Bill was two years older than me. He was a roughhouse, he loved playing, and he was strong as a damn bull. Had hands like cast-iron.

All my brothers were great athletes. Lester was the greatest.

The first time he picked up a bowling ball, he bowled a 300-game. Lester would hit foul balls to my grandson in the stands every time. The Brooklyn Dodgers sent for him to try out, but the day before, he hurt his arm and zilched it.

In high school I weighed about 140 pounds. I was a water rat, a lifeguard. I've taught maybe 300 people how to swim. My first house I bought I had a swimming pool.

My first girlfriend was an Italian girl. I was very welcome in her family's house. But if I'd been down South, I'd have been wiped out.

An influx of Southerners started coming into my neighborhood; they were different from us. One family came in, about eight boys and eight girls. I had to go to a linguistic center to learn how to understand them. They'd say, "'spute." I had no idea what they meant until I learned that "spute" was "dispute."

I enlisted in 1949. The Army said they had a quota system - I didn't know what the hell they were talking about. They sent me home to put on eight pounds, that's how skinny I was. They told me they'd notify me.

In 1950 I changed my mind, but the MPs came and got me; everyone on the block was watching. I said, "I've got a job now; I don't feel like going." They started laughing, said, "Excuse me! You enlisted, you raised your right hand last year."

I was sent to Fort Dix New Jersey. That's when I found out I was colored. I had been "cloistered." Brooklyn was always mixed, my friends were always mixed.

Six white fellows went down on the train together with me. A captain came on the stage at camp, said, "Listen up. Everyone on this side goes to the 69th Training Battalion; everyone on that side goes to the 68th. And you colored boys will go to the 364th."

I'm like, "What?" I was never defined like that before. I was very upset.

I started learning a lot about the outside world. A lot of guys in my company were straight from the South. A lot of what they went through, like lynchings, I had no knowledge of, except reading the *Amsterdam News* [*a black New York paper*].

I took basic training and leadership school at Dix. I was GI all the way, brass polished, shoes shined. When I wore that uniform, I wore it right, and I wore it proudly. We wanted to be known as #1. My training company commander was Captain Steven Mayo - we called him "Mayonnaise" - a World War II veteran. He was slim and light-skinned, looked like an American Indian. A hard-nosed son of a gun. He was a tough dog, but he was fair. If he took a liking to you, you were in good shape.

Captain Mayo tagged me one day. The chaplain was having a garden party, and he needed young men to escort the ladies. He told me to get two other guys just like myself. We were exempt from all duties - all the other guys were looking at me funny. But we got compliments and were invited to other things. The week when your family and girlfriends come down, the chaplain was telling my mother what a wonderful son she had.

Here's my introduction to the South - Fort Benning, Georgia. I had never been below the Mason-Dixon Line. The train went straight to Fort Benning, and I was sent to Sand Hill, which was all black. I took ranger training and jump training there.

I didn't know what grits were. I was putting milk and sugar on it. "What you doing?"

"I'm fixing my farina."

I got laughed at about that.

John French (77th Engineer Company):
We traced our family back to Jamestown in 1608, a slave owned by an Irish sea captain. I'm the oldest of 14 kids, born in Alabama in 1932 and raised in Louisville. My father was a preacher.

When I was 15 years old, about 1947, I wanted to join the Service, so I lied about my age. I went up to the recruiting office and passed the test, but I made the mistake of telling my buddy. On the bus going to Fort Knox, here comes my mother, told the sergeant, "That boy is 15 years old."

John B. Holway

The sergeant was very polite. He told me, "Get your damn black ass off this bus."

I told my mother if she would lie for me to go into the Service, I'd finish high school, college, and go on to law school. When I left home, she gave me three books - *High School Subjects Self-Taught*, *English Made Easy*, and *Latin Made Easy*. I stayed on active duty 13 years, and my mother stayed on my ass for 13 years.

I loved the Army, I really did, I loved the discipline.

My first duty station, we were getting ready for inspection, and I was helping a buddy, Lewis, get ready when the officer came through and chewed my ass: Why wasn't I on my own station?

I told him my section was ready for inspection.

"Then let's go look at it." We went around, he looked up at me, said, "Go back and help Lewis," which pissed me off, because he didn't apologize for chewing my butt. About an hour later I saw him coming back with a piece of paper in his hand. He said, "You can put your two stripes on now." That was better than a damn apology.

Clyde Jones (I Company):

I was born in 1932 in Dayton Tennessee - the Scopes "Monkey" trial. You've heard of it? All my people are white and Indians, but we growed up as "colored people."

We had four Spanish-American war veterans from Dayton. That's the real buffalo soldiers! My wife's Uncle Scott and my Uncle Louis were on San Juan Hill. My uncle told me the story: The Buffalo Soldiers took San Juan Hill. Teddy Roosevelt got all the credit, but it had already been taken by the 24th. He had a picture of himself: "You keep this picture and always remember: I was in the big war in Cuba." I've got the picture in my living room.

My grandmother had a clock, had a mantel piece to set on. It donged and donged until my mother died.

My parents were just Tennessee farmers. My two brothers were in World War II. One was in the Normandy invasion, the other was in the Air Corps.

The town had two red lights and two drug stores. A good town to be raised in. Black and white lived together back in those days. Everyone got along real good, everyone loved each other. Whatever we were doing, we'd help one another.

The senior class of our school all joined the Army. May 12, 1950 - that's my birthday. We went in the Army, because there wasn't any work, and we wanted to go to Japan. Japan is the place to be!

Seven of us - five seniors and two more - we all played football. We went to Fort Knox to basic training, and three of us went to Korea. Rod Wilkerson - we called him "Peepsight," because he had bad eyes - was in Fox Company, and Bobby Joe Bennett went to Easy Company.

Wilfred Mathews (K Company):
I was born in 1932, in Lake Charles Louisiana. My parents were just ordinary people, trying to raise six kids. My father worked at a service station. He was in World War I, in the 369th [*"Men of Bronze"*] regiment, and fought with the French. The Americans didn't want to fight with black soldiers, so the French said, "Give 'em to us." My daddy was French and spoke good French, so it didn't matter to him.

I had four sisters and one brother, I was the next to youngest. I went to Catholic school, was an altar boy. I dropped out to join the Army in 1947 when I was 15 - I lied about my age. My mother had three children in college, so I figured I'd help her, and I did. I sent my sisters and brother to school.

Jim Thompson (L Company):
I'm from Brooklyn, born and raised. Ran track - 100 and 440 - in high school and the Police Athletic League. I went into the Army in 1948 at age 16. Took jump training at Benning, then to Germany in the cavalry.

Robert Fletcher (C Company):

John B. Holway

I come from Ypsilanti Michigan, was born in 1932. Seven of us kids, three above me and three below.

My father was a member of the 93rd Division in the tail end of World War I. He served with the French, because they couldn't fight with the Americans. He got all those medals, then was told they were no good, the government doesn't recognize them, so he threw them away.

He worked in the Ford Motor Company and died in 1942, when I was ten, and I had to help my mother out. I started working, washing cars for 20 cents an hour, before they took out tax. I took out a dollar from my paycheck and gave my mother the rest. That's the way I was raised: Take care of the family.

My older brother was 82nd Airborne - there were units of the 82nd that were black. He and an officer got into a fight. He never talked about it, but it was probably in a bar over a woman. He was charged with striking an officer and took a bad conduct discharge.

My father, my uncle, and my older brother had gone into Service. I felt it was my patriotic duty to join. I said, "Hell, I'll go in too." I joined the army when I was 17, went to Japan when I was 17 and went to Korea when I was 17.

I got a surprise. I was in a long time.

When I went in the Service, I made $68 a month and sent $50 home to my mother.

I didn't know what segregation was. Until I went to Lousville Kentucky and they didn't serve me: "Oh no, colored people have to go around back." I said, "What the hell you talking about?" In school you didn't read about it.

Joe Davis (Third Battalion mess hall):
I'm supposed to be from the Sinclairs from Scotland and Ireland. Sinclair was one of the Knights Templar, and they became kings of Scotland.

I never knew my great grandmother's name. They were slaves of Wingate. My great grandmother spoke Portuguese, she could have come from Cape Verde Islands or Brazil.

My great grandfather was John F Wingate, a principal buyer of slaves from North Carolina. He had 18 children.

My grandmother and grandfather had a set of twin girls. My grandmother was working out in the tobacco field and had to have time off to go home and nurse her twins. She went to the overseer of Wingate Plantation, but he wouldn't let her go. The cabin caught on fire, and the babies burned up in there.

That's what set my grandfather off. He killed two or three of his half-brothers and had to escape.

Someone told me the Quakers or the Amish brought him to Pennsylvania. Then he had to sneak back down and get her and brought her back to Pennsylvania - Kittany, 60 miles north of Pittsburgh. There were only about three or four black families loving in the whole town.

I was born in 1933, and I had a bad time in school and couldn't get any help from the teachers. My family didn't have anything, so the Army was the best way out. My military career began in 1948 when I was 15 years old. I lied about my age.

Bob Jones (D Company):

I was born in a small town in rural Louisiana. My father was a master mechanic, owned a garage, but I decided that was no career for me, so I joined the army when I was 17.

I went to advanced ordnance training, and they sent me to Oakland California. We got training as stevedores, but we walked up and down the street picking up trash. So in September '49 I volunteered to go overseas.

Japan

1948-50

The 24th Infantry - the "Deuce-4" – was all-black with a history that went back to the Indian wars of the 1870s. In Korea it was one of three regiments assigned to the 25th Infantry Division. The other two, the 27th Wolfhounds and the 35th Cacti, were white. The 24th Regiment is often confused with the 24th Division, which was also fought in Korea. In the following pages the term "24th" will refer to the regiment.

There was little fraternizing between the Deuce-4 and its brother regiments. It had its own camp at Gifu near Mount Fuji.

Generally, occupation duty was fun for all U.S. troops, black and white. Japan was exotic, life was pleasant, the girls were pretty. The officers even lived in an old castle with a moat.

The authors of *BSWA* [*Black Soldiers, White Army*] went into detail about the high rate of venereal disease in the 24th Infantry, implying that the black soldiers were over-sexed and running wild in the brothels. The statistics seem to back this portrait up. However, all the GIs in Japan, black and white, were healthy young guys in their late teens and early 20s, and almost all dallied with the girls.

Joe Davis:

The VD problem was not exaggerated in a way. Some soldiers didn't know how to read or write. Thirty percent had venereal disease. In fact, the VD rate throughout the Army in Japan was very, very bad. But people blamed a lot of things on our one regiment.

If the Deuce-4 had a high VD rate, it points an accusing finger at their officers, who apparently did not enforce hygiene and discipline rules. When Lieutenant Bussey, a black officer, took over the 77th Engineer Company, attached to the 24th, it had the worst VD rate in Japan. His first sergeant announced, "The next guy who gets a dose of clap, I'll beat within an inch of his

70

life. Then I'll write a letter to his wife or mother." The rate fell to zero. If Bussey could do it, why couldn't every commander in the Far East?

Many black GIs, like many whites, tried to marry their Japanese sweethearts, although the Army threw road blocks in the way. Some applications were pigeon-holed for two years. Countless GIs left their lovers and children behind and never returned. The women and kids were subject to intense prejudice, especially the half-black kids. Rejected by their fathers' country and their mothers', they grew up to fill Japan's prisons and its death rows.

The VD figures reflected another major weakness of the 24th: The officers - mostly white from lieutenant to captain, and all-white from major to colonel - were considered a cut below those in the white units. An assignment to the 24th was looked on as a stigma.

Joe Davis

We were getting officers the whites didn't want – "he must have done something wrong." A lot of them didn't give a damn, then when the troops didn't do certain things, they'd blame it on the troops. But it was bad leadership. That's one thing the Army tried to keep silent for years.

The 24th was a hellhole. It was run like a prison. You couldn't go through the main gate without throwing your arms up and getting shook down like a common criminal. You had to be in bed for bed check at 11 o'clock. If you had gone to the bathroom, you had a lot of explaining to do to the CO the next morning.

They treated you like you were some kind of a stupid ape walking around. Black officers treated you even worse! You had a lot of sergeants the same goddam way.

Then again, you found some officers who were well-educated and firm and fair.

Even the officers' mess was segregated. White officers ate on one side, black officers on the other.

Bussey:
> The regiment was loaded with cowardly and inept officers who were not acceptable in white units. Some of them should not have held commissions in the Army at all.

Most wished only to get out of the regiment as fast as possible.

From General MacArthur on down, very few leaders, white or black, put emphasis on military readiness, not to mention intelligence. When North Korea attacked the South in July, 1950, MacArthur and his staff would be taken completely by surprise, as they had been at Pearl Harbor. (So much for the general who boasted that he "knew the oriental mind.")

The 24th had one outstanding claim to fame. It cut an impressive figure in the Tokyo parades in front of the Imperial Palace and MacArthur's headquarters.

Jim Thompson:
> We pulled a lot of guard duty, paraded up in Yokohama, spit and polish stuff. I enjoyed it, myself.

Donald Womack:
> Our troops weren't welcome in the 27th or 35th Regiment areas. And we weren't welcome in Yokohama or Tokyo, except for parades. We had our own band, with a special way of marching.

Richard Sanders:

George Bussey was the guidon [flag] bearer for L Company. Captain **Montgomery** would say, "'Forward, harch!' and he'd goose-step. It was very impressive.

Sergeant **Alonzo Spencer** of the 77th Engineers said his weapon was polished until it glistened. The rifles dazzled the spectators, but they were only for parades and useless to hit anything with, which became clear when the unit was rushed to Korea. Other divisions faced the same problem, and, like the Deuce-4, paid a heavy price when the war broke out.

Most of the men remembered their duty fondly.

Albert Kimber:

It was great duty. I was 18-19 years old, and it was brand new to me. I enjoyed it tremendously. I surely did.

Donald Womack:

Gifu - I loved it. Of all my years in the military, that's the only place I loved. Because it was Japan! I could talk Japanese just like I'm talking English. If I happen to be around people talking Japanese, it comes back.

I had a wife, or a sort of wife - Aiko, a school teacher from a well-to-do family. Her father was an alderman. But he didn't like me, because I was a *kokujin heitai* [*black soldier*]. The Army wouldn't let me get married either. You know theold saying, "If the Army wanted you to have a wife, they would have issued you one."

We had two kids, and the Japanese don't like mixed blood children, especially black. I got along with Aiko's mother, but her father would get on her, and her mother couldn't do anything, because in Japan the man is the boss.

Aiko would come back to our home, crying, and I refused to let her go home alone. But when we got there, her father raised hell at the top of his voice in Japanese. I got up to defend my wife. When I spoke to him in Japanese, his mouth went down to his belt buckle.

"Never come back in this house!"

She had no place to go, so I moved her into a house outside the base. We'd go to the town on the base of Mount Fuji. I'd bring *Mama San* little goodies, like eggs, and she would hide us. When the Japanese police and the American MPs would come, she'd hide me in the comforter [*futon*] chest with the comforters over me.

Bob Jones:

Mount Fuji put us in condition. But some guys on the boxing team and football teams didn't have any infantry training. They volunteered for sports so they wouldn't have to go to training.

Ellis Dean:

I took jump training in Sendai. They thought I was Puerto Rican. When they found out I was a Negro, that's when they shipped me to the 24th.

My future wife, Kazuko, was a typist in headquarters. Her father was a member of Parliament.

I was a pretty good athlete, excelled in four major sports, and I was pretty well known throughout the Eighth Army. I held the Army high jump record, 6'3 inches. I was 5'11½.

In 1949 I played baseball against the DiMaggio boys - Vince and Dom - in Yokohama and Tokyo. I talked to Lefty O'Doul, the manager of the San Francisco Seals.

"Big Boy" **Howard Williams** was all-Service heavyweight boxing champ - Army, Navy, Air Force. When **Levi Jackson** came to the regiment, Williams sparred with him and said, "This is a young dude can take over from me." Jackson did take over and became the all-Army champ.

Captain **Eldridge Carter** was a good basketball player. I was officiating a game, and I called a foul on him. He questioned me. It happened again, he questioned me again. I said, "You're out of the game."

He said, "You can't do that. I'm an officer."

"You're still out of the game."

He respected me after that, because I had guts.

One day outside the PX a white second lieutenant wouldn't salute him. Carter said, "You're not saluting me, you're saluting these tracks [*captain's bars*]."

Our colonel, **"Screaming Mike" Halloran**, saw that. That was it, man. He said, "You stand at attention as long as the captain wants you to." I had a good rapport with Colonel Halloran. But, in order to make general, he had to leave the regiment in '49.

Joe Frederick (Regimental Heavy Mortar Company):

Gifu had been a Japanese air force academy with runways and hangers. "Camp Majestic" was the actual name. It was like a little military academy.

We took our duffle bags over to the tailor shop, and a Japanese seamstress made the uniforms fit perfectly. All the members of my company were pretty proud soldiers. We had an enlisted parade every week, no officers at all.

In the mess hall we ate family style at tables. We even had a pianist; one of the cooks played during dinner hour.

I really enjoyed it, especially when you had a chance to go out to town. I didn't feel any harassment.

Bussey

Donald Womack called him "a go-getter... Stuck up for his men." Charlie was "a big-chested, *gung-ho* guy," a fellow air corps cadet said.

He was born in 1921 in the farming town of Bakersfield California.

It was a disgustingly prejudiced place at the time. Even in kindergarten I became aware that there was something wrong, that I wasn't treated like the white kids, the oriental kids, or even the Mexican kids. I was always in a fight; I was walking around with a fat lip.

Bussey's father had served in France, and his grandfather, an ex-slave, had fought in the Wilderness with Grant, on the western plains, and in Cuba. He carried three arrowheads in a pouch and one more around his neck. The old man, in his eighties, in a tattered army coat, drove a rickety buckboard wagon, and six year-old Charlie used to climb up beside him to listen to tales of the old days.

My other granddad was a Methodist minister and graduated from college back in 1887. He built churches in Bakersfield, Riverside, Pasadena, and Santa Monica. A relative founded Voorhees College in South Carolina before the turn of the century, and my uncle became the first black Supreme Court judge in California.

Prior to the Depression, my dad was a railroad mail clerk. But the Civil Service was different then, so when the Depression hit in '29, this became a white boy's job, and Dad had none.

Times were hard from then on. I'm not one of those people who talk about the good old days. The hell with them. I'd hate to go through them again. I worked in the fields from the time I was nine or ten, picking cotton, corn, all kinds of fruits. I got paid damn little, cotton went for one and a quarter cents a pound then.

When I was 17 a friend and I rode freight trains all the way to Detroit. In Ogden Utah there was a wheat harvest on, and we bucked 100-pound bales of wheat. We were there about ten days and made $30 - that was big bucks. In Nebraska we worked shucking corn for three dollars a day, room and board. So when we got to Detroit, I had 57 bucks, a king's ransom, it seemed at the time.

Then we went up the St Lawrence river and out to sea on a "rust bucket." I'd never seen the ocean before. I shoveled coal eight hours a day, the toughest way to make a living. About 400 miles west of the Azores, the ship threw a bearing, so we laid around about ten days, did some drinking, and the little money I had earned was soon spent.

We stowed away on another ship heading back to Norfolk, hopped freight trains, and hoboed our way home.

Stoking boilers is a hard way to make a living, so I finished high school and went to Los Angeles City College for two years. College cost five dollars a semester, and I had a hell of a hard time raising that five bucks.

I applied to the U.S. Army in the middle of '41. Of course I was treated with the utmost discourtesy. I was disgusted and wrote to Eleanor Roosevelt, who responded within three days and apologized for the segregated nature of things and told me there was a program for black fliers in Tuskegee. As a result, in September 1942, I had an opportunity to go to Tuskegee for flight training.

Flying was exciting; it was tremendously rewarding, and there were very fine, high-type people, some with masters' degrees. I was one of the few who didn't have a college degree, which was consistent with my age.

The town of Tuskegee itself was not a good place to be in. They had a sadistic sheriff named Pat Evans, who loved hassling black soldiers, and we got hassled at every opportunity.

A fellow cadet, Harry Shepard, called Bussey aggressive and straight-forward:

There was no hesitation about anything. And he was outspoken; he gave you his views without hesitation. A lot of people didn't like him because of that, but he and I "bought" each other, warts and all.

Another class-mate was Daniel "Chappie" James, a huge man, who went on to become America's first black four-star general. He and Bussey didn't get along, and Charlie admits that "I got slammed against the wall" a few times.

In Italy Charlie flew with the vaunted Red Tails, whose commander ordered them not to go "hunting" for enemy fighters, trying to become aces, but to stick with the bombers and protect them with their lives. Bussey bitched at the order but obeyed. He shared one victory, the first one ever by the unit. He claimed another, but he was alone in the sky and his gun camera jammed, so he had no way to prove it.

After the war Bussey went to college and joined an army reserve engineer unit. That's where he was when he went on active duty. He arrived in Japan, and a skeptical colonel said he could have the engineer company if he could build a Bailey bridge. The last candidate had failed. Charlie had a week to do it. He'd never seen one before, but he read the manual, and a week later it was finished. Bussey got the job.

Womack:

Bussey didn't like inspections. I was always in trouble. still drank a little, and one day they inspected Bussey's jeep, and his driver had a bottle of Japanese Suntory whiskey in the glove compartment. I was sitting in the back, and I took the blame for it - I wouldn't let Bussey get blamed. I lost my stripe, but I got it back later.

The commanding officer, Hollerin' Mike Halloran; called colored troops "my black children." But we couldn't get close to most of the officers, because they got rotated out, so when you got in combat, you didn't even know them.

One time we were on maneuvers on Mount Fuji, and an earthquake hit. The daggone ground broke open, big enough to hold a deuce and a half [2½-ton] truck, like a Tarzan movie, and I just knew it would swallow me. Or a typhoon. We would tie the tents to a deuce-and-a-half, and it rained so hard, the truck was laying on the tent!

LaVaughn Fields:

I'm the corporal who was doing the dance in Charles Bussey's book, *Firefight at Yech'on.* When Lieutenant Bussey took over the company, anyone caught fighting would be court-martialed. **John Van Ness** was hung over from the night before, and I said, "I got a couple of bottles of wine, but don't kill it all." He took a big drink, and I said, "What the hell you doing?" and we got in an argument.

When Bussey's jeep came up, someone said, "Here comes the Old Man!" so I started hugging Van Ness in a sort of a dance step. [*According to Bussey, they tumbled out of a second floor window.*]

Bussey said, "What the hell are you guys doing?"

I said, "I'm showing him a new dance step, we're going to the cabaret tonight." He didn't believe it, but he told me later I was such a good liar, he let it go.

John French (Engineers):

Japan was a different culture, and I really enjoyed it. I wasn't just downtown looking for girls, I was hitting the books. The guys used to laugh and joke about me and the books.

Ralph Hubbard:

I got lost in Camp Drake, the "Repl Depot" [*for replacements*]. A sergeant told me to go into the supply room and get a mattress and told me what billet I was in. That's the last anyone said anything to me. No one sent me anywhere. Almost three months, no work details, no nothing. But I got paid; so someone must have known I was there.

Tokyo was a little like Mississippi or Alabama to me, with a lot of white soldiers. I stayed the hell away from them.

Unlike a lot of guys in Japan, I went places and talked to people. I went to the Tokyo opera [*kabuki*] house and saw my first Japanese opera. A young lady from Finland explained to me what it was about. I didn't understand it, but I liked it - the color, the flamboyance. I wanted to soak up the flavor.

I met a guy, Dobie Hildenbrand, who had been there awhile. He used to "borrow" a jeep - I guess the statute of limitations has run out now - and go all over the place. He took me around. We went up to Sendai [*about 300 miles north*], where the Japanese marines trained. I watched their training, and I was impressed! It was like they were wearing cardboard collars.

One day I'm walking near the Dai-Ichi Building in Tokyo [*MacArthur's headquarters*], where he had his parades, and I'm looking around like I'm at Coney Island. A black master sergeant came up, asked my name. "Where are you assigned?

I told him Camp Drake.

"No, young man, where are you *assigned*?"

"Camp Drake."

"How long you been here?"

I told him. "No one told me otherwise."

"Come with me." We went into the building, into the records room. "Young man, you're AWOL."

"Excuse me?"

"They got you down as AWOL, you're supposed to be in the 24th."

"No one told me anything."

The Deuce-4 was based in Gifu, so he drove me in a jeep down to Gifu. The day we got there, the band was playing a new rendition of "St. Louis Woman" by W.C. Handy. It was so fantastic, I just got goose bumps.

The First Sergeant, **Fowlkes**, said, "Young man, where have you been?"

I told him - I was scared as hell I'm in trouble.

He said, "How AWOL can you be if you got paid?"

I was in M company, heavy weapons - "Mighty Mike." The company commander was Captain **Voight** from Louisiana, a railroad man. I had to sit there and dutifully listen all about the railroad, for god's sake, as if I cared.

I was in the 75 recoilless rifle or the .50-calibre machine gun platoons. The .50 was the biggest machine gun. The guys in the infantry companies didn't know anything about the 75 or the 81-mm mortar. We boned up on all of that, including the "squirt gun," or flame-thrower.

I spent seven months in Japan. In the barracks and out of the houses of ill repute - I didn't know what the hell they were. My brothers had taught me about baseball and basketball but not about that. Some of the younger guys drank like hell in the bars. My god! You were careful not to stand near open flames with their breaths.

Richard Sanders:

They decided I was going into M Company with the machine gun platoon.

I went to Japanese language class in the evening. After you would finish there, you'd go into town and try your hand at Japanese. I could speak it so well, I didn't remember English. Three or four years ago I was in Hawaii speaking Japanese. I always wanted to take my wife back to Japan for two or three more years and learn the language better.

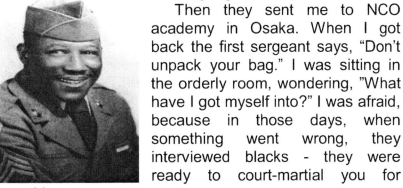

Then they sent me to NCO academy in Osaka. When I got back the first sergeant says, "Don't unpack your bag." I was sitting in the orderly room, wondering, "What have I got myself into?" I was afraid, because in those days, when something went wrong, they interviewed blacks - they were ready to court-martial you for anything.

The company C.O. said, "Let's go over to battalion." Battalion said, "OK, we gotta go up to regiment." I was trying to figure out, "What's wrong?"

The regimental commander, Colonel Halloran, an old fellow in his 60s, was hollering. He said, "We're getting this new weapon called the 75-mm recoilless rifle [*an anti-tank weapon*], and we're going to send you and a major to school in Yokohama. You come back and teach the rest of the regiment." They made me platoon sergeant of the 75-recoilless platoon.

Jim Thompson's cousin, **William Thompson**, was also in M Company. He grew up as a fatherless kid, who was found shivering on a park bench in Harlem. The Reverend Harry Eva, founder of the Home for Homeless Boys, took the 15-year old to the home for a hot bath and hot supper. The boy had "unusual character." Eva said. "He was helpful, cheerful, and willing." He also had a beautiful singing voice and became a soloist in the choir, as well as head worker in Sunday school.

Willie wanted to join the Army, but, Eva worried:

He he was so small, I really didn't expect the Army to take him. But when he came back in his new uniform, he was so proud, and I told him he'd make a good soldier.

In Korea Joe Davis knew the old street-tough youth.

Thompson and I were in the Pioneer Platoon before I got transferred to the kitchen. I used to sleep in the cot next to him. He was a pretty nice guy, a good sort for a guy, didn't steal or anything, didn't drink or smoke.

But he did fight. He had that temper. He was a rowdy guy if anybody messed with him, just like when he was in New York. He was transferred from company to company, because he was always fighting. He went from headquarters company to M company for fighting in a crap game.

Jim Thompson:

I didn't know him until I got to Gifu. He was two years older than me; I was 18, he was about 20. My mother wrote and told me I had a cousin in Gifu in K Company, and we palled around together.

Nathaniel Nicholson (Battery B, 159 FA):

They called me "Milk Man." (Do you really want to hear that story?)

I was on guard duty, and they were supposed to save me some chow, but when I got off, they said they had no more, so I had to walk another two hours to the mess hall with nothing to eat. I was in front of the mess hall and put my gun down, went in the window and got me a quart of milk.

When I climbed back out, the officer of the day was waiting for me with my rifle in his hand. "Where were you? The enemy could have taken this away from you." He put me under arrest.

They gave me a court martial the next day and fined me the cost of a quart of milk, about $20, including the cost of transportation from the States.

Everyone laughed at me and called me "Milk Man." When I got separated from the Service, I had to pay that $20.

My best friend, **James Burnett** (on the left), was in the bed across from me, and his mother used to send him a package every month with rum cake and other things. He would give me everything I wanted except the rum cake.

Burnett:

I was from New York, and my mother was pretty concerned when I went to Fort Bragg. She was scared to death. She said, "Oh, Lord, you're gonna be killed." But I never had a problem with prejudice. Never did. Get off the train, take a bus to go to camp. That was it. I never went into town. I couldn't tell you what was around the corner from the train station. Never had a prejudice situation, because I never put myself in the way of it. I never wanted to go gallivanting. I was never a bar person, hanging out. Go straight home. I had a good life. I didn't know what suffering was. I went along with the program.

In Japan Nick and I buddied up together, I guess because we were both from the Northeast. Everyone else was from Louisiana, Texas. I had to adjust to their speech: "What language is that?" Nick would just say, 'I can understand them." He learned from listening to everyone.

Nick was a very friendly guy. He'd talk to a door knob! He knew everyone and where everyone was. He would disappear and come back, disappear and come back. That's why he was always in trouble, because he wasn't where he was supposed to be. He was in another barracks, talking to someone. Our captain would ask me, "Burnett, where's Nicholson?"

I'd make up a story: "Oh, he's in the motor pool."

He'd say, "Go get him and bring him here."

"I'll take care of it; he'll be ready, sir."

Have you ever read the comic strip, "Peck's Bad Boy?" Nick was like that, always into some little bit of mischief.

Nicholson:

Burnett saved my life. I had just learned how to drive, and I slipped a jeep out unauthorized to go to Mt Fuji, just to sightsee. When I tried to turn, the jeep fell off the road. I couldn't get it out. On Mount Fuji there were little balls of lava, just like sand, and the more you tried to pull the jeep out, the more the lava just pulled it down. I missed three meals. They could have court-martialed me and given me 20 years.

When Burnett found me, I was on my bunk, all nervous and exhausted. "Nick, where's the jeep?"

I mumbled.

He said, "Come on, let's go!"

"I'm tired."

He picked me up, carried me to his weapons carrier [*similar to a pick-up*], and I pointed the way. He hooked a chain onto my jeep and pulled it on out, and we went back to camp. I jumped in my bed. He said, "No, you're not. You're going down to the motor pool and clean that jeep and get all the mud off. The lieutenant is going to court-martial you if you don't clean it up. Clean that jeep up, of you'll be in real trouble."

Burnett saved me. There wouldn't be any more story if it weren't for that guy.

That was Easter Sunday 1950.

Memorial Day. I was on guard duty, supposed to be at the guardhouse, but I was at the barracks instead, playing volleyball. Sergeant **Alonzo Roberts** came along, said, "You're supposed to be at the guardhouse." He sent me to the barracks, but I hit the door and went back and played volleyball.

He came back, said, "Didn't I tell you to report to the barracks?"

"I *did* go to the barracks!"

He hit me on the lip with a riding crop he always carried.

Colonel Halloran heard about it and found my lips had swollen up and wanted me to have Sergeant Roberts court-martialed.

I said, "No. He has 20 more years to stay in the Army to retire, I have three."

Ellis Dean:

I had orders to go to the States in '50, but they had a big track meet in Tokyo. General **Walton Walker,** the CO of the Eighth Army, asked General **[*William*] Kean,** the CO. of the 25th Division, to try to get me to stay and represent the Eighth Army in the meet. I had orders cut to leave the 18th of June, but they said they'd cut new orders to leave after the track meet was over. I said, "OK, I'll get another trophy to take home with me." I was that cocky.

Burnett:

Four or five of us hung out together. We'd go to Nara, the nearest town. I'd say, "Bring Nick with us." He'd take our wallets so we wouldn't lose them. Next morning he'd say, "Here's your wallet... Here's your wallet."

June 24. Nicholson:

Saturday night we went to town drinking and drinking. I don't drink, but I paid all their bills and put them in a rickshaw and brought them back home so they wouldn't be AWOL.

War

June 25.

Nicholson:

Sunday morning at ten a.m., I was outside the theater, which was also the church, and all the drinkers were in there singing. Something came to my mind, and the Spirit of the Lord said, "If those boys can drink and go to church, why can't you?" So I went in. They gave me a program, and on it was the 23rd Psalm.

That was ten o'clock. At two o'clock the Korean War started.

A few days later we got marching orders to Korea. We put all our personal belongings in a footlocker, to hold until we came back. I didn't see it for a year.

All the miraculous things that happened to me happened after that.

Sanders:

The siren went off. Everyone was supposed to come back on base, and they locked the gate.

"What's going on?"

"The North Koreans just invaded South Korea, and you're going."

Oh God, and I thought I'd just stay in Japan three years and I'd be going home!

"You can leave all your packs here. Come back and pick them up when we get back to Japan." We thought we'd be two-three weeks, then back to Japan. I never did see those bags again.

Meanwhile, in the stadium in Tokyo, Dean remembered:

Over the loudspeaker, it said, "Attention, all military personnel! Attention all military personnel! The track meet is cancelled as of now. The track meet is cancelled as of now! Report to your respective units immediately."

We didn't know what the hell Korea was.

I went to the Yokohama Embarkation office, and they said all orders to the States are canceled; they couldn't do anything about mine, the Division would have to do it. I said, "Well, I'll just go back and get new orders."

Division told me they couldn't do anything, go back to the 24th. Nobody was there. The adjutant said, "There's nothing we can do. Report to Head and Head [*headquarters*] Company."

The first thing my first sergeant said was, "Dean, since you can throw footballs and baseballs, I want to see how far you can throw those grenades."

Albert Kimber (I Company):

I had 14 days remaining on a three-year tour when the war broke out. Instead of coming back to the States, my whole outfit was committed to Korea.

Wilfred Mathews, (K Company):

I was scheduled to be on the next ship to come home when the war started, and they gave us an extra year of duty.

There were two groups ahead of me. The first group all went back to the States. The second group got turned around halfway in the ocean and were sent back to Japan. When I saw those guys come back, I said, "Man, if I'd gotten that close, I'd jump off the ship and swim the rest of the way." We made a joke of it.

Robert Fletcher got to Japan about ten to 15 days before the war broke out. "Where the hell is Korea?" he asked.

Jim Thompson:

When we got orders to Korea, I remember my cousin came to my company and said, "Don't worry, I'll take care of you." (I wasn't worried, because I didn't know what the hell

87

was going on.) That's the last time I saw him.

Davis:
    They put us on trains. All the Japanese girls came out with babies and everything else and waved us goodbye.

Dean:
    A lot of guys didn't want to get on that train. Japanese girls laid on the railroad tracks, and the MPs wouldn't allow us to get near them. The Japanese security had to get them off.

Womack:
    Aiko came on the train in one of my uniforms that she had cut down to fit her. They called me and told me she couldn't go with me.

A few hours later Engineer Lieutenant **William "Benny" Benefield's** wife and two children arrived from the States. But the train was already halfway to the port.

Nicholson:
    All my artillery training came on the train to Korea. Sergeant Roberts became my tutor and told me all I needed to know about being an F.O. [*forward observer*]: "You're the eyes of the artillery. You can't see your target if the enemy is shooting at you, so keep your head down until the shooting stops." Had I pressed charges, he would not have been on the train to teach me.

Some of the battalions were sent to Sasebo port opposite Korea. The third battalion was sent to nearby Moji.

Davis:
    At Moji they had us in a warehouse. There were no guards, no fences. They issued us live ammunition, and the guys ran wild, shooting up the town. There were a few rapes.

Some of the cooks and I stayed in that little warehouse where we were, with the mess equipment.

I went to town and got some ice cream and two bottles of beer for one of the guys. A bunch of soldiers were running crazy, but no one bothered me. I didn't even have a weapon. I looked around, got the beer, and ate my ice cream on the way back.

[*Was anyone killed?*]

I really don't know. I hope not.

I came back and went to sleep. They were sending patrols into town to round up the soldiers. As soon as they got everyone rounded up at two o'clock, they woke me up and put us on a Japanese boat to Pusan. They said, "You want to shoot, we'll send you to a place where you can shoot!"

The Army kept that damn thing a secret and got us the hell out of there.

Albert Kimber recalled, "We left on a flat-top fishing boat. It was raining, and we slept on top all the way."

'But there wasn't much sleeping," Dean said. "Everything we saw on the ocean we thought was a submarine."

III.

Death in the Furnace

Deuce-4 Hits the Ground

July 13. The 25th Division was the second one to arrive in Korea. The 24th Division had arrived a week earlier. Out of shape and under-trained, it was already being badly mauled.

Wilfred Mathews (K company):

By the time we got there, the 24th Division was wiped out. Just one division wasn't enough to stop those people, Then *we* caught holy hell. They wiped our ass up too before anyone else came over.

Albert Kimber (K Company):

We had to wade in and hold our weapons above our heads. From there on it was pure hell.

Sergeant **Tom Johnson** from New Orleans came ashor with the `59th Artillery Battalion. He was eligible for discharge in a couple of days, and his commanding officer asked if he wanted to go home or stay and fight. 'I'll stay and fight," a said.

Bussey: "When we got to Korea, the only maps we had were the back page of Stars and Stripes." And no trains were moving – the engineers were on strike. Luckily, one of his men had driven a train before.

I was anxious to get into it, so I said, "There's a marshalling yard over there; get me a train. I want an engine, 12 flat cars, five or six passenger cars, a kitchen, and everything else we need, and I want it here by noon!"

Colonel **Horton White**, the new regimental C.O., warned him, "You're going to jail."

"We're here to fight a war," Bussey retorted. "We can't fight it unless we get there."

Kimber:

The only duty Colonel White had was with MacArthur's "whaling expedition" in Japan, but no experience in combat.

By 12 a train chugged onto the siding. Bussey said the regimental executive officer [*second in command*], Lieutenant Colonel **James Bennett**, unrolled his bedroll, smoothed it out, and lay down: "Oh, my heart!" While the whole company watched, a medic was called,` and the colonel was carried away and evacuated to Japan. Then the whistle blew, and "we took off for Kumchon."

Eventually the Korean engineers returned to their cabs.

Joe Davis (3d Battalion):
We got on our train in Pusan - the windows were all shot out from when the 24th Division got shot up, just like you took a machine gun and shot them as the train went by, and blood on the floor.

Ralph Hubbard (M Company):
We took cattle trains that had slats across the sides. We nailed canvas on it and we huddled in there, all jammed up. "Where the hell are we going?"

Jim Thompson (L Company):
Our engine was all shot up, and we had to get out and push it over the mountain. The whole battalion got on the side and pushed.

Albert Kimber (I Company):
We were totally unprepared. All the white outfits had brand-new everything. We had the same weapons we had been training with, playing soldier in Japan. Some of the guns exploded. When we tried to ie them. But we kept them for the first ten months. We tried to salvage weapons and parts to keep going.

We were short of everything. I was a [*.30 calibre*] light machine gunner, and I remember going to Korea armed with a .50-calibre [*heavy*] machine gun, because the .30 didn't have any decent spare parts, and they couldn't keep us supplied with ammunition.

We got to the top of one hill, and the first thing is dig in and get ready for a counterattack. You could see them coming up right on top of us. But we weren't in a position to hold, because we didn't have any ammunition. We literally picked up rocks and threw them.

They accused us of running. It didn't make sense to run. Where would you run to?

Timmons Jones (E Company):

We weren't treated like a fighting unit. We had an insufficient diet, and we didn't have proper clothes. The white troops would get showers periodically. There were no showers for us; we had to wash in rivers. We had C-rations from World War II, and weapons that were no good, and old ammunition.

Richard Sanders:

We had been given four .75s in Japan, but we had to cannibalize two of them to make the other two work.

LaVaughn Fields:

We had a lot of older equipment from the Second World War. Our old bazookas wouldn't penetrate the Russian T-34 tanks; we had to aim at their tracks. But if you missed, you were in deep yogurt, because he'd turn his guns in your direction.

When we got the larger 3.5-inch bazookas, that's when we started knocking the tanks out.

Lloyd Collins:

We were the only full regiment that went to Korea. The rest of the divisions were all down to six-man squads. We had 12 men. So the load fell on our backs. We were the backbone.

They gave us all new officers. One was Lieutenant **Kirkson**, our platoon leader. At a schoolyard somewhere we were sitting down and suddenly got under fire. That was the last I saw of him.

Joe Frederick of the regimental heavy mortar company took one look at Korea and decided:

This is a place I had no business being in. I made a conscious effort to forget everything about Korea.

And he did.

Ellis Dean (Regimental headquarters):

We boarded a shot-up train to Taegu and assembled in a schoolyard. That's when we started fighting. We weren't dug in, and mortars started coming in, and when those mortars popped, it was a fearful thing. We didn't know *where* to go. We scrambled. Guys were trying to hide. I did it myself - I was scared as hell! I hid behind a jeep, which was probably stupid. That was my baptism to battle as a young dude.

The battalion commander, Major **[*Eugene*] Carson**, was standing up like Patton under the mortar fire. He shouted, "Stop running! Stop running! It's only a few mortars. Keep going! Keep going!"

You had some damn good officers and some bad officers. There were a lot of beautiful Caucasian officers, and the men respected them. But there were a lot of bad ones too. Once the men have confidence in their officers, they'll follow them.

Fortunately, I was in headquarters under the guidance of Curtis Pugh. In combat he was a warrior.

Some days later I was sent to A Company. The company commander called Headquarters and asked, "What are you doing, sending Dean to a rifle company? He doesn't know anything about rifles." But they put me the first platoon with Corporal **Herb Wanca**, who taught me how to fire the 81 mortar. That's when I became a soldier.

Jim Thompson second from left

Richard Sanders (M Company):

From Pusan, we loaded up on trucks, and away we went about 50 or 75 miles north. We had no idea where we were.

We went off looking for the North Koreans, and we didn't even know what the hell they looked like. We did patrols up and down the road in a ¾-ton truck [*like a modern pick-up*], supporting the third battalion, looking for targets of opportunity.

We were a lot of young people, our first time out. Anything we thought moved, we'd shoot. If we didn't see anybody, we'd still shoot at it. We killed a lot of trees.

After we'd been there two or three months, we weren't so trigger-happy, you don't want anyone to know where your position is.

Curtis Bolton (C Company):

I was a Pfc. **Willie Williams** was the first guy got killed in our company. It was an ambush. Someone said, "See those tanks? How many rounds do you have left? Open up with two rounds, see if you can hit that tank." We saw smoke. We used everything we had in our arsenal and put it up on that hill.

John B. Holway

Somebody said, "Sir, we can't hold this hill." We were all waiting anxiously. The Exec Officer [*second in command*] said, "Let's withdraw, let's withdraw!" It was like a stampede. We scrambled for cover and ran into dead Koreans. When we held up and tried to re-group, my company had 32 men left and two officers.

Lionel West (Battery A, 159th Artillery):
I went to Korea as a corporal, so I was one of the lowest-ranking NCO's in charge of a 105-gun section. When the infantry can't see, like a rainy, foggy night, that's when the artillery fires; we may fire all night.
Captain **LaVon Smith** was a very good man. You have to be a slave driver.

Timmons Jones (E Company):
We didn't have a platoon leader, and I was a sergeant first class, so they gave me the platoon, and I remained with it the entire time I was in Korea. Sergeant **Millidge Blocks** and **Hubert Richards** were my assistants.

Curtis Womack:
We had that "Let's go get 'em" attitude, and we went. The infantry would use us to back up patrols. A lot of the firefights the 24th had, we were part of them.

Ernest Collier:
I was considered an old soldier among those kids.
My first chance to see the enemy was around Taegu. The North Koreans stayed on high ground, and when we'd cut across the valleys to get to them, they got behind us, and we had to fall back.
I was wounded three times.
The first time, they got behind us - who could tell who was who? I made it back to the hospital for about three weeks. They patched it up. As long as they don't hit a bone, you were OK. Didn't bother me too much. A couple days off, and back up to the front.

The second time they hit us one night. They wore those damn tennis shoes, you couldn't hear them. That's when I got hit in the shoulder with a damn burp gun. I patched that up myself. Flesh wounds heal really fast. I got a guy to dress it and just kept going.

Ralph Hubbard:

My eyes were wide open, like a little kid. I didn't know anything, nor did anybody else.

Was I scared? I got scared the day I got there and never got over it until I got home. How many miles away from home were we? I'm here with people shooting at me, and I'm shooting at people. It's happening, it's not a game. I started seeing bodies - heads off, things like that. Then I started seeing guys that I knew, and that really did it.

Right after I got there, we were in reserve in Taegu. We were looking at a North Korean burp gun. It was a clumsy-looking thing, like something you made in your back yard from old parts of vehicles. The barrel was misshapen-looking. It had a square-looking middle part, where the shells went in. The side had a flap. If you lift it up, it flips open and you can clean inside the trigger housing, which also allows the hammer to slam forward. But those guns were very unsteady - touchy. If you hit the plate on the side, the gun went off.

Everybody was looking at it. I did too with a guy named **Waters**. We called him "Mezoo," which means "water" in Japanese. A man named **Emery** was holding it, trying to show how to open the plate. **Teddy Burns** said, "Oh, give me that," and tried to reach for it. It went *Brrrip! Brrrip!* and cut Mezoo in half.

I was about ten feet away. The look on Mezoo's face! It was surreal looking, like slow motion. Mezoo looked down at his mid-section, looked up at the guy, and looked back down, said, "Oh my God." All this was a split-second.

Emery turned white. He stood frozen. His bowels let go in his pants. He was crying. Mezoo was his best friend. He just flipped out. He was no good to anyone after that; we shipped him home.

It traumatized me too - a guy I knew so well. I didn't go to sleep for a couple of days after that.

Robert Fletcher (C company):

Until we got reinforcements, we were fighting with about half our full strength.

My platoon sergeant was **Jerry Morgan**, one of the nicest persons I ever met. About 200 pounds, he was also in World War II and Vietnam and taught me how to fight, because I didn't have any advanced combat training.

He was always checking on me to see how I was doing. Until the day he died in 2006.

In our first ambush, up above Taegu, we were in trucks and got hit extremely hard by mortar fire. The North Koreans were very good with mortars. They practiced so long, they didn't need four or five rounds to find the range. They'd take that little hand crank and spin it. The first round was right on.

They'd hit the first truck and the last truck, then started picking the others off.

A lot of us went into the rice paddies, and they opened up with burp guns. It was very effective. I'll be honest: The North Koreans were very good fighters.

But we had better weapons, and that equalized it. The North Korean burp guns couldn't reach us. But our machine gun reached out, you didn't have to be right up on them. Our M-1 rifle would reach two miles and go through five railroad ties, but you had to have the right elevation, windage, and pray for a lot of luck.

I was very lucky. Within the first two or three weeks, I had bullets go through my jacket, but I never was hit. I felt it sting my skin - take my sweater off, see a little bruise mark: "Damn, that was close." That's all you said and kept going.

The second time we got hit was below Taegu. Machine-gun fire.

July to September 15 it was constant fighting every single day.

Squad leaders got killed so fast, you really didn't want to know their names. I don't remember who my first company commander was. The last one was Captain **Bemus Stanley**, a wonderful man, considerate of everyone, not only thinking about himself. He was a regular army master sergeant, but we needed a company commander, and they gave him a battlefield commission.

The Koreans always fired at the officers first. They didn't know that in the American army, if the officers are gone, the sergeants take over, if the sergeants are gone, the corporals and privates take over. Later, in POW camp, they asked us, "How do you fight without officers?"

We'd say, "We don't know, we just take orders and fight." We didn't tell them our secret.

We never left wounded. We went back, and the North Koreans had taken their testicles out, put them in their mouths, and shot them in the back of the head.

That's why you didn't remember guys' names. Sometimes I can talk about it, some days, I can't.

One of the first skirmishes was reported by the black reporter, Jimmy Hicks of the *Baltimore Afro*-American (hereafter referred to as BAA):

SFC **Roy Johnson** of Augusta was driving an ambulance jeep back to the aid station in Taejon when he ran into three tanks.

I stopped my jeep about 50 feet away, when all of a sudden one opened fire, hitting me and another GI. I wasn't armed, because medics don't carry weapons [*under the Geneva Convention*], so the best thing I could do was escape, I started crawling and saw a Korean tank-man approach with his pistol drawn. This is was when I played dead. I didn't know yet that my hand had been shot off.

After about ten minutes, which seemed like hours, I peeked to see if he had gone. But I shouldn't have. He looked straight into my eyes and without saying a word fired three shots into my body. He missed the vital parts – as you can tell, since I'm here to tell the story.

This is when I *really* played dead. About 20 minutes, it must have been. He kicked me to see if I was still alive. Then another jeep ran into the path of the tanks, and they shifted their attention to him. This was my chance to escape.

I was in a lot of pain. To keep from bleeding to death, I used my good hand to take the torn sleeve and make a kind of tourniquet. I gave myself a jab of morphine and crawled to the other jeep and managed to drive away, and another GI got me to the medical station.

Another of the wounded was Joe Louis' cousin, Pfc **Robert Barrow**, Far East Command bantam weight champ.

According to BAA, **Howard Jackson** leaped aboard a loaded ammunition truck with a .50-calibre machine gun and for four hours rained fire into the enemy. Bullets pierced his truck's ammunition load, which could have caused an explosion, but he continued his withering fire until the Reds fled.

Captain **Curtis Walton**, battery commander:
I saw bullets ricochet off his gun mount. That took plenty of nerve in my book.

Jackson was recommended for a Silver Star.
July 17. Nathaniel Nicholson (159 Field Artillery Battalion):
I stayed on the front line ten months. I was assigned to C Battery most of the time. [*A battery was the artillery equivalent of an infantry company.*] I had more front-line duty than anyone else in the battery.

Each battalion had its own FO. (forward observer). I was driving our FO They'd pull one off, and another lieutenant would become forward observer for three weeks, then they'd switch them around again. But all the rest I got was a day and a half.

At 19 I was fearless. I had to be. There was no other way to handle combat except to face it head-on.

So many miraculous things happened to me. C Battery got into a lot of trouble, but I was usually someplace else. To this day I marvel at the opportunities the enemy had to kill me but could not or did not. There were maybe 20 incidents when my life was saved. I'll mention as many as I can remember. All the miracles took place after going to church the day before the invasion.

I also got busted three times.

The first was at Yongdok. I was the jeep driver for the forward observer, and I told them my transmission was leaking and I wanted some oil sent up to the front line. A tank was stuck up there with its tracks off, and we were trying to get it free. The infantry wanted some artillery, and when the tank got free, the F.O. said, "Let's go!" My jeep got stuck in second gear. No oil. Nothing but steel in there.

They said I was responsible. I got busted from private to recruit. I was ordered not to drive any more and was banished to the mess tent.

Burnett:

They put him on KP. That's the last thing you want to do to punish Nick, because he loved the kitchen. And I'd get a little extra serving on my tray.

Wilfred Mathews:

I didn't know where I was half the time. We were taking a town, and the fighting got furious. I was a machine gunner, and they didn't last too long. I got hit by artillery in my left chest and had three pieces of shrapnel in my kidney.

My experience with the hospitals wasn't too good. I went through several aid stations and two hospitals, and they wouldn't even touch me. I didn't get touched until I got to Pusan, where they put me on the ship to Japan. It took from the 19th of July to the first of August before they operated.

I stayed in the hospital a little more than a month. I was the only black in the ward. A colonel came by and gave everyone a Purple Heart but me. He just passed me by. It's on my record, but I've never been presented one.

Meanwhile, not far away, the 24th Division was being cut to pieces. Its commanding general, **William Dean** [*not to be confused with General William Kean of the 25th Division*] was separated from his troops. He was wandering, lost, dazed, and alone, when the North Koreans captured him. It was perhaps the most humiliating day in the history of the U.S. Army since Pearl Harbor.

Curtis Womack (Engineers):

We were sent to find out what happened to the 24th Division. Took a platoon to where they were supposed to be. We found them in a box canyon, in their sleeping bags. The leadership didn't take the high ground, and the Koreans surrounded them and jumped down on them.

LaVaughn Fields:

We rescued a half-track. Bussey did that. We went in the 27th Wolfhound Regiment area, reconnoitering, and ran into some white soldiers who said they had to give up their half-track. The North Koreans had snuck up on them and overwhelmed them. We had BARs [*Browning Automatic Rifles, a lighter version of the machine gun*] and put fire on the enemy. We ran them off, and the white soldiers [*from the 27th*] took the half-track back.

The Army desperately needed a victory.

Yech'on

July 20. The 24th Division commander, General William Dean, was caught by the North Koreans, wandering on foot, looking for his troops. The third battalion was sent to take the cross-roads town of Yech'on. What followed was the first real fight of the war for the Deuce-4 and one of the most controversial, revolving around the fighting engineer commander, Charles Bussey.

John French (77th Engineers):

Lieutenant Bussey was a straightforward, cocky son of a bitch. I was 18, he was 28; to me he was The Old Man. When we got into combat, we found out Bussey wasn't scared either.

Joe Davis:

When we got there, Yech'on was all lit up like a Christmas tree [*from the artillery*]. We got our asses run out of there.

Donald Womack (77th Engineers):

One night we were in a weapons carrier on patrol. We turned the damn corner, and there this damn Russian tank was! Oh my goodness! We had to back the hell out of there. We were in that village during the day, but it wasn't there then. That night we go back in the village - *whew*! I needed to change my underwear.

The job of taking Yech'on back fell to L Company under Lieutenant **Bradley Biggs**, the Army's, and possibly the world's, first black airborne officer, with over 360 jumps. A squad of engineers was in support. The third platoon under Lieutenant (later brigadier general) **Oliver Dillard** (who also became a general) went to the left, while Biggs headed straight for the town. Biggs said he was about it to cross a rice paddy and a small canal when he came under intense mortar fire.

One of the Engineers, LaVaughn Fields, was behind him with an infantry squad on a hill at the edge of the paddy:

There was no firing when we went into position, and when we assaulted our hill, at first there was very little resistance. My squad was on the left flank of the platoon and two infantry squads were to my right.

There was a little valley, with many rice paddies and an orchard out front. Lieutenant Biggs was on the right flank, straight out in front of us, not in view of me.

Meanwhile, Bussey had jumped in a jeep to find his platoon. Womak saw him "riding around with his machine gun."

Bussey:

It was just my driver and me, I had no idea the country was as hostile as it was, or I wouldn't have been out there by myself.

There was a big firefight going on. I climbed a hill, and below me was a series of rice paddies which ran the length of a small valley. I saw a column of about two to three hundred men three-quarters of a mile away, coming out of an *arroyo*, dressed in white like Korean farmers. I could have driven away, but if they cut the road, there would be no getting out for our troops.

Yech'on from Bussey's Hill, 2009

I pressed into service three stragglers. I put two men on a .30-caliber water-cooled machine gun. I had an air-cooled .50-caliber, and I got one man to feed me ammunition. I let the column move in close enough so they wouldn't be able to back out, and put a burst over their heads. They immediately took cover, someone blew a whistle, and things started happening! They started to move toward my hill.

Fields:

There was no firing, to my knowledge, before Bussey arrived. Then we heard firing over on the left but didn't know who it was. We had to expose ourselves to look over there, and I could see Bussey and his jeep driver.

The enemy were on the other side of the orchard to the left, in white, posing as farmers - the North Koreans were noted for doing that at that time. Bussey laid a machine gun blast over their heads, and they ducked for cover. Then they attacked.

I yelled, "Heh, that's the Old Man! He's raising hell over there with his .50 calibre." All the fellows in my squad saw him. I saw about 15 of the enemy drop from his fire. If Bussey hadn't taken them under fire, they would have flanked our position. Bussey's the one who drew the mortar fire on my position, because they had to put him out of action.

Bussey:

I was scared shitless, absolutely shitless! I had no business facing that many people. I kept thinking, "God damn it! Why didn't you mind your own business!" I didn't think I was going to get out of that thing. But now that I was engaged, I didn't have any alternative. There was no place to run to and nothing to do except fight. Air combat was sort of a game. Ground combat is not a game - it is dead serious action on the killing floor.

I had a tremendous advantage by being up on a hill, and I had fairly good cover, while they were down in a rice paddy with almost no protection. But they had a mortar, and it put several bursts on us. I got hit early with a fragment in my wrist and another in my cheek. They bled a little, but a small wound was not important at that time.

The mortar also killed one of my kids on the .30 and wounded the other. My big gun got hot and stopped firing. That's when I was in real trouble. I didn't think the .30 could do the job, but there was no other way.

Crouching, he ran to the .30 and resumed peppering the enemy.

Fields:

When the mortar fire came in, of course I ducked. The fire ran Love Company out. One platoon, or what was left of it, began to withdraw through our area and ran through the fire. As Biggs passed through our position, he told us, "Get the hell out of here!"

We took off for the MSR [*Main Supply Route*] behind us and over the crest of a hill.

Womack:

Lieutenant **[*Chef*] Lenon** asked for volunteers to find out where the mortars were coming from. Six or seven volunteered. We found them! We were in the orchard where the North Korean mortars were, so close you could hear the "whoomp" when the shells came out of the tubes.

They were firing at point-blank range, straight up and straight down. And they were very, very good. They could "walk" the mortars right down your throat. They didn't drop three rounds when two could hit you. [*American doctrine was to fire one long, one short; the third one should be on the target.*] The North Koreans only needed two. If the first one missed you, you better move, because the next one got you.

A guy from L Company got hit, and it blew him up. LaVaughn and I were trying to help him. We saw **Gamble**, a medic, and called him to come over. As he was running over to help us, they dropped a mortar round right in front of him and tore him in half.

Then I got hit in the face by a mortar round. [*In the movies the hero clutches his shoulder, sways, slowly sinks to his knees, and pitches forward. That's not how it is in real life.*] It picked me up like the heat flying out of a stove and sent me sailing across the rice paddy and dropped me about eight feet away.

I had fragments in my leg and my side, and one in my eye. It went in from the side of my head and came out through my eye ball. I couldn't see! They took me to the aid station. The shrapnel was in my retina. They could see the front of it sticking out, and they tried to pull it out, but they were tearing my retina, and I went into shock.

They realized they didn't have the right equipment, so they sent me to an airfield to go to Japan. We hit an air pocket, and the plane went down. Scared the shit out of me, and I got my sight back.

At the hospital they went in and pulled a piece of shrapnel out. I kept that shrapnel a long time, until I left Korea. They needed soldiers, so they sent me back.

Meantime, said Bussey:

I continued to fire until the enemy were all still. We found a few of the enemy still alive but badly maimed. Since we were probably 50 miles from the nearest doctor, we helped them on their way as an act of mercy. We made a body count - 258 bodies. It was a grisly business.

"*Thou shalt not kill.*" That troubled me at the time. It's still not a thing I have fully resolved.

The next morning, Biggs wrote, he led a new attack by a different route, quickly eliminated two enemy rifle sites, and took the town in about an hour.

Historian Roy Appleman said he talked to a colonel who had visited Yech'on the next day and reported no evidence of any fighting. That's because the fighting had taken place a mile or more away.

Dillard also denies the story. He was not on the hill with Biggs but says the company took the town with no opposition. He was obviously referring to the action the following day, when Biggs took a different route and indeed did not meet any resistance. That could be because 258 enemy lay dead at the foot of Bussey's hill.

Bussey returned two days later with a bulldozer and gouged out a trench. Villagers rolled the bodies into it as the 'dozer operator, Alfonso Spencer, snapped the picture.

Bussey:

The Division commander, General Kean, came up to our bivouac and passed out some ribbons and told me the Division was going to recommend me for the Medal of Honor. He said as soon as the paperwork was in, he'd forward it.

But no medal ever arrived. More than 60 years later the Army still refuses to recognize his feat, despite the photo and eye-witnesses.

Fields and presumably Spencer gave affidavits, which First Sergeant **Roscoe Dudley** forwarded through channels. The Army cited Fields in a footnote in *BSWA* but give no indication of what his affidavit said.

Fields:

Bussey got a Silver Star [*the Army's third highest medal*]. The talk was he had "another one coming." Sergeant Dudley, later lived up the street from me in California outside of Atherton. About 1983 four of us were on CNN-TV discussing this. Dudley swears he typed up and fowarded the recommendation for Bussey's Medal of Honor.

I knew what Bussey did, because I was there, but my word didn't mean anything, because I was black.

French:

I wasn't at the firefight, I was back at the company, but everyone in that platoon talked about it when they came back. Sergeant Fields said, "You should have been there and seen how Bussey was machine-gunning them down!"

If you've got an officer who's scared, he spooks the whole unit. But an officer with a lot of courage, it flows down. We would follow Bussey into hell with gas-soaked clothes.

Womack:

I didn't see Bussey kill those men, but you couldn't help but know about it. Bussey's jeep driver saw it, but they didn't want to believe him. I was with L Company, and you could tell what was going on. We could see those North Koreans coming toward us.

Why would someone tell him he was going to get an award, then downgrade it? But you couldn't do anything about it.

Joe Davis (Third Battalion):

I didn't see the incident, but I heard about it. There was a lot of talk about Bussey; it went all through the regiment. He was supposed to put a lot of them to sleep that day, killed over 200 men. He was supposed to get the Medal of Honor, but he never got credit for it.

A lot of things happened in the regiment that they didn't talk about. At that time they had a lot of white southern officers

Lieutenant **Carroll LeTellier**, who joined the company July 24, also heard the buzz going around the company. "I heard a lot of talk about it."

If Bussey had received the Medal it would have made history. It would have been:

The first in Korea (Geoge Libby, a GI from the 24th Division, earned one the same day) ...

The first for a black in half a century... .

And the first ever for a black officer...

Bussey was bucking too much history. The Army desperately needed a hero - but a white hero - and they hadn't heard of Libby yet.

Meanwhile, MacArthur and the nation celebrated their first victory.

Fields:

My mother said all the churches were open, praying for the black soldiers in the battle. Congress passed a resolution to mark the victory. The books were written by whites, and we didn't get credit for it. But the victory at Yech'on did happen.

A later regimental commander, John Corley, seized on the fight as a means to boost morale. He affixed to the mast-head of the regimental newspaper the words:

"Remember Yech'on"

Sixty years later the subject of Yech'on raises a high-decibel emotional response from the authors of *BSWA,* who insist that the story is fiction. Authors William Bowers and Lieutenant Colonel George McGarrigle don't even believe Bussey's Silver Star citation, which says "many" enemy were killed.

As for the photo, they said Spencer "waffled" when questioned by a colonel historian. Spencer might have been intimidated by a bird colonel in full uniform with an authoritative voice implying that his story is false and his picture is phony. But when I arrived in civilian clothes and questioned him, he told me in a low, even voice: "If it wasn't the one I took, it's one exactly like it."

McGarrigle insisted that the picture came from another regiment's unit history. He began pulling all the unit histories off his office shelves and leafing through them, finally shrugging that he couldn't find it. He then said the low hills in the background do not match the topography of Yech'on. I visited Yech'on in 2009. To the South is the hill Bussey was on, to the west the massif of Pondok-San mountain, to the north the town of Yech'on. But to the east are low-lying hills not unlike those in the Spencer photo.

Sangju

July 21-30. Next the Deuce-4 was rushed northwest to Sangju to replace a ROK unit and try to stop the North Koreans' onslaught. With the 24th Division wiped out, and other American units still in Japan, the 25th Lightening Division was the only effective force between the Communists and total victory, and the 24th was the only regiment at full strength.

Before moving out, the engineers destroyed everything in Yech'on of any military use to the enemy. They blew up the hydro-electric plant and an eight-span bridge and burned every lumber yard and every rice mill. The engineers saturated the rice with gasoline, threw thermite grenades on them, and lit up the sky for miles around. Then they laid land mines all around the town so the enemy couldn't enter.

Joe Davis:

Someone had stolen my goddam clothes, my whole duffel bag. When the first guy got bumped off in the Engineer company, a friend of mine had his bag, so I took the dead man's clothes and started wearing them. I don't even know the boy's name.

BSWA fills 28 pages with a long litany of "bugging out" by the black troops. It describes how they threw down their weapons and ran by the dozens, even by the hundreds. Sergeants, lieutenants, captains, and colonels - black and white - all repeated the same story: that they were powerless to stop the stampede. According to BSWA, hill after hill was abandoned, because only a handful of GIs stayed to fight.

If true, it was the most colossal failure of command in U.S. military history since 1814, when raw militia were routed by the British in the battle of Bladensburg in 1814. It reflected wasted months and years on Mount Fuji, when incompetent leaders failed to teach military skills and *esprit de corps*. The failure included General Dean, the 25th Division commander, who, instead of leading his black troops, continually expressed his distaste for them.

General George S Patton had put it this way:

A lot of commanders failed to take their objectives. They blamed it not on themselves but on their troops.

How many bugged out we don't know. How many green troops in other units bugged out, we also do not know. But some black troops did flee the field.

The excuses appear empty when compared to the leadership of one company that was never accused of "bugging out" - Bussey's Engineers. If Bussey and his soldiers could do it, why couldn't everyone?

In a celebrated case, a black lieutenant, **Leon Gilbert**, refused an order to take a hill.

Ellis Dean:

I'll never forget the lieutenant screaming and hollering he's not going to fight. A corporal told him, "If you don't fight, I'm going to cut you down with this machine gun."

LaVaughn Fields:

Sometimes people can let authority go to their head, You get these crazy orders, and the only thing you can do is try to carry them out. Gilbert had gotten run off the hill that night. His platoon [*30 men at full strength*] was down to six men, and he told them he couldn't re-take it. It was a big thing - a black officer turns tail in front of the enemy. But

how can you take a hill, man, with about six men?

Gilbert was court-martialed and sentenced to death - later commuted. In World War II only one American had been executed for cowardice. In Korea Gilbert was singled out almost immediately.

Bussey:

Some of his witnesses were not allowed to leave the combat area to testify for him. In a capital case, that was unconscionable. It gave the trial the appearance of a "kangaroo case."

Some GIs told Jimmy Hicks that Gilbert should have lied. Other officers might have saluted, said, "Yes sir," and quietly found a way not to do it.

Hicks (right) heard reports of one officer who sent his men up the hill, while he stayed at the foot. Others went down from their hills to "round up stragglers."

The men pointed out one captain who never came out of his foxhole except to stick his head out and order a sergeant: "Take the names of any man you see coming down the hill." Two hours later, Hicks saw him back at headquarters getting a haircut.

The S-3 is the staff officer who plans and oversees tactical operations. Hicks asked one S-3 major for an over-all picture of the situation.

He replied, "Why don't you go up yourself? You can get a much better idea." I asked him how many times he had gone up.

"I'm not supposed to go to the front," he answered.

Thurgood Marshall, later the first black Justice of the Supreme Court, went to Korea to investigate. He reported that 60 black GIs had been tried for "misconduct before the enemy," "in an atmosphere that made justice impossible." Only four were acquitted.

By comparison, only eight whites from the division were accused of the same offense, and only two were convicted,

Gilbert was sentenced to death. Twenty-three were sentenced to life, another to 50 years. Four men who were given ten-year sentences were later completely exonerated.

Many of the accused never received a vigorous defense. They told Marshall they did not have enough time to discuss their cases fully. One said he saw his defense counsel for the first time on the morning of the trial. Others were not allowed to call witnesses. Trials were rushed through. Two took 50 minutes, another 44 minutes, and one was finished in 42 minutes,

MacArthur's headquarters rejected Marshall's report.

July 25-26. Sergeant **James Simmons**, of I Company was from North Carolina and New York City. He told the *Courier*:

We were in position on the mountain when at dawn artillery shells began pounding in on us from all sides. I could hear small arms fire, and I saw a column of men coming by us to the right, heading for another company's position on a hill to our right. I laid low until they passed us, about ten feet away.

I tried to get my gunner to go after them as they went up the path in a single file, but he couldn't make out where they were. I took over and aimed three bursts at pretty close range with the machine gun. I only saw four of them get up.

Fighting these guys is like fighting armed mountain goats. They're used to climbing around these hills. Going up and down them fast. And no matter how hard you mow them down, they keep coming in waves. Every time a whistle blows, you know a new wave is coming at you

He received the Silver Star.
Bob Jones:

At Sukchon village, my platoon leader, Lieutenant **Roger Brewington**, got hit in the head. Knocked him down, didn't hurt him, but he got shipped back.

I got wounded the next day. Item and Love Companies were up on a hill. We were going to support Item Company with a 75-millimeter recoilless rifle. The enemy got us pinned down, and some officer from Dog Company was in a jeep with two black guys. He had a .30-calibre machine gun mounted on it, and he was pointing out targets. I told him we should get up on the crest of the hill, but some of the men didn't come with us - they refused to come out. He opened up fire on the hill, and the enemy withdrew - the .30-calibre was pretty effective.

That night we started digging in on the hill. The Koreans launched an attack, throwing mortars on our position, and some of the guys panicked and bailed out to the rear and left four or five of us on the hill.

The Koreans were coming over the rice paddy 500 yards away. They were too far away to hit us with small-arms fire, but they were barraging us with mortars. Able Company was with us, holding the hill. But the North Koreans surrounded our position. We had to come off, and some of our equipment was left.

Lieutenant Colonel **Gerald Miller** had just taken over as First Battalion commander.

Colonel Miller was World War II, but he took a lot of hits for treating blacks too fairly and not having enough experience. He wasn't too popular with some of the white officers, because he had never commanded a unit in combat.

We started to re-take Sukchon. I was helping dig a 75 into Company A's defensive line when the North Koreans attacked. The whole countryside was covered with them. They lined up just like in a movie. And they had mortars going, and they had us zeroed. Mortars were raining on us, and Able Company couldn't handle that and left its position, taking Dog Company vehicles to escape. I was ticked off. I had a ¾-ton [*pickup*] with a .50-calibre gun mount, and I was firing over their heads, trying to get them to stop so we could pull the 75s out of the area. We took about 30 casualties in Dog Company.

I was one. I got hit in the chest by a mortar, and I was on my way to Tokyo hospital.

Ellis Dean (D Company):

I was wounded when I was in a foxhole, waiting to advance. Got hit in the leg by a missile and evacuated to Yokohama.

Kazuko visited me in the hospital, and I recuperated back in Gifu and overstayed my leave. Everybody knew me, and the MPs said, "They're looking for you, Dean, you better get back to the hospital." They put me in the pipeline to go back to Korea.

Lieutenant Benefield of the engineers was ordered to clear some mines although the infantry commander hadn't silenced the enemy gunners covering the surrounding hills. His citation says he advanced alone and was cut down.

Bussey:

He didn't have a prayer. There was a hole in Benny I could have put two fists through." He died in agony with the nearest medical station 50 miles away.

It was the first of many instances of incompetence by field grade officers that I was to see.

Benefield was awarded the DSC. His two-year old son accepted it on his behalf.

July 28. History was made when two white lieutenants, both from the South - **Carroll LeTellier** of South Carolina and a graduate of the Citadel and **Paul Wells** of Texas - reported to Bussey for duty. This is believed to be the first time in U.S. history that a black officer was given command over whites.

Apparently none of the three realized he was making history. The relationship was considered a success by all three, who remembered it warmly for decades after. Bussey was enthusiastic about his two new officers and  would write to LeTellier's father to say how much he admired his son. The lieutenant fondly recalls nightly games of poker and hearts in the officers' tent.

LeTellier (left) replaced Benefield. Wells became the company executive officer (second in command).

French:

Lieutenant LeTellier was a young guy, handsome, came out of The Citadel [*the prestigious southern white military school second only to West Point*]. At first I was apprehensive, but I found out he was one of the best damn officers, eager to learn, and a good leader. LeTellier was the type of guy that inspired you.

LeTeller:

In that situation, you could learn to hate quickly, but that whole company treated me royally.

LeTellier is another white officer whom *BSWA* pointedly ignored in its research.

Albert Kimber: (I Company):

My Company CO was **Captain Petrosky** from Hamtramck Michigan. A wonderful officer, loved by his troops. I had a close relationship with him, because I was his radio operator. He said, "This is a form of punishment, being assigned to a black outfit." But he took me under his wing and taught me a lot of things.

I was wounded in my shoulder and treated at a station hospital back in Pusan. Stayed back there overnight and went right back into battle. I got wounded a second time by shrapnel and small arms [*rifle*] fire. That's when I went back to Osaka General Hospital for about three weeks. Then right back to Korea again.

Womack:

The only officer I had a problem with was Lieutenant [**Haezel**] **Peoples** with L Company. He was black and almost got us killed. He was assigned to us because of his complexion [*black*]. He was an ordnance officer. Take an ordnance officer and put him in charge of an infantry or engineer platoon - does that make sense? He took us out on a patrol to set up a minefield. He had his own jeep, we were following in a deuce-and-a-half.

He didn't tell us where we were going. They don't excuse that with the Green Berets. Did you see the movie, "The Dirty Dozen" with Jim Brown? Everyone can take someone else's place. If something happens to the leadership, the mission goes on.

His interpreter starts asking some Koreans where to put the mines in, and they told him. They were probably North Koreans. We were so far off the MSR, we were on a "honey-bucket" road [*used to carry human waste to the paddy*]. We were sitting in the back of the truck when they opened fire on us.

They started dropping mortars on us. He stopped, and we were right behind him. We tried to get the hell back, but you know how wide the path on a rice paddy is? Can you imagine trying to make a U-turn? The truck slipped off the path and went on its side, and we had to pick that damn thing up and get it out. If one of those mortars hit us, it would be all over for us.

They shipped People's ass out to keep us from getting killed. They transferred him to headquarters [*where, when put in the right job, he was highly regarded.*]

Looked like every time I turned around, I was involved in something. I didn't want to think I was a jinx, but ...

We were running through a creek to get away from the mortars. One hit the stream bottom and sent a rock skipping across the water. It knocked all the crowns out of my face. I was spitting teeth. The aid station didn't have any dental equipment, so they sent me to Japan again. The doctors had to pull the roots of my teeth out.

They sent me to the psycho ward, where people were crazy. They'd wake up in the night, hollering, screaming, trying to kill someone in a bunk. I couldn't handle that. I went to the chaplain and cried. I was worried about my kids and wanted to stay in Japan. He said, "They need you in Korea to train troops. "

I said, "I can train them in Japan." But they sent me back anyway.

Disband the Deuce-4?

Reports of mass "bugging out" continued. The Division commander, General William Kean from Buffalo New York, hounded General MacArthur to disband the Deuce 4. He advocated distributing the men among the white divisions.

Ellis Dean:

I had good rapport with General Kean; he congratulated me on my athletic ability. Why would he do something like that? But MacArthur said, "They're going to stay until another unit can replace them."

Kean's motives may have been wrong, but the outcome – integration – would have been good. Carroll LeTellier believes that blacks would have had more motivation in white units; they wanted to prove that "I'm just as good as, or better than, any white soldier."

Actually, Kean ran one of the few segregated units in Korea.

The 24th Division had been quietly mixing blacks and whites. A spoksman said:

We've been drawing Negro replacements since the beginning of the war. There is hardly a squad that doesn't have a Negro. Colored troops in this now All- American Division have done more for the combat efficiency of the Division than Jackie Robinson did for the Brooklyn Dodgers.

The 7th Division fielded an all-black Ranger Company.

The 2d Division had one black infantry battalion with its own black artillery.

The Marines had been integrated for years, although it had no black officers.

When the 3d Division arrived later, its ranks were speckled black and white.

But, one black newspaper declared:

Integration Is Spelled A.I.R. F.O.R.C.E.

In part because of the famous Tuskegee Airmen, it had made the biggest strides in complying with their Commander-in-Chief's order to integrate. Many black veterans of the Red Tails were among the first to arrive in Korea, flying their old P-51s.

One was **Charlie Dryden:**

I was a "mosquito pilot" flying light T-6 trainers. We were the eyes of Tactical Control Center.

One day I detected Korean caches of weapons and had fighters blast them to hell and gone, so a news reporter came to my outfit and asked to ride in my back seat.

The troops on the ground reported getting fire from a hill, and what could I do about it? I started making diving passes at the hill. "What are you doing that for?" he said.

"Trying to get them to shoot at me to see their muzzle flashes," I said.

"*What*!? You're crazy!"

I said, "We do that every day."

Meantime the Americans were ordered down to the Naktong river in the southeast corner of Korea, to the "Pusan Perimeter. There they would make a final stand against the on-rushing invaders. The 24th covered 50 miles in two days, as the engineers covered their rear and delayed the foe.

July 29. Sergeant **David Robinson** saved two wounded men who came under severe fire. When his company C.O. was put out of action, he took over command and led the fight to hold a critical hill for four hours.

Bussey called it "the day I almost killed my dear friend, infantry Captain **William Jackson**"

He led a squad of engineers to blow a crater in a road in order to stop enemy pursuers. They packed 1500 pounds of TNT into a mountainside at a bend of the road as American infantrymen passed by. As soon as a white lieutenant reported that he was the end of the line, Bussey cried "Fire in the hole!" and twisted the T-handle on his hellbox. The blast was "like a crack of doom" until one of his squad cried out, "You nearly killed two men!" - Jackson and a Lieutenant **Morgan**, who were the real rear guard. Bussey rushed to them.

"What are you trying to do, Hoss, kill us?" Jackson managed to joke. Luckily both survived and were evacuated.

But a Russian tank with Korean infantrymen hove around the corner up to the crater-lip, pinning down Bussey's men in 110-degree heat. He and a Corporal **Barnwell** shouldered one of the Army's new 3.5-inch tank-killing bazookas and fired. But that only gave away their own position, and the tank swung its turret around and its 89-milimeter gun barked - "Ka-WHUMP!" But it couldn't hit them.

The foes faced each other in the furnace until dark let the Americans crawl away.

July 30. LeTellier got his baptism the next day. He accompanied Bussey and Sergeant **Woods** to blow up a bridge. Bussey called Woods "a hell-for-leather guy. Strong, tough, ghetto-smart. He gave the impression of not giving a damn, but whenever there was a difficult, dangerous, or urgent job," Woods was the man he turned to.

While some of the men cooled off a river, Bussey set 1500 pounds of TNT, hooked a wire to the hell-box and backed away until the wire ran out. It was too short. LeTellier had seen a colonel get killed in a similar exercise at Fort Belvoir and started running out of range as the men laughed.

Bussey:

I gave the T-handle a vigorous twist. In a moment the sky was full of boulders, some as big as jeeps, landing all around us. Some men ducked and squeezed themselves into tiny knots.

The others raced as fast as they could to pass LeTellier.

In two days the 25th division covered 150 miles to the "Pusan Perimeter." It was the final "line in the sand." There would be no more retreat. If the enemy broke through there, the vital port of Pusan would fall, and the war would be over

Pusan Perimeter

August 1. They reached the southwest corner of the perimeter.

Donald Womack:

The Naktong river had sandy banks. The North Koreans would lay box mines at night, didn't have any metal on them. At 4:30 every morning we were trying to clear the mines out. We didn't want the North Koreans to know we were there, because they'd get up on the hills and shoot down at us.

They were wooden mines. We called them "box mines" or "bouncing betties." When it goes off, it clicks, and you know you have two-three seconds before it jumps up three or four feet in your face. We had to see where the ground was dug up and dig them out with our bayonets. Normally you put a hand grenade on them and let it blow.

Paul Witt was trying to put a pin in one, like in a grenade, so it wouldn't go off. But the pin didn't go in. He heard the click, and it exploded. He jumped up and looked at us, then he started to run. His head was hanging down between his shoulder blades. You know how a farmer would wring a chicken's neck, and it would run around in circles without a head? That's what he did. His body ran, but his head was hanging backward, running, trying to get away.

Battle Mountain

The 25th was rushed to the southern end of the perimeter, the only division that didn't have a river to protect them. And they were guarding the shortest route to Pusan, only 40 miles away. If they didn't hold, the enemy had a clear road to the port and victory.

The Deuce-4 was given a town, Masan, and a rugged mountain, both astride the main road to Pusan. The mountain was hell to counter-attack while carrying full field packs and weapons in temperatures that reached 120 degrees. GIs called it Battle Mountain. It would witness some of the most savage fighting of the Korean - or any American - war.

Robert Fletcher (C Company):
We got direct orders from MacArthur: "There will be no more withdrawals." The First Battalion commander said, "We'll hold until the last straw."

The Communists' object was Pusan by September 1 - we learned that in POW camp - and then the Chinese Communists were going to attack Formosa [*Taiwan*].

The 31st was assigned the flat ground on the left, or northern, sector. Good tank country. The 24th got Battle Mountain.

Reporter Jimmy Hicks went on a mission with 200 men under Captain **Richard Williams,** who had just gotten out of the hospital after being shot in the ear and shoulder. Hicks said it took three hours to climb from the bottom to the top, and he wasn't carrying a full field pack. He wrote that the men's boots were worn to a frazzle since arriving in Korea.

Battle Mountain from the Communist side; the town of Haman lies in the valley beyond LeTellier:

Battle mountain was a hell of a place to defend. We were assigned the most difficult terrain, very tough to defend and very tough to climb. We had only Japanese maps in black and white, so you had to be really good at reading contours [*of hills*] to know where you were. The 27th and 35th had good MSRs [*Main Supply Routes*]; the 24th had to go through the 35th then back south.

We'd lose the mountain at night, go back and get it in the daylight. The Air Force would drop napalm and bombs, the artillery would give them hell, and the line was restored in a short period of time.

We had only Japanese maps in black and white, so you had to be really good at reading contours [*of hills*] to know where you were.

He also remembers sharing his sleeping bag with "three million mosquitoes. They'd bite you through the netting.")

Jim Burnett (159th Artillery):

We were all jammed up against each other. Everyone was issued rifles - cooks, clerks. One guy had never seen a rifle in his entire life!

Nathaniel Nicholson (159th Artillery):

We had a World War II radio, a 70-pound pack with battery. I had to carry that, plus my other gear, up the hills. The battery lasted one hour and kept cutting off. They had to drop us batteries from the air, otherwise we had to operate by telephone, but the enemy would cut the wire.

Burnett operated the radio for his battery commander:

A British ship started putting artillery shells on us, and I had to communicate with it. I was getting the coordinates from the F.O. and relaying them to the ship. Talking to an English sailor isn't the easiest thing in the world. Captain **[Gustav] Franke** thought it was great that I could do it, and the British operator also gave me a "Jolly good show, chap." They gave me a bronze star. I said, "Does this get me home, or what?"

Howard "Big Boy" Williams was the 258-pound former Eighth Army heavyweight champ from Detroit. He had beaten Rex Layne, who would fight Ezzard Charles for the world title. Williams was a veteran of World War II, one of those who accepted a demotion, from tech sergeant (five stripes), to private so he could get into combat. He spent five months in the infantry and won a Bronze Star.

Williams told BAA reporter Fred Leigh:

We were attacking Bloody Peak. Able and Baker Companies had the enemy hemmed in on two sides, so Charlie Company went around and came up through a village, when one platoon ran into an ambush.

127

My platoon went in to give them a hand. Levi Jackson [*who had defeated him as heavyweight champ*] made two trips to bring out the wounded with bullets hitting all around him. On the last trip,

Jackson threw his body over two wounded men. He saved their lives but lost his own. He was awarded a Distinguished Service Cross, the Army's second highest decoration.

It would seem to be a blatant case of racism. In a white regiment, he would have received the Medal of Honor.

Williams:

I covered the retreat of the rest of the men with a BAR, and I got hit six times in my face, my back, and my legs. The North Koreans moved in on me, and I stretched out and played dead. Two soldiers on each side of me were groaning. Both of them got shot in the head. Then the Koreans cleared out.

I lay in the paddy from 7:30 in the morning until dark. Then I stumbled about a mile back down the road to a 35th Infantry road block.

He was evacuated to Japan.

August 3. Nathaniel Nicholson encountered his second miracle:

I was in line at the mess tent, washing my mess kit, when a bomb was thrown in and exploded. The man next to me died.

Nick was unscathed.

The Americans were confronted by an enemy they weren't taught about at Fort Benning.

John French (Engineers):

We were getting fire from everywhere. The North Koreans were in front of us, and the same guys you'd see working in the fields in the daytime were guerrillas firing at you from the rear at night. I guess the North Koreans had infiltrated even before the war started. In the rush of refugees, you couldn't tell who in the hell was who. Guys would sneak to town looking for girls and get killed.

Fletcher:

We dug in and fought with everything we had. I think we lost that mountain 19 times and took it back 19 times. We used to call it Bloody Peak, because you'd get three-quarters of the way up and run into blood.

We were in 28 straight days of combat. I found out later some of the other guys went to Japan on R&R for ten days. We got only two days and only a few miles behind the lines. I was in combat almost four months, July to November, and got a total of about ten days' rest. They called it ten days, but we would have to come back after two-three days, because, hell, the North Koreans broke through and we had to come back and fill up the line, mainly in the ROK area.

I wouldn't give a plugged nickel for 50 ROKs. They were good until dark, then a whole unit on your flank would go. The North Koreans knew it. They'd probe the line. If there's no resistance, they'd come flying through. Someone's got to close the gap; one of the companies of the 24th would go over. But you never read about that. [*But, Fletcher admits, when the Koreans went to Vietnam, they were "pretty tremendous."*]

Ralph Hubbard:

M Company - "Mighty Mike" - supported the third battalion. We used to be spread out a lot, supporting all different infantry companies. Wherever shooting got heavy, we'd pull over there. A little bragging: We never popped a short round in our own area [*that is, never hit our own troops*].

Our company carried 75 recoilless rifles, heavy mortars, and .50-calibre heavy machine guns. We did some serious walking with all that stuff on our backs. The mortar and the back plate it sits on were heavy. **Terry Maston** carried one of them; he was a cousin of singer Sammy Davis Jr.

I ran into my old hard-nosed training company commander, Captain Mayo, in Masan. He was in Company B, and we passed on a hill and stopped to talk. He was scrungy, hadn't shaved. I went over to him. "Captain Mayo?"

"That you, Hub?"

"Yes, sir."

"Mother Hubbard! Oh God, kid, you look good!" He told everyone, "He was one of my recruits. I trained him very well."

We talked for a couple of hours. His last words to me were, "Keep your head down."

He was killed later.

A lot of our sergeants were World War II types, eight or nine years older than us, the "old men" we looked up to. Some of them got battlefield commissions. That's how I found out about the Peter Principle: You can be great, but at the next level you're lousy. We had a couple of damn good sergeants, but as officers they were terrible.

My company commander got a letter from my sister, saying they hadn't heard from me. I was set down in the CP [*Command Post*] and given three sheets of paper and told what should be on that paper.

Sergeant **Herbie Wilson** was in charge of it. He said, "I'm going to write your family," and he started corresponding with my sister.

In August, Wilson got his commission. The colonel was chasing him for about two months, but Wilson wanted to stay with his guys. Finally they nailed him and put his gold bar on him. He looked funny. Guys would salute him. He'd say, "Why are . .? Oh, that's right."

He talked very fast, especially when he got excited. But he was a hell of a soldier. God, he had balls like.... He was smart and had a hell of a sense of humor. Herbie was a great guy, loved by all. He kind of watched over me, took care of me.

After the war he and my sister started dating and eventually married. So he was my sergeant, then my lieutenant, and then my brother-in-law.

Jim Burnett:

One day I could see the top of the mountain. You mark your position with different-color panels. Airplanes were coming in, and they shot the place up something fierce! They're American planes, and those were Americans on that hill. I'm jumping up and down. Of course the pilot didn't see me.

About 20 years ago at a reunion, one of the guys told me, "We called it in on ourselves, because we were getting wiped out."

Thompson's Medal of Honor

August 5. George Bussey (L Company):

The enemy decided to run us out of there. We were fighting all day. The platoon sergeant, a guy from Florida, got killed, so I was platoon sergeant.

The battalion C.O, Colonel **Sam Pierce,** said, "Bussey, keep your platoon here."

That night, in a hard rain, Pierce and his battalion were caught asleep without digging fox holes.

George Bussey:

They over-ran our position. There were 26 guys in our platoon, and we fought them off and ended up with 11 guys. They shot Colonel Pierce in both arms and both legs. We made a makeshift stretcher and got him off the hill down to safety. He put us all in for a Silver Star.

131

Richard Sanders:

One fellow in my platoon, **Willie Hamm**, was firing the .50-caliber from the turret of a ¾-ton truck. I started to get on the back end of a truck, and an enemy shell landed nearby, and I was hit by the damn white phosphorous. It was burning all over my face and arms. See how the skin's burned off here on the back of my hands?

One North Korean shot me in my left hip. I'm on my elbows laying there, when the smallest guy in the platoon dragged me out of the road. I can't remember his name. I look for him every year at the reunions. He might have been killed later, I'm not sure.

More would have been killed had not Willie Thompson [*left*] covered the unit with machine gun fire. Thompson's platoon leader, Lieutenant

Herbert Wilson told BAA:

I ordered my section to set up their machine guns and open fire. The number-one gun was knocked out, but Thompson, the gunner on the other gun, stayed in position and continued to fire, even after the order was given to withdraw. I told him to withdraw with the rest.

Sanders:

We said, "You can't stay here." I went back on the road and tried to get him.

Thompson said, "I'm going to stay here."

Wilson:

I saw that he had been wounded in several places, but he said he wasn't going to move back. If he couldn't get out, he said he was going to take a lot of enemy with him. His squad leader, Corporal **Washington**, and others tried to pull him away, but he fought them off and began firing again. When I left, he was still firing, and the enemy, who were very close, were throwing grenades at him.

The Army's official citation said:
He remained at his machine gun and continued to deliver deadly fire until he was mortally wounded.

Thompson was awarded the Medal of Honor, the first black so honored since 1898 and the first black to receive one in the 25th Division. He also was the first man to receive it in the 25th Division. His mother accepted the Medal from General Omar Bradley, the Army chief of staff.

In Washington reporters looked up Corporal Dennis Bell, 84, of the 10th Cavalry in Cuba, the oldest living Medal of Honor winner, and asked for his story:

Bell:
I Two officers had had taken some men and tried to rescue our wounded, but each time they failed. So I volunteered. I was in charge of a group of men. We got through all right and got them out. It was pretty rugged going, but the buys of the 10th were pretty rough too.

Meanwhile, said Sanders:
Private Hamm received a Silver Star. "Why didn't you put me in for something?"
"We thought you were killed."
I said, "Well, posthumously?"
They said, "We'll write you up." But they never did.
I went to the hospital, and when I came back, the platoon sergeant of the machine gun platoon had been hit. They told me, "You're going back to the machine gun platoon as platoon leader."
The platoon leader [*usually a lieutenant*] is out in front, the platoon sergeant is in the rear looking for

133

stragglers. So the first one the enemy shoots at is the platoon leader. If you didn't have a platoon leader, then the platoon sergeant goes up front, and the first squad leader goes to the rear. But when we lost our platoon leader, they never replaced him, so I was always up in front.

Nicholson:
That night I was in a firefight on a hill with my FO, and we were relieved and called to come down. We came through a town, and the enemy ran us out of there. We had to duck real quick to get back to the CP.

After we got back, there was a disturbance in the town, and my CO, Captain Franke, wanted to send Lieutenant **Mills** with Sergeant **Roberts** and Corporal **Henderson** to go back there on a recon, and he said, "Nick, you're going too - you're the driver."

He had a map printed in Japanese, and it showed two roads, North and South, and he wanted to send us down the South road. But I knew there was only one road, the North road, and the enemy had it. I told him, but he still wanted to send us down the South road. He was going to send me back there where the enemy ran us out and there was only one road? No way. I refused to go.

He said, "Well, you have to go."

I said, "I refuse to go." I disobeyed a direct order.

Franke was furious. He said, "I can shoot you right now."

I said, "At least you'll know where my body is."

They arrested me.

A fellow named **Ralph Hargrave** took my place. By the time they got ready, it was night time and drizzling. Lieutenant Mills was a brand new lieutenant just out of OCS, and this was his first assignment. The CO had no business sending them out with no light when they couldn't see anything.

Captain Franke wanted to prosecute me or get me out of the battery. He called headquarters to see if they would take me, but they couldn't. So he put me on the outpost until the MPs came to pick me up and take me away. He made me carry a .50-calibre machine gun up the hill. It was so heavy I had to make three trips - with the tripod, the barrel, and the ammo. He told everyone, "Don't help him."

That same night they sent a messenger up there: "Captain Franke wants to see you."

James Burnett:

One of the guys came back, delirious and raving. He babbled something about being ambushed. The captain called for Nick.

Nicholson:

He said, "They've all been ambushed." Henderson had come back and told them the whole party of four was severely wounded, and Hargrave was hung up on a tree and shot in the back.

Burnett:

Nick said, "I know exactly where they are."

The captain said, "Oh? That's where you told me not to go? The only reason you're not in jail is because the MPs didn't get here, because everything's in turmoil."

Captain Franke was a very nice man, a gentleman. He could have put Nick in a lot of trouble, but he didn't.

Nicholson:

The captain said, "We need you to go get them," because I knew the way.

I was getting ready to go when the radio came on, said a captain from headquarters had found them. They brought Hargrave back and sent him to the hospital, and they released me from arrest.

For years I kept trying to find Hargrave. In 1999 I went to the 24th reunion, and someone said, "Hargrave? Yeah, I know him; he's my pastor." Pastor! I was on the next plane. He said they shot him in the back and in the legs; he was in the hospital almost two years.

The regimental commander, Colonel White, told Bussey, "Hot Shot, I'm through with this horse shit. I got no ice for my whiskey." He told General Kean, "I'm too old for this." Kean agreed and sent him home.

Colonel Champeny

August 5. White was replaced by **Arthur Champeny** of Wisconsin, the only man to win the Distinguished Service Cross in three wars - World War I, World War II, and Korea, although the third is suspect.

Champeny's first move was to make a speech that "colored people" don't make good soldiers; in the last war they had a reputation for "running all over Italy." But he was going to change "the frightened 24th" to the "fighting 24th."

Asked why he said that, he replied, "I wanted to get them mad."

He did.

One of his next moves was to order a barbed wire fence erected around Charlie Company so its men couldn't run.

Bussey branded the colonel "biased, gutless, and totally inefficient."

Actually, Jimmy Hicks of the *Baltimore Afro-American* had some positive things to say about the new commander:

He is a driver and hard-wrestlng man. I had to get out there at 5:30 a.m. to catch him, and he would stay out until 9 p.m.

Sam Pierce, the third battalion commander, said he'd had enough of the war, and General Kean granted his wish and sent him home.

August 9. Pierce was replaced by the best officer who ever fought in the 24th - Lieutenant Colonel **John Corley**. A West Point boxer and red-headed Brooklyn Irishman, he talked like his home town - "Dese, dem, doze." He had landed in France on D-Day and won multiple awards for bravery. At 36 he was the youngest battalion commander in Korea and was admired by his men as a soldier and a leader.

"He was a tough Irish soldier," LeTellier said.

The Ambush

August 6. LaVaughn Fields:

I got caught in an ambush; we got chewed up pretty bad, lost about 12 men.

Lieutenant Lenon is the hero, not the rest of us. Lenon was a religious man, a very serious person, a very quiet man, seldom raised his voice. He didn't have to raise his voice, didn't have to chew you out. You just did what he said. Everyone liked him. I worshipped him.

John French:

Lieutenant Lenon was a super, super officer. He'd been a first sergeant in the quartermaster in World War II, got out and finished college in Prairie View Texas. I never heard him raise his voice, but he had a "command presence." You wanted to please him. A unique army man, very polite, a real gentleman.

We were doing engineer work in the day, then we had to go up and fill in on the line [*with the infantry*] at night. You did your job and pitched in - cooks and everyone else. Everyone was a fighting soldier, whatever your main job was.

Fields:

The Marines had come ashore on the extreme left under General [*Paul*] Roberts, the day before. Early in the morning our assistant regimental commander told

Lenon to take his platoon and reinforce King Company, who had got chopped up on a hill called Old Baldy. They had three platoons, plus our engineers. We had a .50-calibre machine gun with a tripod on the end. We needed a .30-calibre, the kind that John Wayne stood up and fired single-handed in the movies. But with ours, one man couldn't put it into action alone; I had the tripod; my assistant gunner, **Frank Cunningham**, had the trigger and barrel assembly. Everyone else had M-1 rifles. We didn't have any mortars.

We spread out into two columns, one on each side of the road.

A South Korean company was up on the ridge on our left, supposed to be protecting us. We stopped for noon chow of C-rations, but it was short, because we wanted to hook up. It was high noon, the sun was hot, and we began to sweat. All was quiet except the sound of our feet on the dirt road. Too quiet. There was something disturbing - no birds flying or singing, the frogs were quiet. With hills on both sides of us, it seemed to me like Death Valley.

We stopped to take ten [*rest*], and I checked the top of the hill again. This time the troops there were in brown uniforms. That was funny, but nobody said  anything about it, and we resumed marching.

All of a sudden it started up front. King Company had run into something, and the shit began to fly. By the sound of it, it was big. The call came, "Move out!" and the columns began moving forward again. Sergeant **Robertson** we called him "Trip Ticket," because he had to authorize the bus that took us to town in Japan - began saying the 23rd Psalm: "Yea, though I walk through the valley of death... ."

We could now see that that the objects on the ridge were North Koreans. They had driven the South Koreans off - the South Koreans were known to do that, leave you high and dry. If they had stayed, we wouldn't have been chewed up.

So the enemy was walking by our side. There must have been a good company of them, 200 or more. They had us under observation for about 1,000 yards and followed us until we walked into a horseshoe range of hills, a fantastic place for an ambush with no way out.

We came under heavy rifle and machine gun fire.

Donald Womack:

We should have been up on the ridge, but we were at the bottom and laid down a base of fire so the infantry could get up there. **Jerome Barnwell** - he was a loan shark, you borrowed five dollars from him, he'd make you pay back ten - he was down with us. The infantry put blockers on the left and right, but they didn't stay, they just kept going over the other side, so we were cut off. That's when a lot of the engineers got killed.

Fields:

Lieutenant Lenon was up front with our first squad, which suffered four to six casualties. Lenon shouts, "Keep moving, keep moving! Don't stop, or we'll get it." He said don't worry about him, he was going after the machine gun that was doing all the damage. He began drawing fire away from us.

Lenon stays behind while the rest of us drive up the hill to get over to the other side. He hollers, "Follow me. If I get hit, keep going and leave me; we'll re-group on the other side."

I take my squad and hear several bullets from automatic weapons [*machine guns*] whiz around me. All of us are crawling on our bellies. If you raise your head, you're dead. I crawl past Barnwell and say, "Come on, Barnwell, let's go!" He doesn't move, and a closer look tells me there is no help for him now. He was a good buddy of mine, and I choke up.

Womack:

I didn't have time to be scared. We started going up the hill. A bullet hit me. **Frank Cunningham** had the base plate for the mortar, was on my right. That Korean machine gun was cutting the grass just like a sickle. I was down lower than Cunningham, and a bullet missed me and hit him. He kept calling me, "Mack! Mack!" I realized I had to get to him, but I couldn't. We could just make hand-to-hand contact. Finally, I reached over and got hold of his arms and dragged him up to this little gully, and when I was pulling him, he got shot again, and he died in my arms.

Fields:

I hear Cunningham holler, "Oh, Lord." When I look over at him, I can see he's dead. **Bob Semedo** is also hit and crying for someone to help him. I can't name them all - I can't stop to get their names. To the best of my knowledge, there are six wounded engineers and four dead at that moment.

Womack:

That's when I got hit again. I got hit in my right arm with a .30 calibre [*from a GI rifle*], but who was I gonna blame? It didn't go all the way through; the back end of the bullet was sticking out.

Fields:

I can see a drainage ditch to my right and roll over into it and call for my squad to move into it. It's about six inches deep, but boy, it feels like six feet.

Robert Moss moves in. **George Thomas** follows. I hear **Randolph Gillespie**, who was half-black and half

Choctaw Indian. **Ellis Stephens**, my assistant squad leader, is cussing, so that means they're all right. Someone yells, "They're all in," and we start to move up the hill again.

The SOB with the automatic fire undresses the leaves on the bush I'm under, and I holler for my mother. Then I tell myself, "Momma can't help you now, get your ass moving, or you'll die here." Some three yards away I can see a rock. I move toward it and make it OK.

Thomas is saying he can see that SOB who is shooting, and I yell, "Take him when you can." Now I see him, and I fire. He's down, and Gillespie finishes him off.

Ellis Stephens, unknown, LaVaughn Fields

Now we have some moments of freedom from being shot at, and we make them count. We begin to return the fire, shooting at anything that looks like it might be a man. I'm thinking, "If we're gonna die, we're gonna die fighting."

Benny Cox, the platoon sergeant, gives us the signal to move out. I tell **Gilmore** and **Hays** to bring up the rear and cover us with fire. I see **Carl Curtis**, leader of the first squad. He's my buddy, and I crawl over to him. "How you doing?"

"I'm not doin' good, man."

"Where you hit?"

"They shot my legs."

"Don't raise up or they'll get you."

"Leave me and go on without me or you'll get killed."

I say, "No, I can't leave you."

He says, "I'm giving you an order. If you don't, when we get back, I'll take care of you.

I say, "You think that shit means anything to me now?" He's on his back, and I put both his feet on my shoulders and start pushing him ahead of me.

Womack, my old schoolmate from New Haven, crawls up beside me to help. I send him over the hill to wait for the squad and put down a base of fire at whatever enemy he sees. He goes up the hill and disappears.

I can see the dirt jumping up on the top of the hill, where the bullets are hitting. I tell Curt, "I'm going to have to roll you over the hill." He's raising hell all the time: "Leave me! Leave me!" I take my foot and push him down the other side.

As he rolls down about 20 yards, I tell my squad, "We better go over in two's, because those guys got us zeroed in." So over we go. God is with us - we all make it.

On the other side there is high grass, and we slide down and out of sight. I pull Curtis with me, dragging him down to a cluster of rocks, and look at his legs. There are holes in both thighs, but they don't look too bad. He and I manage to put a first-aid packet on them and settle down to wait for what's left of our platoon,

Sergeant Cox is still at the top, firing. **Donald Hamilton** is with him and has somehow got hold of an infantry assault machine gun [*a .30-calibre, light enough to be carried*] and is raising hell with it as **Ernest Cherry** and Gilmore assist him. Sergeant **Archie Lott** is directing the fire. The barrels of their guns must be red-hot from the cover they're giving us.

Sergeant **Herndon** crawls in behind the rocks, looking bad; he can hardly make it. He tells us "Old Man" Washington - **Earl Washington** of Baltimore - may not make it; he's about 50, his heart is bad, and he's resting behind some rocks. Not long after, Lott and **Henry Jackson** - we called him "Jack" - bring in Washingon. Gilmore now has managed to get hold of a dead infantryman's automatic rifle [*BAR – Browning Automatic Rifle*] and is raising hell with it.

He soon stops firing. The light is beginning to fade, and darkness is settling in. We take a head count. I have two killed and three missing - Womack, **Thomas**, and Moss. **Marcus Mills** says he saw Moss running, with the enemy chasing him, but he couldn't tell what happened to him. I guess they must have bought it. That makes six KIA.

Sergeant Cox is mad as hell. Right now he'd like to kill the infantry company commander. They knew we were at the end of their company, and they left us to look out for ourselves. They got their own asses out and left us and their own dead and wounded behind. There is no excuse for this. They have automatic weapons fire [*machine guns and BARs*] they could have put on the enemy.

We have out-dated weapons. Plus, being chopped up like we are, our automatic weapons are scattered all over the hill. When Cunningham got hit, we couldn't use our heavy [*.50-calibre*] machine gun. I had the bipod, but he had the base plate. Someone in the Pentagon goofed when they assigned equipment to the combat engineers. But it's too late now.

Most of the first squad, except for Curt, escaped. They were the lucky ones. The rest of the squads caught hell.

Darkness is now on us, and we put down for the night among the rocks. Cox is looking around and tells us we are about 100 yards from a village of six or eight huts, over-run with enemy troops, which means we must lay low without any noise at all. We talk about taking them, but there are too many of them to try it.

The men are dead tired, and we take turns sleeping.

A squad of enemy soldiers walks within ten feet of us - they almost step over us. We freeze. I hold my hand over Washington's nose so he won't snore. We are laying like we're dead, but we're ready. We figure if we're going to go, we'll take them with us. If one of them makes a move, his ass belongs to us, but some of us wouldn't be here to tell about it either. Luckily, they don't see us.

Next, loud bangs begin to come from the village, like hand grenades - at least three or four of them. We're all awake now. We see two GIs moving. The enemy is running to the front end of the village, yelling. Then they stop and return to their huts and start putting out all the lights in a hurry.

We can hear tanks coming - it must be the Marines. The noise of the grenades must have tipped them off. They begin to pop flares, the village is lit up, and the tanks go to work on it. More tanks join the action, at least five of them; I can see the muzzle blasts. They must have hit an ammo dump in one of the huts, because the whole area lights up like day. This is better than being at the movies, only it's real. The village is on fire and nothing is moving. The Marines level it.

At first we decided to join the tanks, but being night-time, and with our complexion, they won't know who we are and think we're North Koreans, so we decide not to move until morning.

But at least we get some sleep.

The next morning Sergeant Cox wakes us up quietly and says we are being observed up on the hill by two North Korean officers looking down at us. As we move slowly and stealthily, Cox says, "On three, we'll charge up the hill like we're after them." We move like lightning up the hill. Jack Jackson is helping me carry Curtis. Now I'm up the hill, the two officers take off into the village, and we continue running the other way.

We get onto the military crest [*in front of the actual crest, so they are not silhouetted against the sky*] and proceed toward the Marines. We're high enough to see the ocean and the Marine tanks a thousand yards off. But we'll have to hide from them now; we're too far away to be recognized, and if spotted, we can be targets for artillery or mortar fire.

Cox holds a short meeting, and we decide to start down the hill toward our lines so the Marines will see us and, we hope, keep the enemy off us. Jack and Cox take the point [*front*], Curtis and I are in the center, **Fred Louis** and Mills on the flanks, and Old Man Washington and Lott bring up the rear. Mills still has a full pack of grenades, which will come in handy later.

We're on our way down a ravine or washout, a ditch five or six feet deep, eight to ten feet wide. That provides good cover. Jack gives us the signal and points to an enemy just 30 yards ahead in a foxhole in the same ravine. We've got to deal with him, but this will make our presence known.

While we hesitate, he fires, and we hit the dirt. I hear the bullet pop as it comes close to me. I can hear him working his bolt to get off another one, and I yell, "You better kill the bastard fast!" Herndon comes up to get a better shot. I yell, "Here he comes again," as I see him rise up and see the muzzle blast. The bullet kicks up dirt in my face, and I realize I'm his target.

He fires again and the bullet hits Wash in the stomach and comes out the other side and hits Herndon in the leg. They're both hollering.

Mills is now in action with his grenades, but they hit the tree limbs, and we have to duck from the shrapnel.

The enemy fires again, and the bullet hits me in the ass. I can feel blood running down my leg. I'm howling, "Oh my God, I think I'm hit!" I'm praying to God I don't lose too much blood. You talk about scared! My biggest worry is there isn't a medic nearby.

John B. Holway

Then I reach back, and here's a bullet hole in my canteen - it's water running down my leg. Lott says, "Damn, Fields, another half-inch and you could wipe your ass cross-wise instead of up and down."

I growl, "This is no time to be funny."

I grab my rifle and start firing. I can keep him pinned down until someone else can take him out. I can see Louis coming up on him as Mills gets a lucky hook shot with his grenade that blows the rifle out of the guy's hand. Louis cuts loose, but he's so nervous he only shoots an arm off. Sergeant **Robert Ward** finishes him.

Jack shoots another enemy. He gets his rifle stock blown away by the enemy's burp gun but finishes him off. As we walk past him he moves, and I put him out of his misery.

Jack's rifle is unusable. Because I'm with Curtis, I won't need mine and let Jack use it.

Now we have three wounded. I'll need more help with Washington and Herndon. Wash can't walk, and Herndon can just barely walk, using his rifle as a crutch. And Curtis' legs are beginning to swell from the heat. I tell Cox we've got to move faster or Curt will lose his legs.

We continue down the hill. The point is reinforced by Ward with orders not to waste time and just blow the enemy away.

We see an enemy soldier drop his rifle and run into a cave. We tell Mills and Gillespie to go to work with their grenades. Mills looks inside and says he can't.

"What the hell do you mean, you can't?"

"Because there's women and children in there."

With sign language we bring them and two old men out. Gillespie and Mills throw two grenades, and the job is done.

Gillespie points to an old wooden wagon, and we load Wash and Curtis on it and put straw over them. Stephens goes back up the hill and gets the old men, and we hand-sign them to pull the cart down the trail.

146

Herndon goes with them. We tell him to lag behind, so if the enemy opens up on the rest of us, they won't hit the wounded. He says, "If you hear me shoot, you'll know the old men gave me some shit." Off go the wounded. We're hoping if there are any more enemy, they'll think it's a wagon of hay.

We haven't had anything to eat. We drink water off a rice paddy. The water is real cool. We're filling up our canteens, and on top of the water is you-know-what floating. We bust open the purification pills and hope that will kill it.

Just then, at last safety shows up. Three Marine Corsairs [*fighter planes*] fly over our heads and are circling to check out the cart, because we're in enemy territory and the North Koreans are known to hide ammo or supplies like that. This scares the hell out of us. We know what will come next if we don't do something fast.

Stephens takes off his T-shirt and starts waving it. We take off our shirts and start waving too. On the second pass the lead plane comes in but doesn't fire. The second plane gives us a barrel roll; that means they recognize us. I think it's a black pilot; he looks like it anyway.

As we cross the open valley, they fly six passes low over our heads to show the enemy they're here to protect us. God has smiled on us again.

When we run into the Marines, they search us and ask for the password. We tell them we don't know the password. They're in the Marines, we're in the Army, they're white, we're black, and we've been gone two days. But they still want the password! One Marine tells us to wait and takes off, his buddy watching us like we were North Koreans.

A voice up on the hill hollers, "You asshole, let 'em in. Can't you see they're Americans?"

They have already taken care of our wounded, and Sergeant Herndon has told them we were coming. We wish him and the other wounded good luck before they are evacuated. It will be six months before they return.

One of the Marine platoons had been hit the day before, and a sergeant wants us to reinforce it and fight with them. We say, "No, we've got to join our own company."

He says, "Well, you're going to join us."

An argument starts. Finally a lieutenant says, "No, they've got to report to their unit."

They feed us, and Cox fills them in on the enemy location. The lieutenant calls for fire from five-inch guns on a destroyer off the coast and tells us to direct the fire. We watch as it wreaks havoc on the hillside.

When the show is over, we hitch a ride with a 25th Division truck. The driver says, "Hop aboard, but hang on, because they drop shells on the road, but we'll get you to your unit in one piece," and he puts the pedal to the metal. I don't think that guy had four wheels on the ground at the same time the whole trip.

About two miles away, we saw our company guidon. Boy, did it look good. Even the first sergeant looked good.

Moss and Thomas were there ahead of us, and did they have a story to tell!

They were veterans from the Second World War, and they were like brothers. Thomas had gotten captured. During the night somehow Moss snuck in the village, found the house where Thomas was, and started throwing grenades to get attention. Then he threw one into the house. He pulled the pin - took a chance, didn't he? But you had to know Moss.

Thomas said it almost got him, but, playing heads up, he saw it come through the window and threw it into the room where the guards were - maybe not like they do in the movies, it was probably more like a good kick. He jumped out the same window it came in, and when it went off, they both escaped while chaos took place.

They made it to the Marines and tipped them off that we were still up there. That's why the tankers came up the road, to rescue us. They thought we'd make a break toward them, but we didn't move; we didn't know Moss and Thomas had tipped them off.

When we got back to the company: "The Old Man wants to see you."

Bussey went through the roof when he heard the story. Four-letter words were flying. "I don't believe the infantry ran off and left you!" He jumped in a jeep and was off to 3rd Battalion headquarters. He chewed up the lieutenant [*Haley*] and wanted an explanation why they left us, but Haley couldn't remember anything.

The Marines

August 7: The Marines went into action for the first time on the Deuce-4's right flank. While Bussey watched, Brigadier General Edward Craig, in starched uniform and shiny boots, posed for "Caesaresque" pictures before sending his first regiment up Hill 255 ("Sugar Loaf"), one of the lesser hills below Subok San (738). [*Hills are named by their height in meters.*] He told the Army, "You guys get out of the way. We're gonna take care of this."

Singing

"We're gonna win, by God,

 We're gonna win!"

They marched forward in approved Camp Pendleton formation.

Bussey:

The Koreans were in fox holes, and they were damn good in fox holes. You couldn't even tell there was a fox hole there. The general called in his air support and blasted that hill with napalm. Didn't mean a damn thing. The Koreans crawled back out of the ground like ants. He put 12 man behind each tank and snapped his fingers. But this wasn't Pendleton.

Nathaniel Nicholson:

It was "the Bowling Alley," the Marines' first encounter of the war. The army's 90th Field Artillery battalion and the Triple Nickel [*555th Infantry Regiment*] supported them, and we set up our guns to support them both.

The North Koreans were on the hills on both sides, and the Marines went down the middle between them. The enemy spread out and "opened the door" and let them go through.

Then, all of a sudden the North Koreans closed ranks behind them, and the Marines saw there were more enemy than they had planned on, and they had to fight their way out. The Koreans annihilated them.

The 90th Artillery battalion was attacked. They had to abandon their guns, block the tubes, and explode them so the enemy couldn't use them.

Our radio man, James Burnett, was talking to the airplanes who were supporting the Marines trying to get out of there.

We had a .50-caliber machine gun mounted on the roof of the cab of an ammo truck. I manned that and started shooting to try to keep the enemy off the Marines. It jammed while I was shooting, and a soldier named **"Fransie" Mackey** unjammed it and started shooting until the enemy killed him.

That could have been me.

The first wave staggered back. The general sent the second wave up, and they got halfway to the top before they too had to retreat.

Robert Fletcher (C Company):

Shit, the Marines thought the North Koreans were going to be little toy soldiers. They got their asses

150

slaughtered. We twice had to open a hole and get them out.

The third wave got almost to the top, but it too had to fall back with heavy casualties. At last, Bussey wrote, the general declared victory and marched his men back to base.

As in every war, GIs and Marines had little love for each other.

Hubbard:

They were a pain in the ass, always bragging. We called them "Jawheads." The Navy called them "Bellhops." (We had a few words for the Navy too.) We always used to be at it with the Marines. I used to get in fights:

"You remind me of bananas."

"Why the hell is that?"

"You're born green, turn yellow, and die rotten." And the fight started.

They told us, "In the Marine Corps they teach us to wash our hands after peeing."

We said, "In the Army they teach us not to pee on our hands." That started it again.

The Rescue

August 11. Fields:

We were not the last ones to come in. A few days later the CO received a call from the aid station saying, "We have a man here who is refusing aid until he sees you." Bussey dropped the phone and was gone in a minute.

It was **Eddie Sanders** - "Bebop" Sanders, a tall, thin private. He said he was with Lieutenant Lenon and the other wounded for two days. He had part of his foot shot off but begged Lenon to let him go for help, but Lenon wanted to keep them all together; he knew Bussey would come back for them, but he didn't know when. But after two days he began to doubt it, because he thought Bussey may have thought they were all been killed. Finally he agreed to let Sanders go.

Sanders crawled all night until daylight, then he hid in some bushes but was discovered by two enemy soldiers when they sat down to eat. He played dead, and they dropped rocks on his head to make sure he was.

Bebop always said he wanted to live to see the New York Yankees play. He recovered from the punishment and was able to continue crawling. He got bit by a poisonous snake [which caused his face to swell up] and couldn't use one hand.

At last he saw American soldiers laying wire and called for help, and they got him to the aid station. He refused aid until he could talk to "the Man, Bussey," in those words.

Sanders said Lenon was still alive with about five or six men back up in the mountains. He described their location in the sketchiest of details, but it was enough for those of us who got out to lead Bussey to the place.

Bussey went to the infantry headquarters to ask for help but was told the area had not been cleared yet and he couldn't go in.

He told them to go to hell, in a polite way. Instead, Bussey geared up to go.

We told him one of our problems was that we didn't have any automatic weapons for supporting fire. While stationed at Mount Fuji we had a white ordnance company with us. We got along like brothers and lived side-by-side. Bussey kept in touch with the unit, and it paid off. He gathered up about eight fifths of whiskey from his officers, and away he went.

When he returned, he had a trailer-load of automatic rifles and machine guns packed in grease. The motor sergeant doused them with gasoline to clean them for action. Each squad now had two automatic rifles and two light assault machine guns, and the heavy machine gun had a tripod. With it, if you can see 'em, you can hit 'em; it will shoot about 2,000 yards - that's about 20 football fields.

Bussey called the company together. "I want volunteers to step forward."

The whole company stepped forward, including the cooks. He apologized but said the cooks had to stay behind so we would have a hot meal when we returned. They said, if we eat C-rations, they could go. But he made them get off the trucks.

French:

We all loved Lenon to death - we all went to get him out, didn't we? Absolutely.

Fields:

"Saddle up." The order was passed.

My squad, back to eight men again, had two automatic rifles and a .50-calibre heavy machine gun. That leaves four or five men with M-1's [rifles], so we were heavily loaded for bear.

We moved out. As we passed through our lines, the checkpoint guards were puzzled. "Where you guys going?"

"To get our goddam wounded out, that's where."

They gave us a thumbs-up and hollered, "Give 'em hell."

We drove behind enemy lines, then hiked on back trails around low hills out of sight.

Bussey ordered French and Fields to take 40 men and secure the cliff above the trail to prevent attack from there. French protested. "Sir, I'm just a corporal. You have plenty of sergeants with more experience."

"French, I picked you for this job because I want it done right. I picked Fields for the same reason. Get it done!"

"French was young and ambitious," Bussey wrote, "I knew nothing would deter him." In his book Bussey named it "French's Ridge."

The force hiked through "Death Valley" in blistering heat.

French:

The enemy were running ahead of us going along the ridge. As we came off the ridge, there was a creek running alongside the road. Bussey said, "All right, men, drink up, fill your canteens."

When we turned off the trail to go over the mountain, we were under fire, and we came upon three or four black GIs, killed the week before. They had their hands tied behind them, their ears were cut off, their noses cut off, and there was puss coming out of them. You never saw so much puking in your life. One of my friends had been killed. I took his letters and his watch to send home to his parents.

The CO called a meeting and covered each detail. He told Sergeant Whitaker, "Take the third platoon up on the high ground. Lieutenant **Wells**' platoon, take the saddle [*between the hills*]. Sergeant Green, you take the left side." Bussey took the fourth Platoon with Sergeant **[*James*] Knight** to go in and perform the rescue. "Tell the men to shoot to kill." And he said, "If you fuck this up, I'll have your ass when we return."

Whitaker told me to take my squad up on the high point, "because you know where they are, and you can command the area with the .50. Give a burst of three rounds when you're in position. That's the signal for Knight to move in."

So off I go.

I left the second platoon sitting there and got up on the hill. Once on top we could see about a mile in all directions. I set the .50 up and hollered, "Test fire!" and kicked off some rounds.

That was the signal for Knight and the CO to take off. They went up the hill and down the other side to where the dead and wounded were.

It also brought four enemy up to investigate. A couple more bursts, and it was all over. Minutes later a squad of North Korean soldiers appeared. I gave the command, "Cut loose," and my squad blew them away. The rest took off, I gave the signal for all-clear, and no further action took place during the whole rescue.

French:

We found some of Lenon's guys, who had been hiding over a week with nothing to eat, and we gave them chocolate bars. One man ate his without taking off the wrapper.

Bussey walked around, hunched over, calling: "Chet? Chet?"

We heard Lenon's voice say, "I knew you were coming."

We had a stretcher - I don't know where Bussey got a damn stretcher from - but we got Lenon out on that stretcher.

We were moving fast.

Fields:

We watched as they brought the litters out with the lucky ones on it. The unlucky ones were given a grave, and their dog tags were collected. We wanted to get back before dark, and Bussey did the fastest memorial service you ever want to see. It didn't take more than two minutes, and he said, "Stop!"

155

To my surprise, someone came out of the bushes, waving at the convoy of stretchers. Moss took the glasses and said, "Son of a bitch, you won't believe it - it's Womack!"

He'd been living on pine seeds and drinking his own urine.

I said, "He disobeyed my order and got separated, I ought to kill him for this. Wait till I get my hands on his ass."

Womack had a harrowing tale to tell of the ambush:

I got to the crest of the hill, but when I got to the top, they didn't have blocking on the left and right flank, so I went down into a little gulley not far from the Korean CP on a little foot path. I could hear them talking, but I didn't know how many people were there, so I hid in some hedges and bushes. I was layin' there, and they walked right past me every day - they didn't look at the ground. I was hiding there for a week.

I was drinking piss - I'd piss in my helmet and put purification tablet in it. My mouth was swollen up, and I got tired of pissing in the helmet.

So after a week I crawled down the hill - there was a creek down there - to fill my canteen with water. I left my helmet up on the hill, somone saw it and kicked it down the hill and started shooting at it, and my helmet came bouncing down. If I hadn't been down the hill, they would have spotted it, and I would have been in it.

It wasn't my day to go.

I'm trying to hide and get as small as I could.

Then I went back up the hill, and that's when I made up my mind: I wasn't going to die alone. I was going to take somone with me. That's exactly what I was going to do! That was my intention! I had two hand grenades and pulled the pins out of both of them with my teeth and spit them on the ground. Now I've got two live grenades in my hands. But what was I going to do with them? Got to make sure I don't go to sleep, and I couldn't turn them loose – the Koreans would know there was somone there, and I was gonna get hit by the grenades too. There was nothing I could do with them.

So I reached with my mouth and found one of the pins, about an inch and a half long, like a cotter pin. I rolled it on my tongue and held it between my teeth. I got to make sure it was lined up with the hole on the grenade handle and pushed it back in. Then I did the same thing with the other one.

The next day Bussey's rescue party arrived.

French:

Getting out of there, we came under more fire. Burp guns, basically - if you've ever heard one, you know what it sounds like.

There was only one way we could go out, the same way we came in. It was the fastest way, and you couldn't look for another route, because you were behind the lines already - hell, no one back at headquarters even knew where the hell we were. We were under fire until we got over the crest of the mountain.

Womack:

One of my grenades was bouncing around in the truck bed. When the others saw what I was staring at, they grabbed it and threw it off the back of the truck.

The rescue party returned to camp singing the unofficial company song, "I was on my way to town to see my *musume*" - *girl friend.* As they moved through the checkpoint, the GIs cheered.

But they found Colonel Roberts pacing up and down, fuming.
French:

The colonel was waiting on Bussey's ass: "Where's Lieutenant Lenon?"

"Here, sir."

He asked Bussey whether anyone got wounded or killed.
Bussey said, "None."

That really made Bussey stand out for me. The commander had written them off. Had Bussey been unsuccessful, without doubt he would have been court-martialed. He laid his career on the line to get those guys.

That was my proudest moment in the Army.

Womack:
    We built a bridge and put on it the names of all the guys that got killed.

Fields:
    Six or eight of us got medals. Lieutenant Lenon got the Distinguished Service Cross. Sergeant Knight got the Silver Star. Captain Bussey, Sergeant Whitaker, and I were recommended for the Silver Star, but Division down-graded them to a Bronze Star with a V for Valor.
    For a black person, this is nothing new. If a white boy had done it, it would have been different. Yes, it happened - it happened many times. Who were you going to complain to? There were only a few field-grade blacks, very few black colonels, and no generals.

BSWA devoted only one graph to the episode. The authors were looking for examples of cowardice before the enemy. This was not what they were told to find.
    Whitaker later received a battlefield commission.

French:
    Whitaker was my platoon leader. He knew his engineering. One of the top NCOs I worked under, and when he got a battlefield promotion, he was a hell of an officer.

August 8. The battle for Battle Mountain raged on.
    Jimmy Hicks went on a mission with 200 men under Captain **Richard Williams,** who had just gotten out of the hospital after he was shot in the ear and shoulder.

After a three-hour climb, reporter Hicks noticed that many of the men's shoes were worn to a frazzle after almost daily fighting. The supply officer said he can't get any, but a soldier said he was told they could have all they wanted if he would ask for them.

Robert Yancey (C Company)

I was assistant platoon sergeant of about 30 men. Our company commander was Captain Mayo. He was highly intelligent, short and dark-skinned [*not to be confused with Captain Steven Mayo of B Company*].

We had to dig in, and before you kicked off an attack, everybody fired machine guns, mortars, everything you had. But those North Koreans .were like ants - they would dig right through to the other side of the  mountain, and nothing was hitting them on that side.

Then they'd come back at you like a plague. You had to know where you're at and where the enemy is at. The problem was when they infiltrate the line and get behind you, and you're shooting all around you. It's crazy.

The more you're on the front line, the more you learn to control your fear. Most people got killed because they did dumb things. You'd say, "Stay down," and they'd want to look and get hit right through the head.

We'd go out and lay minefields. One time I said, "Where's **Kincaid**?" and there was a big explosion. He walked back in to get his field jacket. They found only about ten pounds of him. I told the guys, "You don't *ever* go in a minefield for *nothing!*"

159

Many skirmishes you'd see the trucks loading the bodies in, and you ask yourself, "When is it going to be my turn?" But you learn not to question the Man Upstairs. Understand?

Robert Fletcher (C Company):
Two o'clock in the morning they said, "We've got to take the mountain back."

I said, "Sir, they're going to have an air strike in the morning. Then we can go up and take it."

"We'll put panels up" [so the planes won't hit us].

The first thing the Air Force did was bomb and strafe us anyway.

Fields:
With binoculars we could see our men standing on the hill being strafed by American planes in broad daylight. I think five got killed, because they brought five men off the hill.

Albert Kimber (I Company):
I was wounded in my shoulder, and they treated it at a hospital in Pusan. Stayed back there overnight and went right back into battle.

Ellis Dean:
Herb Wanca and I were on a hill directing mortar fire, and we got a message on our phone that we were being out-flanked and to get off that knoll. Herb took off, and they kept shooting at him. I wanted to run, myself, but I couldn't get away.

About six of them captured me. They were North Korean infiltrators, wearing white farmers' outfits. They wanted my boots, and they kept looking at my wrist for a watch, but I didn't have one. Then they pointed which way I should go and let me go.

I couldn't find my outfit. After two days with the 2nd Division, they located the 24th, and I went back. Wanca made it OK too, but he got wounded.

About this time Hicks reported that a North Korean in black face and in U.S. uniform was spied driving a column of civilians to get close to the American position. Other reports also told of an enemy patrol with faces blackened.

Sfc **Raymond Johnson** of Augusta was driving four wounded men in his jeep, when they were hit by machine gun fire. Johnson was hit in his left wrist and fell from jeep. An enemy tank driver fired three pistol shots at him.

One hit my wrist, another hit me in the chest. Then the driver kicked me to see if I was alive. I didn't move. My right hand was completely off. My buddies came and pulled me to safety.

August 13. Company G was pinned down by heavy fire. A medic, All-Army heavyweight boxing champ Levi Jackson, threw himself over two wounded men, shielding them. It cost him his life, and he was awarded the DSC. (Why not a Medal of Honor? If he had thrown himself on a grenade, he would have received one.)

Engineer Road

August 14. Supplies took a long trip from Haman north, then back south to Battle Mountain. Bussey decided to cut a more direct road from Haman.

Fields:

We were building an escape route, under sniper fire some of the time, at night basically.

Intelligence let us down. For over a week we were getting a lot of air bursts and wondered what the North Koreans were doing. They were zeroing their guns and waiting until we finished that damn road.

When it was finished Colonel Champeny arrived, shaking his finger: "I told you we didn't need another road!"

During the work Sergeant Alfonso Spencer fell off his bulldozer, crushing his arm, which had to be amputated. First Sergeant Dudley gathered Spencer's equipment, including his camera. Amazingly, when the film was developed years later, it included the picture of the mass grave at Yech'on.

August 15. Edward Cleaborn Jr of Memphis was with a platoon in Company A, which was pinned down by inter-lacing fire. He cleared the ridge, firing until his hands were burned. He wiped out several Communist machine gun crews, and when his platoon withdrew, he covered them.

He received the DSC.

Meantime, Arthur Dudley of the 2d Division's all-black 9th Infantry killed 50 enemy riflemen with his M-1. The North Koreans called him "the terrible one." He told the medics: "Patch up my leg fast," and went back to the fight.

It is not known what decoration Dudley received, but in World War II the famous Audie Murphy received the Medal of Honor for doing the same thing.

August 17.

Corporal **Lawrence Grant** of Baltimore commanded the lead tank in an Integrated tank unit supporting the white 35th regiment. He told Hicks:

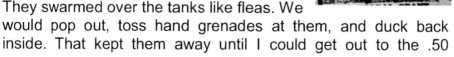

The enemy infiltrated our lines and got behind a heavy mortar company. They over-ran that position and came up behind our tanks.

We swung around and hit them by the hundreds, but they kept coming. We ran out of ammunition for the heavy guns, and the enemy rushed up to the tanks and began sticking small arms inside and firing. They swarmed over the tanks like fleas. We would pop out, toss hand grenades at them, and duck back inside. That kept them away until I could get out to the .50

calibre on top of the tank I cut them down as they came. It seemed like there were millions of them. Their bullets bounced off the tank and machine gun, but they missed me.

When I ran low on ammo, the boys inside handed up a new box. They fought the enemy with grenades and rifles while I reloaded.

We kept fighting, and they kept coming.

When I finally ran out of ammunition, I yelled, "Cover me, I got to reload," but they yelled back: "We're out of ammo too!"

I dived back into the tank. We started to move away, running over the enemy as we left. We got out of there, got more ammunition, came back and re-took our position, killing them as he came.

August 22-23. The North Koreans broke through and cut off E Company. Once again Sergeant Robinson took charge and kept his men in place. They fought off repeated "fanatical" attacks for two days until relief arrived. He was finally given a Silver Star.

The Third Battalion (I, K, L, and M) also came under intense mortar fire. Master Sergeant **Levy Hollis** had a desk job as battalion operations sergeant. Joe Davis knew him well. "he had a big German shepherd dog I used to love to play with in Gifu." Hollis was rank-conscious toward anyone below him, "but he could read maps, and he was a fighter."

He ran out of his tent toward the front, moving constantly from unit to unit, reconnoitering enemy gun positions, carrying ammo and water to the troops, and pointing out targets.

August 24. The battalion was finally forced off its hill. Hollis rounded up stragglers, found weapons for them, and led a counter-attack. In the words of his awards citation, he "inspired the men to perform prodigious feats of arms," and they finally regained the hill.

He was given a DSC.

"He should have got the Medal of Honor," Davis said.

Hollis also received a promotion to lieutenant. He retired as a lieutenant colonel.

Curtis Bolton (C Company):

We came back up to 239 people in our company, because they were sending replacements. One was a white sergeant; only stayed one day and then he was gone: "Oops, we made a mistake."

The Chinese Moon

August 27. A bright orange-red moon rose that night.
John French:
The fight at Battle Mountain was on my 19th birthday. Yep.

We were doing engineer work in the day, then we had to go up and fill in on the line [*with the infantry*] at night. Everyone was a fighting soldier, whatever your main job was.

LaVaughn Fields:

We were out in front of the 159th Artillery Battalion as protection, and we saw some oxen out in front with six and eight legs - the North Koreans were hiding behind them and shooting at us.

That night we called for overhead fire, but no one would support us. The CO of the Division Engineers - the 65th battalion - told us they were friendly troops, and he'd decide whether we needed supporting fire.

We knew it was going to be a long night.

John French:

We were in a schoolhouse, and about 11 or 11:30 at night they started bracketing us [*firing one round long, the next one short – the third one should be on target*]. And they were hitting whatever they were shooting at. We had a slit trench, where we dumped kitchen trash, and when the shells started coming in, I went to jump in the trench, but there were three guys there already.

We were getting fire from everywhere. It was a hell of a fight, hand-to-hand and everything else, the wildest thing I've ever been involved in. Those North Korean son of a guns had some of the best troops. They were determined.

By the time they're on you, you don't want to shoot and kill your own guys, so it was mostly hitting with your rifle. When you get into it with one of those guys, one or the other is going down.

Lieutenant Bussey put me in for a medal.

The fight was murderous.

Bussey:

Garlic, gunpowder, and death.

I heard a man scream, and I was doing a dance of death... Feint, parry, thrust, retrieve, pivot, thrust, retrieve, butt stroke, swing, thrust... poverty, bigotry, hatred, Ku Klux Klan, fire, hunger, and death....

Suddenly, clubbed from behind, my head exploded. Desperately I rolled over and frantically scuttled sideways. My rifle was gone! Trying to clear away the cobwebs, I dragged my hand across an entrenching tool. A little man was stalking me with a long weapon like a scythe blade. I swung the entrenching tool and performed a perfect combat lobotomy, dumping his blood and brains onto my chest. I was sticky and wet and sick.

September 1. The Communists mounted another major attack. This is another story that BSWA barely reports. All headquarters were hit simultaneously at midnight.

Nathaniel Nicholson (159 Artillery):

We were in a river bed. We had no infantry with us, because they had been relieved and had gone back about five miles. The pay truck came, and that night everybody was feeling good. About one a.m. we were listening to records when mortar rounds started coming in - more than 50 or 60 - and blew that pay truck to pieces.

James Burnett;
We were just relaxing when it started, so loud it scared me half to death, I didn't know what to do next. Officers were getting knocked off left and right. Their artillery was deadly accurate.

Bussey:
The first shell hit a kitchen truck, the second overturned an artillery piece.

Nicholson:
We all jumped into our foxholes. The enemy were coming over the mountain. Machine gun fire came from our outpost. That meant they were coming in force. Some of the South Korean troops were unreliable in standing their ground, and a lot of stragglers left their positions without permission. The second battalion collapsed. They sent one company from the reserve up to try to close the line, but the enemy had already broken through.

The ROKs gave way on the right flank, Jimmy Hicks wrote, and an estimated five battalions - 3,000 men - poured through. They reached 500 yards behind regimental headquarters, with "nothing but cooks, and correspondents in reserve." Some men were shot almost in sight of division headquarters.

Sergeant first class **Chappel Hampton** told Hicks:
At day-break, about five a.m., about 80 of them charged a platoon of American soldiers, throwing grenades. I killed several of them, and they kept coming. One of my men got frightened and jumped in my foxhole. This gave away my position.
The enemy slipped around behind me, and It was almost hand-to-hand. They scored a direct hit with a grenade, but I continued to fight for another 15-20 minutes.

Then I felt and found out I had no right leg.

Nicholson:

We started sending artillery rounds back at them. We were shooting everything we had - we even fired smoke shells. They weren't doing any damage, but at least they were keeping the enemy back. We just wanted to make a boom: They didn't know what was coming [*laughs*].

Burnett:

Just about day-break Nick heard someone call for .50-calibre ammunition up the hill. The guy was keeping the North Koreas off our behinds, gave us a chance to get out of there.

Nick jumped up and started carrying ammo up the hill. When he did that, he loosened me up, the fear went out of me.

Nicholson:

Willie Boone and another man were on the outpost, where the road went to a little farmhouse 300 yards away. Boone was holding the enemy off with a .50-calibre. He needed ammunition, and I grabbed two cans and ran through the river bed, down the road, and down another road, to him. Then I ran back.

We never knew what happened to Boone. They never found his body. Some think he stayed there. There's another report that he ran away, but I know that's not true, because I took him ammunition. This was an example of the excuses the Army used, to put blame on black soldiers. I know for a fact he didn't run.

He was listed as MIA [*Missing in Action*]. I have the casualty reports showing his name twice, once on August 31, once on September 1. I don't know what really happened. It's a mystery. One report says he went down shooting. But they gave him no award.

We were down to our last high-explosive shells - World War II stuff. There's a timer on the head of the shell, and you set it to explode in the air just before you think it's going to hit the ground; that way you get more casualties - that was our "smart bomb."

As day was breaking, we started shooting rounds point-blank. We depressed the muzzles and sighted through the tube, didn't use the sights. You're not supposed to fire high explosive rounds with the tube aimed close to the ground, because the rounds already had their timers pre-set [*to explode at a certain altitude*], and they could go off too soon. But that was all we had left.

There was a gully on the other side of the road, and as they raised their heads to come over, we'd shoot at them.

Captain **Lavon Smith**'s battery also depressed its guns to fire directly at the enemy.

Lionel West from Louisiana was only a corporal, but he was section chief of a 105 howitzer in Battery A:

I got a Bronze Star for shooting direct fire. When you've got to do that, you're in bad shape; the enemy is like a running back in the secondary - he's got to score.

We put machine guns in front of the 105s [*artillery pieces*] for protection, but the enemy had broken the line, and the only thing the machine gunner could call back on his radio was, "Fire on me, I'm surrounded!" My gunners took him out as well as the enemy.

My gun was the last defense. It slowed the enemy down. All five of the other guns had gone back. I was still there. If you're the chief, you've got to stay with the gun.

When the section officer set up at the rear, he gave me 30 seconds to move - get the heck out of there.

The enemy shot off the deuce-and-a-half [*two-and-a-half-ton truck*] tires, and the driver went on down the road pulling the gun with both the front tires out. When we pulled into the new position, they jacked that son of a gun up and changed the tires, and we continued to give support.

The same scene was taking police in Battery B.
Burnett:

I asked Captain Franke what to do. He told the artillery to hook up the guns and take them out one by one. They would fire one, hook it to the truck, and take it away. One by one.

Until we got down to the last gun.

Nicholson:

One of the 105 guns was covering the withdrawal of the rest, and I was covering the 105 with a BAR. That one gun and me and three men managed to hold the position until the other guns withdrew.

Before I knew what was happening, they shot the BAR out of my hands, so I threw it in an abandoned ammo truck. it looked like everyone had disappeared except me. I thought, "What did I get myself into?" I said, "Nick, get out of here, quick!"

Finally Captain Franke said, "Close stations! March order! We can withdraw."

Then I saw a truck. My FO, Lieutenant **Ingraham**, suddenly appeared. We found an enemy shell in the radiator, but I turned the key, and it started. It might not have had any water in it, and it ran hot, but it ran.

Captain Franke was in Burnett's weapons carrier. He said, "Come on! This way! This way! Over here!"

The lieutenant said, "Wait! We gotta get the last gun." A bullet came through my window past my chest and went through the big muscle of my left arm, but I could still drive with one arm.

Burnett:

When Nick got shot, it just inspired me more. I hooked up the gun to Nick's truck. As he's driving the gun, the engine got hot, lost water, and blew up. A captain and six of us together lifted this one gun and hooked it to a weapons carrier.

Nicholson:

The captain pulled over so we could switch the gun to the weapons carrier and pull it to safety. Captain Franke said, "Let's get out of here!" They jumped on the shield of the gun, which you could stand on, and I started pulling it out.

Burnett:

Off we went, I didn't know where. The captain said, "Come on, this is the way to go!"

I said, "All right, you're the boss." Sure enough, there was a road, Engineer's Road. The 77th built it precisely for us. There was no other way for us to get out.

Nicholson:

I didn't even know the engineers had built a road, but if they hadn't, we would have been trapped.

One of the builders of the road, Lieutenant LeTellier, was watching:

I remember the artillery coming out, with the last piece being pulled by the commanding officer's jeep, covered by wounded soldiers. That was a once-in-a-life-time moment. It was a classic withdrawal; he didn't leave any of his pieces.

Nicholson:

I was proud to be part of B Battery. We never lost a gun. The Division lost guns. We never lost one.

That morning someone else escaped on Engineer Road - Colonel Champeny.

Nicholson:
We stopped at a place called Horseshoe Road. We had ammunition stockpiled there and we set the guns up again and shot everything we had, from high explosive to smoke.

I was taken to the hospital, and after two days they put my arm in a sling and sent me right back. Thirty guys were admitted, and 29 were given R&R. I was the only one who was sent back to the front.

They also gave me a Silver Star.

September 2. Sixteen hours after the attack began, the Engineers' second platoon was surrounded – 218 men against 600. Captain Bussey and Lieutenant Wells fought their way into their advanced command post. Bussey grabbed the field phone and cranked regimental headquarters, about a mile up the road. A voice answered in Korean. He turned to Wells: "I think it's time to get the hell out of here."

Wells fired one more hail of lead, grunted, and followed Bussey.

When Bussey called the roll, 17 of his men had been wounded, but luckily only two were killed.

The 27th white infantry regiment was sent to help. It also met heavy resistance and called for large-scale artillery support.

Jimmy Hicks reported that three batteries of the 159, plus one white battery, fired a TOT (Time on Target) barrage. Though separated by miles, they coordinated their fire perfectly to land on the enemy at the same moment. The Reds didn't have time to take cover. When the Infantry moved in and re-took the position, they found 250 dead. The next day the guns killed 400 more.

Colonel Clayton's second battalion was surrounded. For two days there was a complete blackout. The situation was so hazardous, even the intrepid Hicks couldn't reach them. Division admitted it knew nothing of the unit.

When the battalion finally made contact, Division said its losses were "moderate." But survivors told another story - they had been virtually wiped out. A day or two later, it became clear that no one at headquarters actually knew what had happened.

Hicks was told that a check of second battalion foxholes produced 80 men. A battalion is about 1,000. The rest obviously were not all killed,

Still, when you can find only 80 out of 1,000. it can only show that the organization has been decimated, disorganized, and virtually broken up.

They have been hit so hard they were routed, and many may have been missing for several days.

There is also the fact that at such times many men break in the face of the enemy and deliberately hide for several days. The 24th is no exception.

Out of countless acts of individual courage, Hicks captured several snapshots:

Corporal **Albert Griffin** of Milwaukee enlisted to pay for college. He was one of five boys, and his parents couldn't afford tuition.

I was in charge of a machine gun, but it jammed and the enemy came at us on our left flank. I gave the squad orders to retreat, while I grabbed a BAR and returned fire.

Griffin suffered six bullet wounds - two in the neck, two in his leg, one round went through his shoulder, and another creased his cheek.

They over-ran me, and I was given up for dead. I lay there wounded for three hours before I got any medical assistance.

Master Sergeant **Wayman Ransom** (Intelligence and Recon platoon) was from Detroit, serving his second tour in the Army. He worked in the Briggs automobile plant before signing up for a second hitch "because it's a better job than I could find in civilian life."

I got sprayed with shrapnel in the face and shoulders, but it was nothing that they couldn't pick out with tweezers.

A day later he was back to duty, when he was hit by a grenade. Once more he walked back to the aid station, then returned to his platoon.

Strap Lyles of South Carolina drove a weapons carrier filled with wounded amid a hail of bullets. The enemy shot its tires, blowing holes in two of them, but he kept driving.

Wade Rutledge of Greenville MS (G Company) had joined the Army because "I always wanted to see the rest of the world." He was killed while covering the withdrawal of his squad.

The infantry re-grouped, returned via Engineer Road, and re-took Battle Mountain. The last big North Korean threat had been blunted.

Nicholson:

That night I went to sleep next to the gun with my arm still in a sling. I fell into a deep sleep, because I hadn't slept in 24 hours. I heard my mother calling me: "Nate! Nate! Nate!" Nobody in the army called me Nate; they all called me Nick. In a flash I woke up and heard the enemy coming through again. We had hung out some brass artillery shells in front of our position, and I could hear them clicking together, *ping, ping, ping.*

I couldn't see anything, so I woke everyone and crawled over to Captain Franke and said, "Somebody's coming up the hill on gun four." I heard them *bang! bang! bang!* on the gun sights with bricks. I said, "Give some hand grenades," and I threw them down the hill, and the enemy finally left, doing no harm. I went back to where Burnett was in his radio jeep and stayed with him that night.

When I told my mother about it after I got home, she said, "I was praying for you."

173

From September 1-5, Hicks said, over 500 casualties passed through the regimental aid station. About 120 more had to be sent to another station. That does not include dead and missing.

Meantime others came back.

Albert Kimber (I Company):

After three weeks in the hospital in Japan, my whole body was wrapped up, from under my arms to my waist, but they flew me back to Korea.

I Company was up on Rocky Crag when I got there. They had just gotten run off that hill - you'd take it today, they'd take it tomorrow, next day we'd go back up there and take it back. I told Sergeant Simmons, my platoon leader, "Man, I'm hurt."

He said, "What's wrong?"

I opened my jacket, and he saw me bandaged up and said, "Man, get your ass back down the hill. Stay down with M Company, man." They were back in the rear echelon, where they set up mortars, and I manned a machine gun to protect the mortars.

It was about three months before I took the bandages off.

Meanwhile, back home, the headline in the Baltimore *Afro-American* read:

Truman civil rights program is dead
For duration of 81st Congress

Three black newsmen – Hicks, Frank Whisenant of the Pittsburgh *Courier,* and Alexander Wilson of the Chicago *Defender,* were riding in a truck which went off a narrow road while trying to pass a line of parked jeeps. It took ten minutes before the driver got his vehicle out, and Col Corley stormed up, cussing the lieutenant, **Charles Ellis**, who was black. "Get that damn truck off the road, you're holding up my whole convoy!" He pulled the bolt of his carbine back and pushed the muzzle into Ellis' stomach.

"Do you realize you're threatening me?" the lieutenant said.

"You're damn right I am, and I'll shoot you too!"

"Would you really shoot me, Colonel?"

"You're damn right I would!" Corley's eyes flashed.

Ellis pushed the gun aside. Wilson said the lieutenant started to go for his own pistol but thought better of it. He motioned to the driver to turn the truck around, to report the incident to Colonel Champeny.

Corley cooled down and patted him on the back: "Lieutenant, I've got to apologize."

"You can apologize to the regimental commander!"

Then Corley "really blew up." "I've apologized. Isn't that enough? What's your name? ... I'll fix you! I'll fix you!"

Seventeen EM who watched the exchange rushed up to Ellis and offered to be witnesses.

Wilson reports that Champeny came upon the scene and said he'd take the matter "under advisement."

(BSWA did not say a word about the incident. Ironically, many GI's thought Ellis "sucked up" to whites too much.)

No action was ever taken, however.

The next day Champeny was out, and Corley was in as the new regimental CO.

Corley Takes Command

September 6. Colonel Champeny received a slight wound. (Donald Womack says he shot himself in the foot.) He was given a DSC, and put in charge of training Koreans. However, he was soon relieved from that job and sent home, where he was promoted to general.

Colonel Corley took over the regiment. It was one of the best things that happened to the Deuce-4. Said white Lieutenant Lyle Ryshell of Company A: "Instead of telling them they would fail, he told them they could win."

September 7-9. On Corley's first day, the enemy drove F Company off its position, but it counter-attacked and won the hill back. Then the North Koreans hit K and B Companies, and Corley called for the 27th Infantry, the famous Wolfhounds, for assistance. They fought for two days but couldn't re-take the hill. Next Corley asked for the 35th Infantry [*the Cacti*] to help. But they also suffered heavy casualties in the rugged terrain and asked permission to withdraw. Corley had no choice but to call off the operation.

However, General Kean put the blame on the 24th and begged the Eighth Army commander, **Walton Walker**, to de-activate it as "untrustworthy." Walker did nothing.

Major **Melvin Blair**, of General MacArthur's headquarters, replaced Corley as head of the third battalion.

Blair was a former sergeant, who got his second lieutenant's bars in the 10th Cavalry, a black regiment. In World War II Blair had volunteered for the famous Merrill's Marauders in Burma. His patrol was pinned down by machine gun fire, and Blair crawled alone behind the enemy and shot the gunner with his carbine. Three days later two of his men were wounded, and again he crawled under heavy fire and brought them back. He won two Distinguished Service Crosses, second only to the Medal of Honor, plus a Silver Star.

Joe Davis:

Blair was a little short, well-built around the shoulders, sandy brown hair, a good-looking man. He was a pretty good soldier, he was no goddam dummy. He knew what he was doing. He made lieutenant colonel right quick. I used to work in the officers' mess. He was very quiet at times, but he could make life miserable for you if he wanted to.

Carroll LeTellier:

Blair was not one of my favorite guys. Everywhere he went, he went with a cameraman, you'd think he was running for president. He borrowed an assault boat from us and got some of his battalion members to paddle him to shore, with his cameraman taking pictures. He put his boot in the water like he was making an assault crossing.

Pugh's Fight Above the Clouds

September 14. One charge often made against the Deuce-4 wqas, "Man, dont get in that regiment. If you get wounded they'll never come and get you out."

About 0330 the enemy delivered heavy attacks against Charlie, Item, King and Love Companies and knocked them off their positions. According to Ellis Dean: "Curtis Pugh saved Colonel Blair's ass."

It was called "the fight above the clouds."

Blair called for volunteers to protect the left flank on Razorback Hill, a 15-foot-wide ridge west of Battle Mountain. Jimmy Hicks interviewed several survivors - Sergeant **William Winters** (Cleveland), George Bussey, **Thomas Birton** (Houston), **Willie Belcher** (Virginia), **Timothy Jackson** (Texas), **Alley Waler** (Houston), and **Howard Jaren** (Chicago).

They beat off several *banzai* charges Two enemy tackled Blair, who called, "Pugh!"

Dean:

Blair was surrounded, and Pugh went in to get him. Man, he killed some guys! Choked two to death. They had to pry his hands from around their necks.

Blair fell off the edge and climbed back up. "I just couldn't leave him there alone." He rallied the others to help Pugh fight his way out. Then they picked up the dead and wounded and began a three-hour retreat. Finally their ammunition was gone, except for Pugh's BAR and Blair's pistol, which he emptied, then threw at the enemy.

Pugh remained 100 yards behind, covering their rear, though Blair called on him to leave his position. "Hell, Major," he shouted "I'm having fun!"

Blair shook his head: "He's the greatest fighting man I've ever seen."

Blair recommended Pugh for a Medal of Honor, he got the DSC instead. MacArthur personally pinned it on.

BSWA mentioned Pugh's award but said nothing about how it was earned. (One of the knocks white officers often made against the 24th was, "Man, you don't want to be assigned to that regiment; if you get wounded, they'll never come and get you out.")

The regiment also began getting replacements, though most of them were truck drivers and other non-infantry troops.

Floyd Williams (A Company):

I was in a bath and fumigation outfit in Okinawa, but when I got to A Company, someone gave me a rifle and said I was in the infantry.

Lieutenant **Lipman** was the A Company commander. How cool he was under fire. The platoon leader was

Lieutenant Ryshell, Sergeant **Nollie** was the platoon sergeant.

I was *gung-ho*, no doubt about it - I had seen too many John Wayne movies.

One day when I had just joined the company, a plane had caught some

North Koreans on a little bitty hill, and there were dead bodies all over. You'd see all those bodies lying around bloated, and you'd stop near them and eat your dinner. You learned how to control your mind.

We had a guy called "Sleepy" - I don't remember his real name. He could go to sleep anywhere. We'd sit down, he'd go to sleep. At lunchtime I remember Sleepy going to sleep on all those bodies. We'd say, "Wake him up when it's time to go." He got killed later on.

Guys would come up and tell me, "When things get rough, don't feel fear, you do what you have to do, be calm." The worst thing in the world is to see men panic, especially in the infantry.

Fields:

We were on line 92 days. They recommended us Engineers for the Combat Infantry Badge, then retracted the order, so we didn't get anything.

However, the ordeal was about to end.

Inch'on

September 15. MacArthur sent the Marines and the Army's 7th Division on a surprise landing on the west coast deep behind enemy lines. It was the most brilliant move of his career.

Womack:

They wanted me to jump at Inch'on. The 187th [*parachute regiment*] wanted me, but I didn't want to leave the engineers.

The outfit did have one black member - Lieutenant **Richard Robinson**.

Caught in a pincer, the Communists bugged out from the South, and the Americans raced after them to catch them between a hammer and an anvil.

For six weeks the North had thrown everything they had at the Americans, but the Deuce-4 and the other Yanks held. After six brutal weeks the North Koreans were exhausted, out of supplies, and not one inch closer to Pusan. Much of the credit goes to the 25th Division and the 24th Infantry.

Jim Thompson (L Company):

At the end of the month we had the mountain. We had whipped the North Koreans - we had really whipped them.

Corley informed all troops:

In 60 days of continual combat, you have withstood roughness of battle which I have not seen in five campaigns in Africa, Sicily, and Europe with the First Infantry. You have held your ground against superior odds. The first victory was yours at Yech'on... Other units have not been able to accomplish what depleted companies of the 24th have done.

I am proud of the Blockhouse Busters.

The statistics tell the story. The Deuce-4 lost more blood than the other two regiments combined:

	Killed	Wounded	Total
24th Infantry	258	796	1054
35th Infantry	154	381	535
27th Infantry	117	382	499

Source: 25th Division Command Report, October 1 1950

There are three possible explanations:

1. General Kean, deliberately or not, was giving the Deuce-4 the most dangerous assignments while protecting his white units. "They were trying to get rid of us," black GIs muttered.

2. If the 24th was running away from enemy, apparently the 35th and 27th were running even faster.

3. - and I think the correct one - far from running from the fight, the men of the Deuce stood and fought. They paid the highest price and got the smallest thanks. If so, then General Kean badly mishandled his Division. If he had been color blind,

he might have conducted his tactics more efficiently to the benefit of everyone in the Division.

Fletcher:
    When I read those history books, I get infuriated. If it wasn't for the 24th, Pusan and Korea would have fallen. The load fell on our backs. We were the backbone.

When the *Afo-American* asked MacArthur to comment on the performance of the 24th, the general issued this reply:
    The 24th Regiment is a symbol of the courage, tenacity, and effectiveness of the colored troops... I have only words of praise and applause for them.

The men held up two fingers for victory. Their new motto: "We've got it made."

Autumn Pursuit

September 19. Kean called on his troops to put pressure on the enemy so they couldn't send reinforcements to the north. The 25th attacked, with the 24th in the center attacked west then north to clear the enemy from that part of South Korea. But the North Koreans could still put up a vicious resistance. The second battalion lost 55 men the first day; three days later the first lost 62.
    One company of the third battalion, under Captain **Nathaniel McWee,** jumped off and met heavy resistance. "I know those men;" Corley said, "they'll have that hill in three hours."

Jimmy Hicks:
    Corley is being well received as a fighting man, despite the incident with Lieutenant Ellis. He has completely won the hearts of the men with his fair-mindedness and fighting ability.
    He has revamped the morale of the regiment, which, though depleted and tired, is now back up to its former

fighting peak. He did this through disregard of rank in assigning officers to command positions, praise and awards for men who do a good job, and severe discipline for those who lie down... He is obviously proud of the way his troops are performing.

September 22. An enemy mortar attack left 60 men killed or wounded. C Company was hit hardest.

Robert Yancey (on the right):

C Company was always out front. A Company might be on the flank on the right, or B Company on the left. But we were spear-heading the rest of the regiment. And we didn't have the top equipment.

We would be in skirmishes: Fight, take over a hill, and move on ... fight, take over a hill, and move on.

The more you're on the front line, the more you learn to control your fear. Most people got killed because they did dumb things. You'd say, "Stay down," and they'd want to look and get hit right through the head.

Corporal **Willie Bennett** was driving a truck-load of ammo. "A couple of enemy up in the hills opened up on us, and one of them had a burp gun." Bennett tried to outrun the shots, but when they began hitting right in front of the truck, he and his assistant driver jumped out and ran down the hill. "The truck disappeared with the loudest noise I ever heard."

When they went back, "the only thing left was the steering wheel, dangling on a bush."

LaVaughn Fields (Engineers):

A battalion of North Koreans surrendered. It was either run north and get shot or stand there and surrender. They chose to surrender.

The 89th Tank Battalion, Sheridan medium tanks, was one of the lead elements of the 25th Division. If it didn't look like a bridge would hold, we'd send the tanks across on a bypass. Lieutenant **Nordstrom** was commanding Dog Troop of the 89th. He was white and was wonderful to work with. He said, "Just get me where I want to go." And we did.

Ernest Collier (G Co):

My third wound, they took me out, around Seoul, the first time I ever saw my whole battalion together. We were pushing them back and they pulled us back to rest and re-group, when the North Koreans brought these big heavy mortars.

They needed a forward observer, and of all the people, the only one who had a pair of binoculars was me, so I was singled out, or the binoculars singled me out, and they sent me up as an FO. I was calling the shots pretty good, but they spotted me, and they lobbed one in on me. I got "creased" - that's what they called it in the cowboy movies. Hit me in my legs, tore my leg up.

What was that crap - "You're going to be home by Christmas"? It was two or three Christmases before I got home. They sent a specialist to do a skin graft. I spent three years in Letterman Hospital in San Francisco. I lost the calf of my right leg and part of my foot.

Donald Womack (Engineers):

Every morning we picked up mines that were placed on the road at night. The enemy made them out of wood, a box with explosives in it, and dug a hole. The detector wouldn't pick up wood, so we'd look for piles of dirt and use bayonets to locate the mines.

Sometimes they would booby-trap them with long wires; you'd pick one mine up, and all of a sudden way back down the road - *boom*! - it would blow the tracks off a tank or blow the trestle off a bridge, and then the road was blocked, and you got a crater you gotta fill up.

The Koreans were up in the hills shooting down. A white lieutenant was walking around on the road like some kind of hero. I'm laying flat on the road. The bullets would come through the mud and land near me. I cussed him: "Get the f- off the road!"

I found someone who had died and took his BAR belt. I put two magazines of ammunition into each pocket. I used it on single shot until somone was charging toward me. I used it with such proficiency some people didn't know it was an automatic rifle. I named it "Rabbit." You know how fast a rabbit is? I wrote that on the stock - "Rabbit."

The Deuce-4 ran into atrocities not reported in the history books.

Clyde Jones (I Company):

The North Koreans were mean, bad, and tough as pig iron. But they were good soldiers. Hard to kill, just didn't give up. They were trained that way. We weren't. At a school house they left 16 or 17 Americans, all white, with their heads blown off, sitting beside the road, where we would see them while we were walking by. I was an 18-year-old boy. That's when I became a man.

They had castrated some Americans - we saw one man come running down the road. The North Koreans had tied others to trees with barbed wire in their mouths so they couldn't talk. Or they were tied on the ground with barbed wire, hands and feet, land mines around them so we couldn't move them or touch them. One was hanging in a tree; he didn't have any clothes on, just skin. They piled up about 20 Americans they had killed on the side of the road like fence posts for us to see. It was sickening.

They say I cried when I saw them; maybe I did. We kept going, and the older soldiers kept telling us, "It's just war."

I had three knives, one in my boot, one in a New Testament over my heart, and a bayonet. The old 24th believed in carrying a razor as a last resort to fight with. I had no razor at that time, everybody else did. I soon got one.

Fields:

We found ten or 11 GIs executed in the head. We vowed to take no prisoners, and we didn't for two days. We got word the North Koreans had a group of American prisoners 30-40 miles up the road. Nordstrom said, "We'll overtake them." So we ran all night instead of bedding down. The next day around five, we caught up with them.

They had left the prisoners in a big barn. Sergeant **Da Rogier** was on the lead tank. He was the first one off and ran up to the guard. He mumbled something in Portuguese. The guard nodded his head and opened up the gate. Then they blew him away. When other guards came, we slapped them around and killed them. They dropped their weapons and started surrendering.

We ran into the barn looking for the prisoners. At first we couldn't see them, it was too dark. As we opened the door and let some light in, we saw about 80 Americans, all from the 25th Division, laying in the straw. At first they didn't believe who we were, because we were black, and they just looked at us. Then it dawned on them, and they let out a yell. There was a lot of hugging.

We found the guards and turned the prisoners loose on them.

Womack:

We gave the guards' weapons to the prisoners, and they started shooting them up - they tore those assholes up. They got even!

Fields:

That was before General **Wilson** [*assistant division commander*] and the big boys arrived, and said we were violating the Geneva Convention and we had to stop.

Joe Louis was fighting Ezzard Charles that day, and we listened to the fight on the Army radio. [*Charles won in 15 rounds to take the undisputed heavyweight title.*]

September 29. In Washington President Truman gave MacArthur the green light to move into North Korea.

Clyde Jones:

We started walking north with little resistance. We burned down the first city we came to, someone set a house on fire, and it burned everything to the ground.

Floyd Williams:

We moved up into some town and got off a cattle car and were just standing around when a guy asked the guy next to me, which way to D Company [*Heavy Weapons Company*]?" I turned around, and believe it or not, it was my brother, **Albert!**

I didn't even know he was in the military! He was a year and a half younger than me. He and I were pretty close - he was one of those guys who liked to have the center of attention. So I asked about a transfer into D Company with him.

Womack suffered a third serious wound:

I crawled under a deuce-and-a-half [*two-and-a-half ton truck*]. The North Koreans walked the damn mortars up to the truck, and it got hit. *Boom!* I'm under there. All my right arm was on fire, I was beating it with my left hand. The skin was just rolling off.

They put me on a jeep going to the aid station. They had to tie me down, because I was trying to jump off. They had to give me morphine and put me in the hospital in Japan and thought they might have to amputate this finger. They taught me how to squeeze a ball and play ping pong to use that wrist. I became pretty good at it.

October

The Deuce-4 was back to full strength, but most of the new men were out of shape and not infantry-trained - truck drivers, supply people. There were even enough black replacements to send some to the white 27th and 35th regiments. A black captain, **Milford Stanley**, was put in command of C Company over white lieutenants.

Ralph Hubbard (M Company):

I found myself two different times when I thought I would be a POW, sure as hell.

The first time we got to the other side of the Han River [*south of Seoul*]. Three of us - **Walter Map** from Pennsylvania, and **Forrester** from Georgia - were carrying the three parts of the 75. They were heavy as hell; everything the Heavy Weapons Platoon had was heavy - the 8.1" mortar, the .50-calibre machine gun, and the 75. That's why they call it the Heavy Weapons Company. It was no misnomer. I weighed 146 pounds.

When we could, we'd get a-hold of a *papa san* and let him carry it on his A-frame on his back.

Anyway, we couldn't run with these damn things, and we were trying to keep up. We could see guys' heads bobbing up and down ahead of us, so we weren't concerned when it grew dark.

Pretty soon we were hearing a lot of foreign language I couldn't understand. I squinted, but I couldn't really see. Weapons are starting to be fired. We could tell they were North Koreans from their burp guns: *Brrrrip! Brrrrip!* If we heard burp guns to the left, we'd take off to the right.

There were big trucks coming through, and they weren't ours. We covered up our weapons and stayed off the road. When we saw them pushing soldiers with beards onto the trucks, our stomachs dropped down to our ankles.

We got quieter, if that's possible. We stayed on the ground in the hedges, about four feet high. It was 20 degrees, and we were cold.

It was getting into darkness when a company of North Koreans came walking 25 feet from us. We could tell them from the heavy garlic smell, *kimchi* [*garlic*] - my god, you could smell it all over the area.

I dived in a rice paddy. Now I tell my daughters the ingredients of the rice paddy - you're covered with she hit - but once you dive in there, you lay still. Don't breathe. We stayed low, and they never saw us. They moved north, but I had no way to scout the area, so we lay there half a day just to be on the safe side. It was one of the more harrowing days of my life. Later, when I became a platoon leader, I said, "You *never* let the rest of the unit out of your sight." That was a must!

That evening, just as it was getting dark, we met an I&R [*Intelligence and Recon*] patrol from the 27th Wolfhounds. We scared the shit out of them, and they scared us. We said, "We don't know where the North Koreans are." We didn't care what was on the other side of the mountains; we had too much heavy equipment to be scouting. They took off.

I thought we should start pushing the North Koreans hard while we had them on the run. You get to be quite a general, pissing and moaning, but a lot of times you're right. But we finally started to kick some ass, yes we did.

Clyde Jones:

At Seoul they sent us to Kimpo Airfield on guard duty. Came a big rain, and we were all standing near a fire trying to get dry. A Korean - we thought he was friendly - walked up to the side. We didn't pay too much attention, and he dropped this grenade on the fire. I was about to turn my head when it went off and hit me from the right side. I went down to the ground. I didn't quite know what was going on. "What happened?" I thought I was dead.

The medic took the shrapnel out of my head. The best thing America ever made was a band aid. He stuck it on my head and said, "You'll be all right." It never bothered me again. I've still got the scar.

He ran up a hill. We took off after the guy, and he ran under a fence at the air base. We didn't catch him, but we found a little headquarters - beds made with mattresses or straw. We got ten of them in fox holes there. Like everyone else, they were frightened.

Two men came by on a motorcycle, went about 100 yards and turned around. They were the intelligence for the North Koreans up on the mountain - whoever came down the road, they'd report it. They told me to knock one off his motorcycle with my rifle, and I did - I've been shooting since I was six years old; they called me Hawkeye.

The other one ran down into a tunnel under a house, half the length of a football field. They had a radio station down there to report who went up the road. GIs - "tunnel rats," we called them - went in there after them. Ten or 15 Koreans would come out of one hole, the soldiers would go a little more, and ten or 15 more Koreans would come out the next hole. Twenty-nine came out in all. Like Tennessee moles. Three of them wouldn't come out, so they burned them up.

We began to run down guerrillas. They were surrendering, and we had more enemy than we could do anything with.

The North Koreans had women fighting along with the men. They were tough! They shot American men, and the Americans shot them. This lieutenant said he was going to court-martial anyone shooting them. But I never saw any more of him. War is war.

Next town, still in South Korea, a *papa san* came out and motioned to us that the North Koreans had some women and children down in the school house. This guy came up with a flame thrower, went in the backside and burned it half-way down.

They started coming out. The soldiers had these little kids in their arms for protection - one of them had this little boy - and they were going to kill them. We were laying on the ground, couldn't shoot, so we stood up and ran with fixed bayonets, and they dropped the kids. One ran into the village, and we found him and killed him.

All the people got out of the school, and that thing blew up - they had stored some explosives in it.

MacArthur Blunders

October 3. The Americans reached the 38th Parallel. South Korea had been liberated. That's where the Korean War should have ended. In fact, that's where it did end - three years and 25,000 more American deaths later.

Their deaths can be blamed on the megalomania of one man, Douglas MacArthur. He boasted that he "understood the Asian mind." Yet he was caught napping by the Japanese at Pearl Harbor, he was surprised by the North Koreans in Korea, and was about to be caught asleep again by the Chinese.

MacArthur talked grandly of clearing communism out of Korea - perhaps out of all Asia. But Premier Chou En-lai warned that China would not tolerate U.S. troops on its border (any more than we would tolerate Chinese troops on the Rio Grande). The Revolutionary veteran, Marshall Peng Dehuai, was dispatched to Mongolia, backed by tens of thousands of troops. In total secrecy, they entered North Korea.

Unaware, the Americans captured Pyongyang, the North Korean capital. That would have been another perfect place to stop, where the Korean peninsular was most narrow and defensible. But the generals just renewed their race north.

The regiment welcomed a champion back.

Big Boy Williams, the boxing champ, had been shot in August and sent to Japan with six bullets in his body. But protesting that "they can't do this shit to me!" he went AWOL and hopped a plane back to the front lines. Weighing a mere 183 pounds - 75 below his fighting weight, Williams still carried one bullet in him.

They said it would work its way out, but I couldn't wait, so I took a razor blade, sterilized it, and hauled the little rascal [*sic*] out. It's one of my prized possessions.

AWOL charges were dropped. Instead, he was welcomed by General Kean personally, promoted to master sergeant, and awarded the Silver Star.

"He was a leader all the way, always out front," Yancey said; "he didn't believe he could be killed."

October 25-30. A Republic of Korea [*ROK*] corps was ambushed by 10,000 bugle-blowing Chinese and was knocked back with 75% losses.

Australian troops ran into a major North Korean counter-attack - apparently the North Koreans hadn't been wiped out after all but had simply been pushed back. The whole point of the Inch'on landing had been to catch the North Koreans between a hammer and an anvil. Instead there was no anvil – the Marines and Army troops were all racing north toward the China border, eager to win the glory of being first. Truman had ordered that only ROK units could approach the Yalu river border, but his generals ignored him.

In the West Walker's 1st Cavalry Division and the 24th Infantry Division advanced to within 20 miles of the river. It reported capturing Chinese-speaking enemy.

MacArthur refused to believe it.

A unique fight in the history of cavalry warfare unfolded, Mongolian ponies against American tanks. After three days of hand-to-hand combat, the First Cav fled, warning, "Whoever says they're not Chinks is crazy."

November 1-6. The first Soviet MIG fighter jets were spotted. A ROK regiment was surrounded. In the west the Chinese threatened to outflank General Almond's I Corps. Chinese over-ran the 24th Division and hit the Aussies. A Marine battalion was hit hard and trapped; it would be known as the "lost battalion." "World War III has started," one Marine declared.

Still MacArthur insisted there were only 30,000 Chinese "volunteers" in Korea, "maximum." We now know there were at least 200,000. He said he would clear them out in ten days and promised that his air force would "slaughter" them.

Then the Chinese disappeared; Peng ordered his men to lie low and suck the Americans deeper into his trap.

November 9. At Kaesang, back near the 38th parallel.

Bussey:

I drank all I could get hold

of in those days and was getting cases of booze every week from Gifu and shared it with my NCOs - my officers didn't drink, they were clean livers. Corley [*on the right with General Kean*] had stretched his own supplies thin, and one evening we got above the 38th parallel and stopped, and he said, "Why don't we toss a few?"

I said, "Fine."

After several belts, according to Bussey, Corley turned to him and said, "You probably wonder what happened to that recommendation for the Medal of Honor."

"You know, General Kean promised me that thing."

"Well, I'm agin it." Corley said he approved it for a Silver Star, the third highest of the army's four medals for bravery. He said Bussey deserved the Medal of Honor for Yech'on, and the Distinguished Service Cross for rescuing Lenon in the Valley of Death. Instead he agreed to only a Bronze Star, the nation's lowest, for the latter. "If you were white you'd have gotten them both - "you killed more men than Audie Murphy and John Wayne combined."

According to Bussey, Corley said he would also have OK'd the CMH if Charlie had been killed or an enlisted man. But a living black officer with the blue ribbon around his neck could be a dangerous inspiration to black kids.

Bussey took a long pull on the bottle and said he called his boss a bigot and a bastard. "Of course "that was the end of our drinking."

There is no way to confirm the story. Others I talked to had positive comments on Corley as a commander. Yet the story could be true. It was consistent with America's racial attitude of that time.

The tragedy was that the two best soldiers in the 24th could not get alone with each other.

John B. Holway

Ambush at Kaesang

November 9-10. Meantime the Deuce-4 was still clearing the enemy from the South. Company A was ordered to relieve a ROK unit just above the 38th parallel.

Floyd Williams:

Late in the afternoon, Company A moved up to take a town near Kaesang, which is now in the DMZ [*Demilitarized Zone between North and South Korea*]. There were a lot of North Koreans in it.

On the way in, one of the North Koreans fired on us. I managed to fire at him, but he was a long distance away and went over the crest of the hill, and I don't think I got him.

Next morning we had a little sporadic fire, but the enemy was way out of range, and we took the town with very little resistance.

Late in the afternoon they sent trucks to take us back. Someone accidentally fired a weapon, and they told us, "Unload your weapons," which was not the smartest thing in a combat zone.

We passed South Korean police coming up to secure the town. There must have been some North Koreans behind them, but they didn't have uniforms, and we didn't know one from the other, and we didn't pay them great attention. They were on the left and right, especially on the right front - a lot of them.

Two or three miles farther, they hit us with rocket-propelled grenades and everything else. They had a beautiful ambush set up - flat ground and no cover. Within a minute bullets were flying everywhere, and people all around us were getting killed.

Bob Jones (A Company):

I was sitting in the back of a ¾-ton truck [*similar to a pick-up*]. **Harry King** was sitting next to me over the

194

wheel when we hit a mine. He got blown apart - decapitated - and it blew me off the truck, floating through the air. The medics picked me up covered with blood. We had ammunition on the vehicle; for some reason it didn't explode.

I had abrasions on my back and a couple crooked vertebrae. But the pain let up after a while. As I got older they found out I had a cracked disk. They put me in a jeep and took me to a clearing station.

Williams:

Things were happening fast. I saw Sergeant **McRoberts** take a bullet. A guy named **McGruder** was right in front of me; I saw the bullet hit him. **Thomas Cordell**, a real nice friendly guy, had been in our platoon and got transferred out. He was visiting a friend and got killed.

They were all stacked up, dying fast. Those North Koreans had a base of fire an ant couldn't crawl through.

The truck stopped on the road, and most of the men jumped off on the right. Most of them got hit, because there was no cover. **Clyde Williams** - we called him "Big Philly" because he was from Philadelphia - and I jumped off on the left.

Someone said, "Fire! Fire!" but most people didn't have their rifles loaded. I managed to get mine loaded, but it kept jamming. Somebody jerked it away from me - maybe he didn't have one. I rolled over, but I had trouble moving, with all my heavy clothes on.

Wayman Ransom was with the I&R platoon, which accompanied A Company. He told Jimmy Hicks:

A lot of Koreans wearing ROK arm bands passed us, and we let them go. But as soon as they got out of sight, they took off their bands and jumped the platoon ahead of us.

Then they turned on us.

Corporal **John Hicks** (I&R):

It looked like a million of them was coming after us. Sergeant Ransom called for us to run for it, but he didn't. It suddenly dawned on me what he had said some time ago:

"Buster - that's my nickname - one of these days they're going to make me so damn mad with their *banzai*, I'm going to make one of my own."

He jumped from his position and walked into the enemy, firing and swearing ... I called him, but he didn't stop.

Ransom:

One of my squad leaders managed to get a machine gun into action, but we were in an open field with no cover, and I got hit in the knee. A Korean officer ran up, and he and I tangled for my rifle.

Then I caught four shots from a sub-machine gun and fell down and played dead. Next thing I recall was some Koreans trying to steal my shoes. I put up a fight, but they hit me over the head with a rifle butt and knocked me out.

When I came to, they stomped me around some more and took my field jacket and my billfold and cap. Then they left me... I think they shot anybody they saw was still moving.

Floyd Williams:

It only lasted a little while in the killing zone. Clyde Williams and I got separated from the company and were holed up in a rice paddy by ourselves. I crawled back a few feet. There happened to be a little indentation in the ground, and I rolled into it and got out of the fire.

Clyde Williams had got half his thumb shot off. Neither one of us had a weapon. I told him our only chance was to get to the railroad track about 100 yards away, maybe less. If the enemy is there, we'll try to kill them with our bare hands, because they didn't take any prisoners.

I had no idea where we were, but I took a chance we'd catch up with the company. He didn't come with me, but I crawled through the rice paddies until I got to the railroad and hid in a haystack all night long. I could hear them chattering in Korean and firing every now and then.

With five bullets in him, Ransom lay in the field all night. in the morning the Reds came back through, shooting all the wounded. They saw a U.S. tank battalion, shot him again, and ran.

Williams:

Next morning I said, "Well, I'll try to see who has control here." I started walking and passed little villages. Every village the people would be out observing me. Even though they were flying South Korean flags, they were still frightened. I got lucky. That evening I ran into the 24th. I was all scratched up and beat up, and I had a minor injury in the thumb, maybe from shrapnel.

November 14. Williams finally reached the rest of the regiment:

I was at Division clearing station, and they brought in Sergeant **Nollie** and Lieutenant Ryshell. Both of them were wounded. As far as I know, the three of us - the two leaders and a pfc - were the only ones who survived from our platoon.

A fourth man, Ransom, was also found, frozen but alive. He received the Distinguished Service Cross, the nation's second highest honor.

In all, 50 Americans were killed or missing.

Williams:

I stayed in the hospital about a week, and they wanted to send me to Japan, but MacArthur said the war would be over by Christmas, so I decided to stay and go to D Company with my brother.

Clyde Jones (I Company):

Some things we were told never to tell, but I guess it's OK now. We were sitting on the side of a hill in North Korea. We had a new weapon - white phosphorous hand grenades. They were the size of a Pet milk pint can. You could shoot it 60 yards with an M-1. Captain Petrosky came over, said, "Jones, see how far you can throw one." I could throw a football 60 yards and a "pineapple" [*regular grenade*] 60 yards too. I pulled the pin on it, and I threw it as far as the M-1 shot it out. Yes.

Back home, Althea Gibson broke the color line at the U.S. tennis Open, and Dr Ralph Bunch, son of a barber and grandson of a slave, won the Nobel Peace Prize.

The Deuce-4 mounted trucks for a 130-mile drive north. Their mission: to relieve the 1st Cav.

Clyde Jones:

We went through Seoul and got on a train, and they pulled another train up right beside us. We looked at the soldiers, and they were black, from Ethiopia.

Sergeant **Trives** was an old man, was going to go back. We all were privates, but they had to put someone in charge. He said, "Jones is the man to put in charge. We're making you sergeant." I was surprised. He said, "Do the best you can do."

November 15. The thermometer sat at 29 degrees below zero when Bussey and his driver climbed in a jeep for a staff meeting with Corley. Peering through the icy windshield, they saw "a little buck-toothed Korean woman" struggling under a three-foot bundle on her head.

She waved and beckoned him to stop. Then she reached into the layers of clothes she was wrapped in and brought out a three-year old baby on one hip. She dug through some more and produced a one-year old on the other hip. Both began bawling as the freezing air hit them.

She groaned and, standing in a puddle, which the men didn't understand, handed the kids to them and motioned them to help her into a ditch, where she squatted, softy moaning, while they retreated.

Then they heard a whine and a cry and saw her wrapping her new baby in some rags as they extended their hands to help her up. They drove her to headquarters and turned her over to the aid station.

When they arrived for the meeting, Corley was livid. "Where in hell you been?" he demanded. When they explained, "he actually smiled" and suggested they get an ambulance to take the woman to the next village. They did. But she refused.

Bussey:

She walked by me, gave me a helluva smile, walked right past the ambulance, and padded down the road.

November 19.

Curtis Bolton (C Company):

Things were going pretty good. We went right through the North Korean capital, Pyongyang, with no resistance hardly. Kids were waving flags and hollering. Civilians in the towns would throw kisses. But if the enemy had kept on fighting, they would be waving the other flag. They couldn't help it. They were in between, just trying to stay alive.

Sometimes we had orders to burn up whole villages. I couldn't understand that. People had lived there for centuries. But we were told, "We don't want the enemy to use the houses."

MacArthur had given the order that we would go to the Manchurian border. Said once we reached it, that would be the end of Korea, and we could be rotated home, so I wanted to reach the border as soon as possible.

Clyde Jones:

We got a new white major at battalion headquarters came to visit us. "What do you need?"

"We need some new rifles. Our old ones aren't very good, half of them work, and half of them don't. Here's one here - want to try it out?"

All we had to keep warm was a poncho, but it saved our lives. I'll tell everybody: It kept the rain off you. If you laid down in the water, it would keep the water off you.

North of Pyongyang we went up on a mountain, jumped off the truck, and hit the ground running. Got into the woods. Nothing there.

This corporal came up, said, "Who's in charge of the second platoon?" Everyone turned around and looked at me - I was a private, just acting sergeant. He told me he'd take charge and to wait for orders to attack the farm house.

He stuck a hand grenade in his belt, and it came out. He had knocked the pin off. You could hear two clicks, or pops. It takes four seconds before it goes off. He grabbed it to get it off of him, but it blowed his stomach out, and his eyes rolled back in his head. His buddy also tried to get it out, and it blew up in his face, and he fell over backwards. Oh, Lord have mercy! It was the first time I ever saw a man die. I can tell you to this day how it looked.

We went down to a reservoir, and that was the beginning of "the Petrified Forest." There were trees, and we hadn't seen too many trees real close together. I'm a hillbilly, and I told them, "Something's wrong."

"What's wrong?"

"Look in the trees."

The whole mountain was "petrified." They took maybe 100 North Korean men and put them in fox holes on the side of the mountain, where we could see them. They looked like they were alive, but they were all dead. A whole mountain full of men! They had trails where you could walk through them. We thought they had guns, but they had sticks. It's using psychology on you.

Captain Petrosky told us, "Stop where you're at. Back off of that hill, or you won't forget this for the rest of your life."

But I never will forget it.

Anyway, the war was over - that was the rumor: The North Koreans were wiped out. "Oh, man, we'll be home for Christmas."

While the 25th Division was mopping up in the South - the original purpose of the Inch'on landing - the rest of the Army was hundreds of miles north, rushing toward the border with China. The original idea was to catch the enemy between the hammer and the anvil. But the anvil wasn't there.

"First outfit to the Yalu will be the first one home." The message raced through the Army. Defying orders from Washington, MacArthur sent the Marines and 7th Division on a race to be first. The 7th Division won. When its 17th Infantry (my future outfit) reached the bank, the officers gleefully pissed in the water as General George Patton had famously pissed in the Rhine five years earlier. Marshall Peng must have noted the ceremony, and that bit of schoolboy horsing around may have cost the division dearly in the days that followed.

Douglas MacArthur was sending his army to its worst disaster since he had abandoned it at Corregidor in 1942.

IV.

A New War

The Killing Cold

The GIs did not carry maps or thermometers in their packs, thus when they came to a major river, some assumed it was the Yalu, and when the temperature plunged, they thought it was 30 below. It may have been.

The Americans lost as many men to the bitter cold as to the enemy. According to Edwin Hoyt (*The Day the Chinese Attacked*), each American GI was issued:

long woolen underwear
2 pair of woolen sox
wool shirt
wool trousers
cotton trousers over the wool
 insulated shoe packs inside the boots
 pile jacket
 parka with hood
 trigger-finger mittens.

This was the uniform MacArthur was bundled up in when he flew from Tokyo to Korea. But it was not the uniform the men of the Deuce-4 were wearing when winter struck. *BSWA* says 90% of the regiment received either

one fur jacket,
one fur cap, or
one pair of gloves.

BSWA also says the 24th got the same clothing as every other outfit, but it gives no source. The men of the Deuce-4 tell a different story.

Jim Thompson (L Company):
We didn't get our winter gear. They said we were moving too fast, it would catch up with us. Yeah! Some got gloves, some got a field jacket. But the 27th and 35th, they all got theirs. That was so goddam prejudiced. From

the git-go they didn't want to be bothered with us. I think they were trying to get rid of us.

Robert Fletcher (C Company):

They preached to us, "We'll be back in Japan soon, don't worry about it." A lot of the winter clothes were sent back to Japan, and later they were back-packing them to us, but they never caught up with us. I had no winter boots, no woolen socks, no cap with earflaps. A lot of guys died.

Clyde Jones (I Company):

We didn't have anything but our [*summer*] field jackets. We took out our ponchos, and put them on, but we were still cold. One side of your face was frozen, the other half was thawed out. You had to breathe through your nose, you couldn't breathe through your mouth - it would freeze right there in front of you.

James Burnett (Artillery):

Oh, God, you talking about cold! I prayed to the Lord: "If you don't let me freeze to death, I don't care if it's 900 degrees in the shade, I'll never complain about it being 100 in New York. I'd say, "Yes, it's hot, but I love it!"

Robert Yancey (C Company):

They called us "the Frozen Chosen." Y9o eyes would tear up, and the tears would freeze on your face and drip down on your scarf. We'd take the ice off our scarf. When guys were exhausted, they had to lay on the ground with nothing underneath them. Some of them never woke up.

You didn't have any gloves. Your hands were so cold you couldn't even pull the trigger. You couldn't fire with accuracy, you had to fire what we called "harassing [*un-aimed*] fire."

We'd pull a truck up, let some gas out, someone would throw a match, and you'd see 200 guys trying to get near that fire! Good God, it was cold! I said, "Lord, if you ever let me out of here, I'll be a different person." I don't know how often He told me I lied to Him.

Wilfred Mathews (K Company):
Some guys didn't even have a field jacket. All I had was a [*summer*] fatigue jacket. We didn't have any sleeping bags. So we just laid our blankets down and laid on the snow until morning. We couldn't sleep.
They called it "frost bite." I called it freezing.

Ralph Hubbard (M Company):
There is only one word to describe Korea in the winter: "miserable, miserable, miserable." Compared to the South, the North was always gloomy.
How much time did I spend in Korea with a roof over my head? Down south we were in schools or things like that. Up north we were not in something that even *looked* like a roof. That whole winter we didn't set foot under any cover other than a shelter-half [*pup tent*] or parts of buildings.

Yancey:
The first thing you do as assistant platoon sergeant is check your men's feet. You'd sweat when you'd work, and you'd slosh and felt like you were walking in water. You've got to stay on the men, make sure they're changing their socks. They're supposed to change them daily and rinse them with water. You pin one pair to your chest and wear the other pair. But sometimes they get so doggone lazy, so you've got to stay on them and maintain some form of personal hygiene in the field. You've also got to keep them moving.
If you get frostbite, they can court martial you.
Trench foot is like leprosy, there's no pain, it just rots away, there's nothing but numbness. One guy, his toes came off with his sock.

Albert Kimber (I Company):

My toe nails and finger nails came off. I was sent back to Pusan until my hands and feet were thawed out, but my toe nails and finger nails came off.

Donald Womack:

When you get frost-bitten, your bones rub against each other - knees, wrists, elbows; you can hear them rubbing.

The 25th Division official figures for frostbite through February eloquently tell the story:
27th Inf 200
35th Inf 240
24th Inf 659

This is clear evidence that:

1. The 24th was not issued the same winter uniforms that the other two regiments received, or

2. The officer corps once again was not up to the calibre of the white units'

It's miraculous that every man was not frozen to death. The incompetence reached to the highest levels.

The GIs threw away their steel helmets in favor of wool caps with ear muffs if they could find them. Many also discarded their entrenching tools, the small shovels they carried to dig foxholes; they were useless for chopping the solidly frozen ground.

One man seemed to be an exception.

Hubbard:

I'm a "sweater" - sweated like hell. It helped me stay warm. The other guys used to get pissed at me. Below zero, sweat would be running down my hands. I *wanted* to catch cold so I could go back to the rear to the hospital. I tried opening my coat. I couldn't get a sniffle! I was trying, God knows!

Yancey:
The Chinese each carried a sack of rice and dried fish, and they could stay in the mountains indefinitely. But a GI isn't conditioned to it. He needs a hot meal or he'll go batty.

They put me supervising the pack train. Climbing over mountains wasn't easy, so we had Koreans who carried our supplies on A-frames. There were three of us - me and a corporal and a warrant officer - one in the front, one at the rear, and I was in the middle. If you didn't do that, they'd run off with your stuff.

Frozen stiff, the men slogged painfully north. But not everyone walked.

Davis:
We were going up north, and Colonel Blair was riding in an ambulance. It's cold as hell, and he's in an ambulance! He liked his comfort.

"Closing the Vice"

MacArthur announced a major offensive, when his two pincers, east and west, would join to "close the vice" on the Reds. It would end the war, and his career, with glory. He even announced when it would be launched – the day after Thanksgiving.

Marshall Peng read all the American press dispatches to keep abreast of everything the Americans were planning. The reporting was accurate, but security was lax, writes Edwin P Hoyt. "And the biggest security risk was General MacArthur."

Grateful for the tip-off, Peng ordered his troops to give way and let the Yanks through.

November 21. The 25th Division received orders to move to Kunu-ri on the Ch'ongch'on river 70 miles below the Yalu.
LaVaughn Fields:

We were close to "MiG Ally," where the Chinese jets would fly across the river later.

No one even thought of the Chinese army that was massing on the border. We began running into them, but they were scattered here and there in Korean clothes, not in their own uniforms. I had a cap with a red star on it, which I got in a warehouse raid.

November 22. Floyd Williams reported back from the hospital:

I stayed in the hospital about a week. They wanted to send me to Japan, but MacArthur said the war would be over by Christmas, so I decided to put in for a transfer to D Company, Heavy Weapons Company, with my brother.

I got back the day before Thanksgiving.

November 23. Thanksgiving.

Joe Davis (3rd Battalion cook):

We had Turks fighting with us, wanted everything cooked in butter; we had to boil the damn turkey in butter and water just for them.

Nathaniel Nicholson (Artillery):

I came down from the outpost for a rest, and I was sleeping in the cooks' tent the night before Thanksgiving, and the tent caught on fire. The turkeys were cooking, so I ran in and pulled two turkeys out in a big pan and covered them with a tarpaulin until the next day. Everyone thought the turkeys were ruined, but I told them, "I got turkey!"

"You got *turkey*?"

And I pulled the tarpaulin off.

The cook said, "I'll cook some rolls." They gave it to the officers and sergeants - of course I got some too.

My CO had given me an assignment - two men to make a run to Inch'on and replace two 105 tubes [*barrels*] and a breechblock. The whole Army was

210

heading north, but the three of us went south. We got in our truck just before the Chinese attacked.

Fields (Engineers):
We were in reserve and had time to goof off. I ran into a cousin I hadn't seen since Japan. We ran down to the medics and got a jug of Canadian Club - they called it "medication" - and we went up in the hills and got loaded. That jug, by the way, cost $55. So next day my head was not too clear at best.
But it cleared up in a hurry!

November 24. Bob Jones (D Company) returned from the hospital just in time to join the 24th as, to the roar of artillery, the Allied army jumped off. It was still ignorant that 19 Chinese divisions lay in wait.

The Deuce-4 was assigned a rugged, mountainous sector with deep snow-filled gorges dividing three snow-covered peaks. It's orders were to keep up with the units on the low ground on either side. The 24th was aligned from west to east with the First Battalion, Third Battalion, and Second Battalion. On the regiment's west was a tank-heavy task force named Dolvin. On the east was the black 9th Infantry regiment of the 2d Division.

Because of the mountains and intense cold, radios often didn't work, and battalions often didn't know where their companies were. There were few roads. Trucks broke down and couldn't bring up supplies, so the companies had to rely on Korean porters. Still, the 24th moved one or two miles ahead of the others. They knew something that MacArthur didn't.

Yancey:
There were a lot of indications the Chinese were there - from the First Cav and the Koreans - but the generals wouldn't listen to them.

Clyde Jones (I Company):
We saw the Chinese with little bitty horses like Shetland ponies, with white canvases over their packs.

That's the way they carried ammunition, on horseback. The Chinese were little people, but these were bigger than I was, and I'm six foot. They were *big* dudes! - the biggest Chinese I've ever seen in my life. They called themselves Mongolians; they were a different breed of Chinese.

Someone said they rode camels. I said, "Oh my goodness, I never heard of anyone riding camels!" I guess there were thousands of them. Every road had them. They didn't attempt to fire on us, and the next day they disappeared; I never saw them any more.

Thompson:

Our recon people were bringing in prisoners. The Koreans and Chinese all looked alike to me. (They say that about us blacks too.) People back at 8th Army were saying they're Korean. But those guys weren't Korean, they were Chinese!"

The first day the 24th gained about five miles against little resistance. C Company moved out a mile or two ahead of the rest of the regiment.

Womack:

The Chinese came in sneakers and insulated pajamas. We were looking down on them, they saw us and we saw them. A bullet could have killed them, but we were told to let them alone. They told us: "If you don't get fired on, don't fire on them." The Chinese walked past us, and two or three days later, they were behind us, and we had to fight to get through them.

Fletcher:

Every division had a spear-head company, in front of the rest. C Company was always out front. That means we got shot at before anyone else. Our object was to make contact with the enemy and report how many troops we ran into. We would radio back, "No opposition," and they'd move the front forward.

Yancey:

They put me supervising C Company's pack train. Climbing over mountains wasn't easy, so we had Koreans who carried our supplies on A-frames. There were three of us - me and a corporal and a warrant officer - one in the front, one at the rear, and I was in the middle. If you didn't do that, they'd run off with your stuff.

Yancey:

The Chinese each carried a sack of rice and dried fish, and they could stay in the mountains indefinitely. But a GI isn't conditioned to it. He needs a hot meal or he'll go batty.

China Attacks

November 25.
Yancey: "All of a sudden all hell broke loose."

Williams:

We were on point and went up a little draw. That was as far north as we ever got. Here come the Chinese, blowing bugles - no one told us they were there! I'm counting Chinese by the thousands, but I didn't know they were Chinese then.

Fields:

As usual, our squad was attached to Captain Nordstrom's troop of the 89th Tankers. The tanks were out in front, and we were beginning to head into hilly terrain. Then the column stopped, and the tanks began to fire at the hills to our front. All the quad-.50s *[four heavy machine guns]* were firing. Something big was going on.

We always had a spotter plane up, so if we ran into something, the infantry would pull forward and go to work. The plane came in low and dropped a message: "Many Chinese soldiers to your front. Pull back." God bless that spotter pilot! If it hadn't been for him, we would have walked right into 20,000 Chinese, and we had a spearhead of only two battalions, or only 800 soldiers. Good thing someone saw him drop the message.

They were running right at us, and they kept coming, like a crowd coming out of a football stadium. The hills in front of us were crawling with them.

The tankers took up defensive positions, firing on the hills. The artillery FO captain also lost no time. Within minutes they were firing on the hills with everything - 155s, 105s, and eight-inch guns. Was that a show! And we had a ring-side seat - in fact, we were almost part of it! It was "a show of death." I'll never forget it.

Jones:

About 9:30 they hit us.

I went to a U-T [*Tennessee*] football game once, 100,000 people doing the "wave." That was like the first time I saw the Chinese. Here they come! They got to the foot of the hill. There were too many of them - wave after wave after wave. They were all over us, shooting mortars. We began to see, I'd estimate, 5-10,000 of them; we were about 200 men in our company.

"Hold at all risk!"

But the odds were against us. There were too many, we couldn't do anything with them. We had so many casualties, no way in the world we could hold.

"We got to get out of here!"

They pulled us back. The last company out was Item.

There was a rice paddy, and we had to go across it 100 yards to the next hill. Two medics were carrying men on litters, and we helped carry them out.

214

Fields:

The Chinese were getting slaughtered, but they kept coming. They wore light-colored quilted uniforms. They had no rifles but plenty of grenades and were throwing them at us. They wanted our rifles; when they killed a GI, they kept his weapon.

Womack:

The second wave didn't have weapons, they'd pick up the weapons carried by the first wave when they got shot.

Yancey:

The Chinese were using beetle nut, they were all hopped up. Red and black beetle nut - their mouths were black or red. You shot them, but if you didn't hit a vital spot, they were still coming at you.

They had the manpower, but we had the firepower. That's the only reason we survived. If they'd had the firepower, they'd have taken us all out.

Fields:

You had to slow down your rate of fire so your weapon wouldn't over-heat. By the fourth wave you had to break the .50 down [*into components*] and run off the hill. If the gun is too hot to carry, destroy it any way you can; you sure as hell don't want to leave it for the enemy to use.

Clyde Jones:

About 9:30 they hit us.

I went to a U-T [*Tennessee*] football game once, 100,000 people doing the "wave." That was like the first time I saw the Chinese. Here they come! They got to the foot of the hill. There were too many of them - wave after wave after wave. They were all over us, shooting mortars. We began to see, I'd estimate, 5-10,000 of them; we were about 200 men in our company.

"Hold at all risk!"

But the odds were against us. There were too many, we couldn't do anything with them. We had so many casualties, no way in the world we could hold.

The CO said, "China's in the war. We don't know how many men. Get out of here! Pull back!"

We had to run for our lives - they called it "withdrawal." Wasn't any vehicles, so we just ran. They pulled us back. The last company out was Item.

There was a rice paddy, and we had to go across it 100 yards to the next hill. Two medics were carrying men on litters, and we helped carry them out.

Running all day with a heavy pack on is hard: "I'm going to take this pack off. I'm tired!" My buddy got his mess kit shot off him. We ran until dark, five-six o'clock that night, going as fast as we could, and finally got out of range of them.

James Burnett:

Everything was in chaos. Our unit got pinned down. I got my radio hooked up with the Air Force, giving them information about where our units are. One pilot said to me, "We're going to strafe the area. Tell them when we come overhead to just get up and run." I thought this was a little odd. I said, "Will you repeat that message? I have to be sure."

He repeated it.

"Roger, over and out."

I told **Charles Jenkins**, our forward observer, to get up and run. He gave me the same response: "Would you repeat that?" I repeated what the pilot told me: "Get up and run!"

They did exactly what the pilot told them to - they picked up and moved it out. Along the line, that got misinterpreted as running away, but that was absolutely the directive the pilot gave me.

I wouldn't say "retreat," but we were backing hard out of there! We were moving fast. The Chinese swarmed on us. We'd stop and set up and fire for a couple of hours. Set up, fire, move.... Set up, fire, move. We'd move four or five times a day in that freezing cold. We were getting murdered.

Williams:

We had no idea where we were going. They dropped us food late in the afternoon. We got what we could and kept going south.

Wilfred Mathews:

The Air Force made an air drop to us, but they dropped it in enemy territory, and we had to fight to go get it. Everyone came back with ammunition but no food. We had to go back there and finally get our food. We went about three days without food and had limited ammunition.

Fields:

The infantry withdrew, some running, some walking, passing through our positions and heading south.

We also started to get out of the hills, because they had caught us in a ravine, and the tanks couldn't maneuver there. It would be easy to ambush us, because there was no room to turn around or pass a stalled tank. We wanted to get into more open territory and make a stand and give our other units time to head south. So they started leap-frogging back, firing at the same time, keeping the enemy in front of them.

The FO continued to call in fire, and his jeep stayed behind to cover our withdrawal.

We were setting up road blocks to slow the enemy down - laying mines, blowing bridges, whatever we could. We tried to stop them with explosives, creating ditches and craters as big and as deep as we could - anything that worked.

Womack:

The engineers were the last American unit to head south. We had to pick up stragglers. The infantry took our trucks and jeeps away from us, because they didn't want to be trapped. If we had to leave one, we would booby trap the seats. The gas tank was underneath the seat; we booby trapped it with phosphorous grenades.

Six Chinese divisions poured through the Allied line, often through ROK units, and fanned out in the rear. Peng was about to capture MacArthur's pincer in a pincer of his own.

Fields:

We didn't know it at the time, but the whole 8th Army was withdrawing. Also the X Corps [*Tenth Corps, made up of Marines and GIs to the East*].

Word came later in the day that a full Chinese army was in front of us, to drive us out of Korea. They almost succeeded. In all, the Chinese sent about a third of a million men, but it looked like more, because they came at us in waves.

Then all of a sudden the Chinese stopped. We were lucky, because we were almost out of ammunition. Boy, did we learn our first lesson: Keep plenty of ammo and make your shots count, or you may not be around for the next attack.

We settled in for the night on a hill, where we had a good view of the terrain and the Chinese would have to come out in the open to get to us. We bedded down and picked up stragglers, even whole companies. They were hungry and tired, and we gave them all the rations we could. They were our troops, so what else could we do? The whole Army looked like hell. Someone said he had never seen the American army look so bad.

We registered fire on all possible targets. [*That is, the mortars and artillery fired in advance to get the range and direction, and gave each target a number. Later the*

218

forward observers could call the number, and the gunners already knew the correct settings.]

November 26. The Chinese hit the 25th Division and the 2d Division, on its east flank, simultaneously.

Thompson:
We were stretched thin. We were cut off. We started pulling back under fire all the way back. We were just as orderly as everyone else - everything was in disarray. We would hold at night, then start leap-frogging the next morning to get out of there.

That's where all the lying came in: "You guys would run." I never saw anyone running. You could hardly walk, less run! Where the hell you going to run to? There's an outfit in front of you. What you going to do, run over them? But the rumors kept coming. We said. "What are you talking about? We covered your flank. If we're not here, you get over-run."

Mathews:
I do believe we were left up there. There was no way all of us could have gotten surrounded like that if we had all been together. We were left out there alone and had to fight all the way back.

About the second day I had no food at all and didn't even have a full belt of ammunition for my machine gun. Every time we got attacked, you had to make sure there was a target before you shot. If not, you wouldn't have anything left.

It took us about a day to get in touch with somebody, and the Air Force made a drop. But the chutes landed back where we had come from, and we set up a task force of guys to go back and get it, and we were supporting them from a hill.

K Company had a few captured, but most of us came out. We were squashed in between the enemy in front of us and behind us. If we moved too fast, we'd catch up with the enemy, and if we moved too slow, the enemy was going to catch up with us.

Colonel Clayton also lost contact with regimental headquarters but contacted the 2d Division by radio and told them he would try to break out after dark and join its all-black third battalion. The 9th regiment commander, Colonel **Sloan**, wrote:

During the evening, E and G Companies withdrew to our position. They were immediately fed, re-equipped with rifles, and steps were taken to round up and evacuate approximately 150 casualties.

The other 150-200 men were organized under the battalion commander, Lieutenant Colonel **D.M. McMain**. "They repulsed an attack in an excellent manner."

One GI in the 9th Infantry, Second Division, Private **Charles Rangel** from Harlem, recalled:

When night fell, the Chinese troops came out of the dark in waves. For two or three nights we listened to the constant blare of Chinese bugle calls and stared at the flares they would send up. Tension rose to a crescendo with the eerie bugle blare, which seemed to get louder by the hour.

We saw a lot of GIs fall over, frozen to death as they tried desperately to stay awake. When planes came over to bomb, the enemy disappeared into deep tunnels in the coal mines above us.

General Kean took C Company out of the First Battalion and attached it to Task Force Dolvin. That may have contributed to the later confusion as the battalion lost contact with them.

Kean ordered the Division to pull back. As soon as darkness fell, units began fighting their way back against heavy Chinese fire.

Charlie Company of the First Battalion was under attack, and Corley desperately tried to call it to order it to pull back. But it never got the word as its radios failed.

Charlie Company's Ordeal

Fletcher:

That night we got hammered. Our radio froze, and all we got was some garbage, like static. A and B companies, on our left and right, pulled back five miles. They also ordered us back, but we never got the message. So we didn't know we didn't have anyone on our flanks. We were up there by ourselves. We couldn't withdraw, because we were cut off from the rear and the front.

At the foot of the mountain was a road that went north, then swung back south. We were going to get on the road, but we got pinned down by two machine guns at the crest of a hill, and they forced us back.

We hadn't eaten for two or three days and didn't have any ammunition. The Air Force tried to drop some, but in the mountains you get cross winds, and the supplies would drift half a mile away, and we'd see the Chinese run out and get them.

November 27. Curtis Bolton (C Company):

Early that morning we started receiving fire and got down in a defensive position. 'Copters dropped some kind of message telling us to move back, but we should have gotten it two or three hours earlier.

The firing got more rapid. Finally the Chinese were coming in real rapidly. Our executive officer was behind us to direct fire. We were looking and listening, waiting on his command.

He said something, and as I turned my head to hear, I got shot right through my right ear. I was unconscious for a few seconds, and one of the guys, **Herbert Williams**, took two men and carried me back to a lower part of the hill and put a bandage around my wound.

All at once, more fire started coming, and they had us running like driven cattle. We kept down and tried to get back where the 'copters were. Some of the guys were shot in the legs, so walking was painful.

The Chinese drove us into a little Korean shack, 19 of us with seven or eight rifles between us. The others had lost their weapons. Some guy said, "Look, they're all around the shack."

Sergeant **Pugh** [*not Curtis Pugh*] said, "They'll burn the hut down. I'll go out," and one of the guys said, "I'll go with you, Sarge." They put a rag on a stick, and he gave orders: "No one shoot." Everybody obeyed.

Fletcher was with the compny commander:

Captain *[Milford]* **Stanley** was hit and badly wounded in the left shoulder and left hip. He took a handkerchief, and he and Lieutenant *[Howard]* **Eichelsdoerfer,** the only other officer left, walked out. After a few minutes they came back.

The captain said, "They're giving us a choice, either fight to the last man, or surrender." He asked the men, "How much ammunition have you got?" Some were down to one clip [*12 shots*]. So he says, "If we surrender, we stand a 50-50 chance of going home. If we fight it out, we know we're not going to make it. So tell the men to give me their choice."

I went back and told my squad what the C.O. said. Ninety-eight percent said, "If we stand a 50-50 chance, sure." I didn't feel like it - I was 17; nothing could stop me, as far as I was concerned. At 17 you had ego. Thinking back, it was foolish.

Lieutenant Eichelsdoerfer said, "Field strip your weapons, take the firing pins out and break 'em or throw them in the water." We did. "Put your hands on your helmets and walk out in a straight line."

Bolton:

Miles Lampkin didn't want to go out. He said, "I don't want to be captured," so we covered him up. The rest of us went out with our arms up. I never saw him again.

The Chinese came out of the bushes and trees; they came out of everywhere. They motioned the way for us to go, and we went along at a rapid pace. One guy was shot in the leg, and the Chinese said, "We'll have to shoot him if he can't keep up."

He told me, "Don't carry me," because I was bleeding pretty much myself.

Our planes were doing some pretty good jobs in the rear. The hills were lit up. We were hoping they wouldn't put any of their fire on us. We used aluminum mess kits, trying to throw a damn signal up to them.

Fletcher:

I got interrogated. I said my name, rank, and serial number. "What company?" - he spoke English very well.

"Name, rank, serial number."

He asked me three times. Then he said, "You're the 24th Regiment, your battalion commander is Colonel Miller." hey even had our radio call signs; Colonel Miller was "Red Rooster."

I said, "Sir, can I ask you a question? How many Chinese are here?"

He smiled and said, "Thirty thousand of us. You're at division headquarters."

"What if we hadn't surrendered?"

"None of you would be alive. Our orders were, surrender or annihilation."

"Are we going to get any food?"

He said, "Yes, we'll feed you later." We didn't get fed until that evening - boiled cracked corn. That stayed our diet the whole time we were on the march. Once a day. We went from 3800 calories a day to 360.

When we surrendered, only 139 of us were still alive. Out of that, about 39 survived.

BSWA would call C Company's capture another black mark against the Deuce-4: They didn't bug out fast enough!

Luckily for him, Yancey never did get back through the Chinese lines to C Company.

Yancey:

The 25th Division wrote a book, *Korean Stories*, and said our whole company was lost except for a few. But 25 of us got out.

The Air Force tried to drop food and ammunition, but the wind carried it into enemy territory. Captain **Mayo** gave the command to break up into small groups and infiltrate the lines and make it to friendly forces. I never saw him after that, I don't know if he was missing in action or got killed. A great man, a great soldier, a great infantryman.

[There were two Captain Mayo's. The C Company commander was short and black; B Company's was tall, thin and almost Caucasian.]

General Kean finally rushed the vaunted 27th Infantry out of reserve and into the battle. Why had he waited so long? Until then the 24th and 35th had taken the full fury of the attack. One company from the 27th was quickly over-run, as C of the 24th had been; another was severely penetrated. But no criticism was leveled against either of them.

Sergeant **Gibson** of D Company's machine gun platoon was a "quiet, shy-acting guy," according to Floyd Williams:

One night he was riding in a ¾-ton and they left him up on the hill. He battled all that night by himself. Next day they sent someone up to get him.

Fields:

The 2d Division [] is getting chopped up. Their losses are horrible as the Chinese blew through on way south. The 503rd Field Artillery [*another black unit from the 2d Division*] bore-sighted their guns and fired point-blank at

224

the on-rushing men. Bodies were flying everywhere; they stacked the enemy up. They fired until their guns wouldn't fire any more.

Easy and George companies of the 24th were in the middle of it.

Colonel McMain (9th Infantry):

After the regiment had been ordered to withdraw, the two companies were placed in a new defense line in depth. After the Chinese had over-run the forward elements of the third battalion, they were surprised upon running into E and G companies. As a result of their action, the Chinese onslaught for the first time was halted. It was by this action that my right battalion was able to hold the temporary defense line long enough to permit the 23rd Infantry to occupy a new defense line further to the rear.

The above information is furnished as an expression of the fine work these two companies did while temporarily under our command.

In the Third Battalion Corporal **Earl Phoenix** of Mike Company, though badly wounded, blasted away with his machine gun until his ammunition was gone, saving his squad from being cut off and over-run. He was put in for a Medal of Honor, but it was down-graded to a DSC.

The Hospital Tent

Clyde Jones:

The hospital was in the middle of a field the Chinese were running through, and they over-ran it like a western movie - ran over the tents like a stampede of cattle. Didn't even stop.

According to Charlie Bussey, Corley dragged him out of his cot after a long day on his feet. The colonel slapped a map with

his pointer: "The Chinese have set up road blocks here and here. And they've over-run the medical clearing station here." Bussey's orders: Clear the road blocks and rescue any survivors from the clearing station.

"What about some tank support?"
"We can't get any in at night, but come morning we'll get you some - if you can hold out."

Bussey called for two platoons under Lieutenants Robert Green (left) and David Carlisle, both fresh from West Point. "Carisle was a brilliant guy," LeTellier recalled, "but he had a chip on his shoulder. "

LaVaughn Fields:

It must have been at least below zero that night. Dead-ass from lack of sleep, we moved out. At least we could ride most of the way and cat-nap before we reached a large school yard.

From there we walked in two columns. My squad is lugging this big .50-calibre. It's a monster. Stevenson has the barrel, **Robert** Moss has the tripod, and **James** Newsom has the trigger housing. The gun weighs 90 pounds, not counting the ammo. I have two belts of ammo around my neck. I swear, I'm going to shoot half of it up so I won't have to carry it all the way back.

Jake Ford lit a cigarette under his poncho. Then it happened. A shower of bullets hit the road, and we hit the ground. "Fields, pick up!" It meant go into action with the .50. I gave the order to set it as fast as we could. **Randolph "Dizzy" Gillespie** - who was half-Choctaw, half black - and I set up our weapon.

I yell, "Up and cut it" - that's Negro talk so the enemy won't understand. Away we go! Between the bursts I hear the enemy hollering. We saturate his position.

The first platoon moves out to check the target, and we get the order to break the gun down [*into its three components*] and move out. We stop often to listen for noise that might mean ambush. We pass an ambulance over-turned with four dead GIs inside.

The halt sign is given. We could use a good rest, but this was one very short one. The captain laid out the plan of attack just around the next curve. When we got there, we could see a fire. Because of such a dumb stunt, the Chinese pay with their lives.

My third platoon was sent up the hill over-looking the enemy. Robert Mills wanted to use his hand grenades on them - you could always count on Mills, he always had a few grenades in his pack. We will open up after we're sure they're Chinese and not GIs. There were eight of them, one squad, eating some of our combat rations from the vehicle they shot up. We're waiting for the "Go," which will be a flare to light up the target.

There it goes! We shoot everything we can.

At last they reached the clearing station. They had no idea what they'd find. Bussey wrote, "I could hear the cries of patients, wounded and dying." Carlisle's platoon surrounded the area while Green's men entered. They found many GIs, doctors, and nurses lying shot. In an over-turned bed lay a man in traction in excruciating pain. "The place looked like a slaughter-house. There were blood and bodies everywhere." The air was frigid. There were no lights. "The sobbing and wailing was heart-breaking." Doctors and nurses had run out in the night.

Fields:

We began to call them: "Come back, we need your help!" Slowly they crept out of the dark.

Then we became like bloodhounds, looking for Chinese under bushes, in holes, wherever we thought they might be hiding. I clipped my bayonet over the muzzle of my rifle. This was going to be personal; I wanted to *feel* it. I asked God to forgive me.

I didn't say anything to my squad, but I could hear the clicks of their bayonets also, almost as if I had given the order. You have to be in the right state of mind to use the bayonet, and I was ready. Someone found three Chinese. Not a sound was made or a scream heard, except something that sounded like an Indian war cry. I found a Chinese with his head cut off. Others had throats cut from ear to ear.

At daybreak I thought I saw **George Thomas** give Moss the sign of a hand across his throat, and Moss nodded. I didn't see anything myself, and I didn't ask any questions.

The whole episode was covered in a couple of lines in BSWA. Bussey gives it seven pages.

November 28. A cook from battalion headquarters was making a chow run, bringing hot coffee and food to the front.

Joe Davis:

The Chinese were shooting down at us from both sides of the hills. You could see yellow flames coming out of their guns, giving everyone hell. We came through the first ambush on the first run, drove right straight through it.

Then, like fools we went back again, and they were waiting on us. All hell was breaking loose. Those bastards had at least three machine gun nests up there, shooting down and blasting us. You could see bullets smash all over. I saw truck-loads of dead.

The jeep driver got nervous and stopped, whether from shell shock or what. We were trying to tell him, "Keep going! Keep going," but he just panicked.

There was a .30-calibre machine gun on the jeep. I got on that gun for maybe five-six minutes, got shot in the arm and the mouth. Knocked out about ten of my teeth and came out the left side of my lip. Took half my jaw off. A bullet hit my neck. Then I hid behind the wheel.

I was sitting in the jeep and got shot across my back. I jumped out of the jeep and ran back where the tank was.

Then Colonel Blair came out of nowhere, wearing fatigues, a turtle-neck sweater, no hat, just like I was. He runs and jumps up on that goddam tank, opened the top, and went down inside. He turned the tank toward the side of the hill, and knocked those machine guns out. I don't know why he never got credit for it.

They say Colonel Blair was a coward. He was no coward. No coward is going to jump on a tank with that machine gun nest up there. He was a hero. I'm a witness to that. I was behind that tank. I never told anybody until you. The only other witness was Master Sergeant **Jackson**, the field first sergeant of Third Battalion headquarters company. He died a couple years ago.

The other jeep had made a wrong turn and about 30 minutes later made it back to headquarters and turned the report in that we were caught in an ambush. Luckily, recon tanks came to get us and saved me. Colonel Blair sent me back to the regimental aid station.

Twenty-thirty minutes later, the medical officer, Captain **Edgepath**, a big, light-skinned fellow, looked almost Caucasian, was sick with pneumonia and came by in a jeep.

I said, "I'm all messed up, I've got to get some aid."

He said, "Get in the jeep."

Another guy with us was on the tank and died when we got to battalion headquarters.

The two ambulance drivers who brought us down there got killed on the way back.

We made it all the way to the division aid station. Hell, me and Edgepath laid side by side out there, out in the cold, on litters because they didn't have any room in the tent. The doctors just couldn't work with so many at once.

They shipped me by truck to Pyongyang, where the Russians had built a big hospital. My mouth was all ragged. They didn't even have beds. I asked a nurse, "Are you going to give me a spinal injection?" She said no. A lieutenant told me I shouldn't be asking that question. I told him to go to hell.

Going into the operating room, the Koreans who were carrying me took the boots right off my feet. I don't remember anything after that.

I woke up on a hospital train going to South Korea, and a guy was giving me a penicillin shot. They gave me a blanket, and we all got on a truck to Kimpo Airfield near Seoul. We could see the wreckage of Russian planes, lines of refugees, and fires all around Seoul.

They flew me to Japan and took out half my jaw.

I was wounded November 28. On December 15 I was sitting in my mother's dining room.

MacArthur wakes up

MacArthur finally understood the reality. "We face a new war," he intoned. Back home papers screamed, "DISASTER." President Truman announced that that he was considering nuclear weapons

In eastern Korea General Ned Almond of X Corps was still ignoring the obvious: "Don't let a bunch of Chinese laundrymen stop you. We're going all the way to the Yalu!" It must have been the stupidest speech in a war of stupid speeches. Captured Chinese POWs boasted that they would wipe the Marines out. "Arrogant and blind," as historian Clay Blair wrote, Almond resolutely "marched to disaster."

In the west, the 8th Army commander, **Walton "Johnny" Walker** understood the real situation and drew a new line 20 miles to the rear. His 25th and 2d Divisions stumbled back toward the Ch'ongch'on.

Carroll Le Tellier:

We were in a town north of the Ch'ongch'on on an east-west road. Blair went up the road to the east and came back in a jeep. He'd just been shot at on the other side of the mountain, and said, "Can you help me find the battalion?"

Bussey, Carlisle, Sergeant **Woods**, and I went with him. It wasn't too far, a half mile, or a mile at the most. Woods thought he heard something and cried out, "Hello!" The answer came back - it was Blair's battalion. He was very thankful.

Across the river lay the town of Kunu-ri and temporary safety.

The Second Division crossed first and occupied Kunu-ri. The 24th would follow.

November 29.
Fields:

If the 2d Division loses Kunu-ri, we'll be cut off. The push could come in our direction next.

Our task was laying mines and shoring up bridge capacity. We have to make sure the bridges can carry 50 tons; if not, we have to find a ford they can cross. Our company was running a ferry site and doing a big  business. Our job was to keep the ferry free to move.

Kunu-ri

Kean ordered his shivering Division to cross the river. The Second Battalion led.

Jones:

"The Ditch" that's what we called Kunu-ri. We walked from seven o'clock in the evening until two o'clock in the morning, when we finally set down. "We got tanks. We'll stop them here." We dug in and got set up.

It was cold, cold, *cold, COLD!*

The 1st Cavalry ran off and left us - MacArthur's favorite bunch of boys. We were trapped. [*On the east*] the Marines also were trapped, but they went out by water; we went out by foot.

Mathews:

We got to Kunu-ri and stretched out. Oh, it was cold! About 45 below zero during the daytime - 65 [*sic*] at night. We couldn't dig a fox hole, the ground was frozen solid.

Next came the First Battalion.

Fields:It was so cold the river started to freeze. My squad with the .50 was in business, was doing a job on the ferry to sink it. The Chinese got mad and fired some mortars at us. We didn't hang around there very long.

Soon the river was frozen - you could walk across it.

Yancey:

You could drive a truck across it. We played leap frog to get across. A machine gun pinned us down, but I was more afraid of the ice cracking than the machine gun, because I couldn't swim.

One of the guys ran back and got the platoon sergeant, "Big Boy" Williams, the old Army boxer - he picked up a basketball like I pick up a tennis ball. He came up with a BAR and knocked out the machine gun and told us, "Get your asses moving!"

(Williams would later be wounded again and went AWOL for the second time. On a hospital plane to the States, he asked to use the men's room at a refueling stop, escaped again, and went back to see his family in Gifu.)

Floyd Williams (A Company):
We got in a little fight, some got wounded. A Korean came out of a little shack. He was trying to help us, I don't think he was involved with the enemy, but there was a language barrier. A guy from Louisiana, light-skinned with a gold tooth, had a bead on this guy, getting ready to blast him away. I yelled at him, "Don't shoot!" because it appeared that he was trying to help us. I took his rifle away.

We pulled back on a little mountain in Kunu-ri and went into a perimeter defense.

The weather got cold - vicious cold. I was trying to dig in, and the damn entrenching tool would bounce up when it hit that ice; it was frozen solid.

I almost wished the Chinese *would* come, because it was so cold, we had no food, we were hungry, no proper clothes, very low ammunition. Didn't know whether your weapon was going to work or not.

My brother, Albert, was carrying a radio for the D company commander. Since he was in the Heavy Weapons Company [*which supported all three infantry companies in the battalion*], he could be anywhere in the battalion. Unbeknownst to me, he was in Kunu-ri too, and we were trapped on the mountain together.

Naïve as I was, I believed someone would come up and get us, or we would get out on our own - I had seen too many movies.

The Third Battalion was next.

233

Sanders:

I walked into Kunu-Ri at night and found the rest of my platoon intact. There was a big auditorium, and the first sergeant said, "Bring your platoon over here, this is where you're going to camp for the night."

I told the men, "Leave your stuff here, go up for C-rations and come back and eat here."

They bedded down, listening to the guns of the 2d Division, locked in combat with the Chinese.

The Engineers were last to cross. LeTellier passed several Chinese soldiers who had been hit by napalm. "It was a grisly sight."

Donald Womack:

The Chinese came across at night and put mines on the bank. Two tanks ran over them, and the mines knocked the treads off. We got a bulldozer and made a ramp for the tanks, and they became artillery pieces, firing across the river.

Fields:

We were told to put up a defense. We drove down the main road until we saw our CO and pulled into a large meadow. The quad-.50 machine guns were set up, and the tanks were setting up a roadblock, then they would pull back at nightfall to help the ground troops. Everyone was on line.

Jones:

We set down in Kunu-ri for three days, didn't have anything to eat, just what we could find. Then they sent "box car" airplanes, and they dropped food to us.

Williams:

The third day a C-119 [*transport plane*] dropped food to us. Some of it was outside my perimeter, so late in the evening they sent us to get what food we could and carry it back to D Company. The Chinese started blowing their bugles - a little sniping, not a full-scale attack, and the Chinese were run off. Next morning when I got up, a few Chinese dead were left out there.

Fields;

The Chinese wanted to go straight down the main road, and we were right on the route they wanted to go. The roads in Korea were very poor and undeveloped. There were no alternate routes beside the MSR. The CO sent out a party to see if there were any other roads at all.

Bussey found a "goat path" west of town about eight feet wide, and his bulldozer widened it to about 16 feet. In the headlong flight that followed, it would prove as valuable as "Engineer Road" had been back at Haman.

Jones:

The Chinese blew bugles in the evening for three nights. They blew *Taps*. Then they blew *St Louis Blues* and *My Momma Done Tol' Me*. Then they played *When the Saints Go Marching In.*

"Hello, Joe! Do you know MacArthur feeds his dog better food than you get? You grow food, but you can't eat it. You ride in the back of the bus. What are you fighting for? Why don't you surrender and come to China?

"If not, we'll see what happens tomorrow."

Sanders:

I said, "Don't take off your shoes, don't pull off anything but your helmet. Put your head on the helmet, put your rifle across your chest, because you might need it quicker than you think. Lie there and sleep as much as you can. If anything happens, you're ready to move."

Fields:

Off in the distance someone was playing music - at this time of night! Someone should shoot that dumb-ass. But there was something about this music: "Heh, that sounds like bugles blowing." We looked at each other. The bugle calls were used to issue commands, but we had no way of knowing what they meant. The bugles are loud and clear.

George Thomas, a veteran of World War II, was cursing and saying, "Load the .50!" He was waking everyone in the platoon to get up.

Jones:

We went to bed at 2:30. They woke us at six, told us, "We don't know what's going on, we may have to do a little fighting."

In the Second Division sector, Charlie Rangel reported:

The infantry that were supposed to protect us had already retreated past us. Helicopters had evacuated some key field officers.

Then they hit. The Chinese poured over the mountain pass like ants swarming, from both sides of the road, screaming and yelling and bugling.

November 30.

Sanders:

Two or three o'clock in the morning, we heard a voice say, "They're coming down out of the hill!"

I said, "Get your weapon and let's move out!"

Everyone was running out of the building. We went to the road. Everybody's wondering, "Are we going in the right direction?"

It was the brightest moon I had ever seen, and I ran out in the middle of the road. All of a sudden this Chinese opened up with his machine gun. The first sergeant, **Don O'Herring**, got killed. God! I could have gotten killed too!

I yelled, "Go back!" and we ran back behind the building, and the gun took part of the building off. My whole platoon got behind me. The Chinese are all over. I'm trying to figure out how the hell to get out of here!

Williams:

Someone said, "Move out," and we got in a file. This is night, it's dark, we didn't have any idea where we were going. Lieutenant **Barnes** - he wasn't even a member of our company, I don't know what he was doing there - but he led us off that mountain in Kunu-ri. He made colonel in Vietnam before he got killed.

Sanders:

We walked all night. We couldn't see where the hell we were, and I had no idea where we were heading - I think we were heading south. The next morning when the sun came out, we finally found other people out of the 25th Division. Everybody said, "What do you think we should do?"

I said, "Shoot the vehicles up and destroy the 75."

We decided we would back up about a thousand yards until things cleared up. We were sitting there waiting, when an L-19 [*light observation*] plane flew over and dropped a message saying, "Withdraw, you're being surrounded."

We said, "Hell, we'll try to get the hell out." We backed up and got behind a rice paddy bank, the only protection we had. The Chinese were up on the hill above us, 200 yards away, shooting down at us. Any time we would stick our heads up, we'd get hit. We could see bodies all over the place.

After 20-30 minutes three tanks appeared in the middle of a field and started shooting point-blank over our heads at the hills where the Chinese were. I tried to get my platoon to move out and get behind the tanks. I told them, "One-two-three. Go!"

Not a soul moved.

I realized they weren't going to move until I moved, so I said, "We're going to try this one more time. After this I'm going. You better be behind me." I ran across the field, and the rest of the men followed me. I lost my helmet and stumbled, and I could see the tracer bullets going above my head. [*The stumble may have saved his life.*] I didn't even look for my helmet.

Something hit me in the right eye, either shrapnel or a rock, and I lost vision in that eye temporarily. Then a bullet went through my right leg. You can picture this: I'm laid out and calling the medic: "Come on, help me!" I'm not going to sit there and wait for the Chinese to over-run our position; I would have been a POW. I was still going to fight. I got up and was walking along behind the tanks, and a guy said, "I think you're hit."

I said, "I think so, too."

Someone in the tank said, "You OK?" But I couldn't ride in the tank, there was just enough room for the tankers.

We walked for miles, I don't know how far. They wanted to send me to the hospital, but I was afraid to go, because they had ambushed an ambulance just before that - I could have been in that damn thing. One fellow in the medics, **Oscar Robertson**, was my classmate in high school, and he fixed my leg up and put a little patch on it. I've still got the patch on my leg.

I felt like a wounded animal, just trying to get away. I said, "I'll walk as far as I can to stay ahead of the Chinese if I possibly can." I walked at least two or three days and never said a word.

Bussey:

The fields were littered with the bodies of soldiers, who had fired a last round or two as they'd fallen.

Fields:

The hills are loaded with Chinese, and they're charging about a thousand yards away. I'm getting the squad up and loaded while Stephens and Dizzy are shooting. Then it's my turn to shoot while they load up.

All kinds of tracers of different colors are flying all over the area. Some colors are armor-piercing rounds, others are for smoke to mark the target. Red Tracers leave a trail so you can see where your bullets are hitting. But when we had time we would pick them out of the ammunition belt, because they also gave away our own positions.

Then we hear the call, "Cease fire and break down" [*take the machine gun apart*]." The barrel is too hot to handle, so I load the whole weapon into the truck. It's a good thing we sleep ready-to-roll - get up, roll up, and you're ready. If you left something in bed, it's in the roll. As we loaded on the trucks, we also took some wounded soldiers who are having a hard time walking.

Soon there's a long column of vehicles and men on foot, all headed south. The men are walking fast but not running. They stop and take a shot at the enemy if they can. Don't turn your back, because you never know what he'll do.

Williams:

Captain [*Gordon*] **Lippman** was also cool under fire. A couple times we had incoming rounds on the road, but he was calm, said, "Move the machine gun over here." He finally made lieutenant colonel. Guess where he died? Vietnam.

Our platoon sergeant, Sergeant **Mimms,** was another good man - a good man. A little, short stocky guy, who would pray before his meal. He didn't panic. He calmly said, "Put the machine gun there," or "move it here beside me." He was killed after I left. He knew a machine gun was out there, but he ran across in front of it. Didn't have to. I never forgot him. He was a real man.

Both divisions tried to crowd onto one road, creating a massive traffic jam, until some were funneled onto Bussey's "Goat Track."

Fields:

If we'd both gone by the main road, we'd have gotten ruined; they would have caught two divisions in one city.

LeTellier:

We didn't realize we were so close to being over-run. Bussey made a great decision, saved our lives. I said we ought to stay here for the night. He said, "No, we're going to keep going until we find some of our units." We left via a north-south road through the town of Suwon. Bussey took us on the right route.

Womack:

The MSR [*Main Supply Route*] was cut off by Chinese fire, so we cut across the outskirts of the city by driving on frozen rice paddies.

Fields:

As we looked back, all kinds of vehicles were following us, so we must have made a good by-pass.

Blair's Lost Battalion

Blair was asleep when Corley phoned him to move his battalion before the Chinese over-ran him. Just then machine gun fire ripped into his CP, killing his sergeant-major. Blair dove under the bed. Then, a black warrant officer, **Thomas Pettigrew**, wrote, he began "hysterically and incoherently" giving orders to defend the headquarters. Instead, his staff all dashed for jeeps in a mad effort to escape. Pettigrew was cited for bravery in leading Blair plus 60 others to safety.

Blair headed for Corley's headquarters without trying to contact his units, which had to fend for themselves.

Company M was over-run.

Albert Kimber (K Company):
We were completely surrounded with no escape route, and they told us, "Everyone get out the best way you can." We were on our own.

Wilfred Mathews (K Company):
We took off but didn't know where to go. The captains didn't know anything either. We walked, crawled, and everything else to get out of there. All that night we didn't know M Company was being attacked on the other side of us. They went through a village, and we went through the fields.

When Blair finally found Corley, the colonel screamed, and Blair broke down crying. Perhaps because of his earlier combat record, Corley did not relieve him. Instead, he ordered Blair to find his men and stormed out to move his own CP farther south.

However, Blair told two officers on the scene to find the lost companies and tell their commanders to handle the withdrawal themselves. Then he also left to move his own command post south.

From a hillside, Blair said later, he watched his troops being cut to pieces as "they ran like rabbits,"

"They would not have run," Pettigrew wrote icily, "had the leadership not failed them ... It was the tragedy of leaderless men."

Blair also said he was driving down the road, looking for his battalion, when he heard voices gathered around a fire singing a catchy song, a parody of Hank Williams' hit, "Movin' On." He stopped and asked what the song was. "Sir," he said one man answered, "It's the official song of the 24th Infantry -- 'The Bug Out Boogie.'"

Pettigrew called it an attempt by Blair to stereotype Negroes as "cowards and minstrel men." BSWA says the song was sung in many divisions, usually with lyrics to reflect on rival outfits:
The Second Division is second to none,
The First Cav is the first to run.

Why blacks would have picked a white country/western song to parody is not clear. However, the story can still be read in several history books, which ascribe it to the 24th.

Actually, it turned out, it was Blair who was discovered warming himself by a fire.

By evening, still with no radio link to Blair, Corley was desperate. Three lieutenants - Oliver Dillard of battalion headquarters, **Alfred Tittle** of K Company, and **Adolph Voight** of M - said they were ordered to find their leader, though why they were in Corley's headquarters and not with their troops is not clear.

Joe Davis recalled Dillard as a second lieutenant at Fort Dix.

Davis:
> That guy was a wizard with maps. He ran the whole damn battalion and saved Blair's ass many a time.

An army light liaison plane was also sent to scour the hills for the missing battalion.

Bussey writes that he had just flopped onto his cot and fallen into his first sleep in three nights when the field phone rang: "I knew some bastard was going to deny me another night's sleep."

It was Corley: "Come up here in ten minutes."

Again the colonel slapped a map. "Somewhere in this area is the Third Battalion." Bussey's job: find it.

"Why do you always choose me to do the dirty work? I'm tired."

Corley: "I'll let that pass. If Blair doesn't get back, he'll be isolated."

Again Bussey said he took Carlisle and Green, who were "on the same wave length" with him. They trudged through the freezing dark and at last walked into Blair's CP.

Meanwhile, the light plane also spotted the missing force and threw a note down in an empty grenade can to "How Able" ("*haul ass*"). That was followed by a second note:

"Imperative you start now."

When Blair finally arrived in Corley's tent, the commander "ate a ton out of him." "You belong in Leavenworth [*prison*]!" he roared. Instead of a court martial, Blair was sent home for "medical" reasons, probably combat fatigue. However, one man stood up for he commander.

Davis:
They say Colonel Blair was a coward. He was no goddam coward, because I know what he did. No coward is going to jump on a tank with that machine gun nest up there. He was no goddam coward. He was a hero.

(After the war, Blair's erratic behavior continued. In 1958 he attempted to rob the Bing Crosby golf tourney at gunpoint. At his trial he called Sergeant Pugh as a character witness but was convicted anyway.)

Williams:
I'm still angry today, because our leadership wasn't too good. There weren't anything but company-grade officers there. None of our majors or colonels were on the line. I never saw our commander, Colonel Miller, the whole time we were withdrawing.

Bob Jones of D Company disagreed:
Battalion commanders usually didn't hang around with front-line troops. Colonel Miller did. He was an OK guy in my book. The last time I saw him, he was standing up in the middle of the area, trying to re-organize what was left of the headquarters. We said, "You better watch out, Sir. We don't know who the hell would be our leader if you got hit."
Colonel Miller said, "Don't worry, they can't shoot." He couldn't show fear in front of black troops. One hell of a guy.

Williams:

We walked all that night, still carrying the wounded with us. We ran into B Company, and in a few minutes the Chinese were firing down on us, but we set up a machine gun and did a little firing, and they disappeared.

In the 9th Infantry, Rangel wrote:

By dawn the attack seemed to taper off, and we made our way south to Suchon past a string of Chinese road blocks... The Chinese were on both sides of the road, as it wound through higher and higher hills leading to a narrow pass. They were playing cat and mouse with us, letting us get a little farther, then cutting off one part or another of our ragtag column. Battery B was pinched off and torn up in an attack after dark. Battery A was cut off, and very few escaped.

The remaining officers decided that there was no choice but to split up. One group would attempt to break through with trucks carrying wounded. They weren't very successful. The rest of us, with the 38th infantry, would try to go through the hills and around the mountain by foot.

I was still clearing the road of dead and wounded bodies to try and keep the convoy moving. We didn't know what the hell we were really doing, with all the people screaming and moaning around us. We could see some GIs being marched away by the Chinese.

It was so unbelievably cold that the blood was frozen in the wounds. I didn't have a rifle. I picked one up, but my hands were probably too numb to fire it. I didn't know if it would work, anyway, because in that cold a lot of rifles just froze up.

There was a tractor vehicle, I guess an ammunition carrier... Something hit that damn thing, maybe a mortar, and all I saw

was orange. I was thrown into a deep gully... I prayed to Jesus, and I heard Jesus say, "Boy, if you want any help, you better get out of that hole." As I pulled myself up, I could see hand-to-hand combat, and the outlines of our soldiers being led away with hands over their heads. Above it all, formed by a full moon, was that mountain.

My heart was beating so hard, I remember thinking people could hear it... I crawled to the other side of the road on my stomach. There were other GIs there, screaming and yelling at me, "What should we do, Sarge, what should we do?"

Rangel was actually a pfc, but he had learned early in his army career that if he carried a clipboard and looked officious, others would assume he had been sent from headquarters to report on what they were doing, and they gave him a lot of respect.

I didn't have the slightest idea what we should do, but I knew we had to get the hell out of there. I was so damn scared, but I couldn't let them know I was scared. I didn't know what to do, but they didn't know I didn't know.

The mountain's crest loomed in the moonlight. I heard so much moaning and groaning and screaming and machine gun fire. I remember the top sergeant yelling hysterically, "You better get the hell out of here." I saw this long-legged, decorated World War II veteran racing across the hill like a mad spider on a hot rock. He would beat us to the other side of the mountain...

Meantime, away we went in the night, desperately afraid of sunrise catching us where we had been, praying for the moonlight to hold back the dawn. I didn't know where the hell to go.

The Longest Day

December 1. Dawn broke on one of the most disgraceful days in U.S. military history.

Rangel:

When the sun finally lit up, we looked down on the most awful sight. We saw dead GIs hanging out of vehicles. We saw dead Chinese while other Chinese poured over those vehicles like ants, trying to take rifles and everything they could get off the trucks.

He also saw planes strafing their own men.

It was like trying to scream in a nightmare. We couldn't yell or signal them, because we were so scared the Chinese would find us.

We were starving and frozen. When we got to the Taedong river, they had all those fires on the other side, burning for us. And there was the biggest raft I ever saw in my life waiting for us. Damn, that was a good sight! There was a field hospital and medics waiting for us. They put me on a cart, and there was a general congratulating me for leading the men through enemy lines, but in my first moment as a war hero, I felt nothing but the shock of fleeing for my life and the awe that I still had life.

Meanwhile, back in the 24th:

Clyde Jones:

We were standing beside this tank, and a colonel got out of his jeep. "My name is Colonel **Call**" - or **McCall**, something like that. I don't know where he came from, he wasn't from my battalion. The tank man said, "I'm sorry, sir, you can't get in, I just can't carry any more in the tank."

"I'm a colonel!"

That bastard got in the tank: "Pull out, and don't stop until you get to the other side of the paddy!" he moved off and left us to be killed.

Ralph Hubbard:

Everyone hauled ass!

We were under a tent-half hung from a tree that gave us some semblance of a roof. I had low-quarter shoes

246

on; I had lost my boots on the train from Pusan. So I was there with my feet on a little Japanese *hibachi* stove to warm them, when the Chinese walked in on us - I mean they walked *in* on us! I don't know how those people did it - and we were supposed to have intelligence. They busted in on us, firing,

We scrambled - we came out running! I left my gun laying against a wall. We were going *south*!

I was walking bare-foot in the snow, about two and a half or three miles. And I was not the only one. Believe it or not, I didn't feel my feet. What the hell could you do?

I saw a jeep turned over. Two dead men in it. I reached down and pulled the boots off one man and stuck my feet in them. Well, he didn't need 'em any more.

A lot of guys, when they took off and ran, the heaviest thing they had was their rifles. M-1s and carbines were laying everywhere.

. . But we never left any of our heavy weapons in shape when we had to leave them. I threw a can of white phosphorous into our 75; it melted the breech like white-hot lead. Did the same thing in the mortar.

I was talking to a guy in the 24th Division, said he took his tripod with him. That wasn't doing any good. He should have left the tripod and taken the gun. I said, "You didn't do shit, you left the best part for them." He got a little testy.

Jones:

I found my company, and we started to walk. The Chinese walked right along with us, just about 100 yards behind, about ten million of them. We stopped for ten minutes, the Chinese stopped.

The ground was frozen, we couldn't dig in the ice, so we just laid on top of it and slept.

Williams:

I guess the whole 25th Division was out on that road. You'd hear screaming from up on the mountain, where the Chinese were shooting down on us. I was lucky, I was always in front of that stuff. Usually we'd pass by, then the Chinese started firing, and we'd hear people screaming back there.

There were wounded everywhere, on the tanks, on the hoods of jeeps, you name it. We were trying to carry them on make-shift stretchers with ponchos and poles. You ever try to carry a man on a make-shift litter? My brother and I were carrying one of them, just a young guy. He was begging us not to leave him.

Mathews:

The Air Force had a little liaison guy, a white guy, in a jeep. We asked that boy to put as many wounded on that jeep as he could. You know, that bastard refused! They couldn't walk much farther, and he wouldn't even take one of them back.

These kinds of things you can't forget.

John French (Engineers):

The Chinese were all over us. You had a lot of hand-to-hand there, a lot of it. Just about every mountain pass, you looked for them. They would try to hit the lead and the rear vehicles.

Williams:

There was no panicking, but we'd keep moving - moving south. They were cold, nasty nights. We'd go from hill to hill, go to a hill and set up, go to another one, set up, trying to make the Chinese believe there were more of us than there were.

No food. Very low on ammunition. Didn't know whether your weapon was going to work or not. And we didn't have many vehicles, because a lot of them were captured or destroyed.

Didn't have any ammunition and no food. We lived off the land, went into houses: "Any food here?" You'd dig holes and look for apples, or eat dogs, and we'd make a meal. I don't know how we got by without winter clothes. We did, though.

Jones:

Tanks froze. Jeeps froze. Everything the Americans had froze. We saw them by the side of the road as we walked past.

We were carrying wounded men. Two medics were carrying men on litters, and we helped carry them out. I was the last man in line at I Company, and I had a 16-year old boy, **Dixon**, who had been shot in the leg. Everybody liked him, he was the company pet. i got behind Dixon and pushed.

Captain Petrosky said "Pull back." Men in litters, we had to lay them down. I had to put Dixon down. I thought his buddy had him. But I don't know what happened to him. Every time I go to a reunion, I ask about him, but no one knows anything.

"Here they come again!" I turned around and looked. Three or 400 Chinese were running straight at us. We fell on the ground and stopped them - the white phosphorous grenades stopped them - for about 15 minutes.

Before they could re-group and run at us again, four P-51s come over there and started strafing the Chinese. When they got close to us, I had an American flag in my hand. I was hit in the head by a piece of metal that fell off the plane, hit me right on top of the head, they were so close to us. "Get me up, boys." They stuck another band aid on there.

All of a sudden the planes raised their noses and picked up and left. When they pulled off, here come 5,000 more Chinese! They were running alongside us and said, "Run, Joe," or "Joe, you prisoner."

Mathews said the Chinese literally ran up behind them and pushed them.

A captain from the Second Division, Sherman Pratt, watched from a hill as the Chinese caught up with the Yanks. He told BSWA;

I could see troops moving in the valley below us. They were too distant to make out, but it was clear that they weren't organized. They were moving around in bunches, this way and that, like chickens in a barnyard, with no direction.

As they got close, one of my lieutenants said, "My God, Captain, I think they're GIs."

Black GIs. Most had no helmets, and few had any weapons. They looked thoroughly disorganized and terrorized. We could see them running and stumbling over the frozen ground. Some would fall and not get back up. We could see one or two of them stop, look back, and fire. Although there wasn't much of that, because so few still had their rifles.

Then we noticed that mixed among the GIs were Chinese. They were running in among them grabbing them and trying to pull them to the ground. We could see fist fights as the GIs tried to throw them off. We saw other GIs hitting the Chinese with clubs or sticks. The wild melee continued for two or three hours.

Why couldn't Pratt and his men go to help? Instead they sat safely on their hill for three hours as though watching the scene in a movie theater.

Bussey:

The generals turned our Army into a leaderless horde, running head-long for Pusan. Our soldiers had lost every bit of confidence in all their leaders, from the commander-in-chief down. I had no idea where we were going or if we'd get there.

The Gap

The Deuce-4 hoped to make a stand along a railroad track, where a train would be waiting.

Mathews:

Captain **Schwartz** asked six automatic weapons men - three BARs and three .30 calibres - would we set up a defense on the railroad tracks until they could get the wounded out. **Edward Burwell** was the machine gunner of the first platoon. He was my best friend in Japan, a very easy-going, slow-talking fellow. And a hell of a machine gunner. I was second platoon gunner. I don't know who the third platoon was, he was a replacement.

The planes dropped bombs, but the Chinese were just walking through them - they just kept coming. There were just too many of them. As fast as we knocked them down, they'd get back up and come at us again.

I tell everybody, we may have the best weapons, but they aren't worth anything without manpower. If they have more manpower, they'll over-run you, I don't care what kind of weapons you have.

We shot at them and laughed at 'em for being damn fools coming at us like this. It was fun while it was happening, it was a joke. Afterward, when you're telling about it, that's when you get scared.

We stayed on the railroad until about four o'clock that evening. After everyone had gotten out, we hauled ass out of there.

But not everyone had gotten out.

Jones:

A truck came by, throwed off a load of blankets. They said, "There's a blizzard coming. Go to the Gap!" There was a train there, about a mile and a half or two miles away. We thought we were going to ride the train.

Captain Petrosky came up in a jeep, said, "Get to the Gap!" We loaded the jeep with wounded men. He didn't leave us until the last man was on the jeep. One man was sitting on his lap.

The rest of us, about 12 or 13, could walk.

We got halfway there, and they pulled another attack on us. The Chinese were everywhere. We didn't get any replacements - they had plenty.

The Chinese were dead shots. You could hear, *Bam!* Just *Bam!* You'd be talking to your buddy, right beside you. *Bam*! Another dead soldier. Three or four minutes later, another *Bam!* Another boy gone. They shot five times. I can still hear those *Bams!* some times in my sleep.

We carried eight bandoliers of ammunition each [*96 rounds*] and we fired five bandoliers for about 15 minutes. That stopped them.

Seven bullets hit next to my foxhole. I jumped up and looked around. No one was there. I was by myself, wasn't anybody there with me.

Herbert T Jones, a master sergeant - he's the man who saved my life. He said, "What in the world are you doing here by yourself?"

I said, "I'm holding the line for Captain Petrosky. He said he'd come back."

"Holding the line!? Get out of here! There are too many of them. Get out of here! I'm too old, I'll hold for you." He was using a .45 and an M-1. He loaded the .45. *Bam. Bam.* Shot eight times and reloaded John Wayne-style. Then he went down. There's no record of what happened to him.

I jumped up, got behind a dike. There were water towers 100 feet high. A medic friend had been shot in the leg. He said, "Jump down here!" I jumped on another man.

"He's dead."

"What?!"

"They're all dead here." There were dead laying everywhere.

I said, "Watch out!" The Chinese came up the wall. We were going hand-to-hand, fighting like dogs, trying to keep them off us. They ·were everywhere, coming like piss ants. "There's too many of them. Pull back!"

Everyone was gone except me, and the Chinese were coming from everywhere. I was the last one. I finally ran into our medic, **Pilgrim**. He was in World War II, in the 92d Division, wore a stetson hat. He came running up, said, "Come on, Tennessee, there's too many of 'em!"

We ran to the railroad tracks. It was dark, about six o'clock, by the time we got to the Gap. We kept moving wounded over the tracks. We moved as many as we could. There was a train there about a mile and a half or two miles away, and we started going down the track. We were carrying eight to 20 men who were wounded, many more than we could do anything with. We got halfway there, and they pulled another attack on us, but we stopped it.

A 2½-ton truck stopped and picked them up. Then they sent a Red Cross truck down and got the last of them. I looked back, and they rolled the wounded in like fence posts.

The Chinese stopped 50 yards away. If they had fired on us, they could have killed us.

A sergeant said, "Is this I Company?"

"What's left of us."

"The Chinese have already got the train. Hit the hill, soldier!" We started climbing. He said, "You're going too slow!"

We were doing the best we could, but we were whipped, beaten down, and tired. "Hell, we've been walking since seven o'clock this morning."

"But you got to go! Get! Get!" I was the first one. The rest of them followed me. He pushed us to the top of the hill. Got about halfway up, and the Chinese broke through at the bottom.

Mustangs laid some napalm "eggs."

There were 75 or 80 Americans up there. They said, "Are you L Company?"

I said, "No, Item Company. Love Company is to the left." About 20 of them. We never did see them again.

Captain Petrosky was pulling people up. They had an ambulance, and they loaded the wounded in, couldn't get any more in. They brought a 2½-ton and put them in.

He said, "Anybody left?"

"No one's behind me."

"I Company, count off!"

There were about 17 of us.

Everyone was standing up, firing. Captain Petrosky told me, "Go tell them to lay down,"

We were starving, tired. Captain Petrosky took two men and got us some chow. We ate that food like hogs, and we felt better. He said, "Sit down for 15 minutes and I'll come back and tell you what to do."

Blizzard

Jones:

We sat there about five minutes, and it commenced snowing. And it snowed, and it snowed, and it snowed. I looked down, and it had snowed about three inches, and we hadn't paid any attention. I never saw so much snow in my life! It looked like talcum powder, just like you take a handful of flour. That's *snow*!

I went to find Captain Petrosky. He said he wasn't going to be a Chinese prisoner, told us, "Stay on this road." The

company commander and everyone else - the whole battalion - just left us, 17 men. I came running back on the double, told the rest, "Come on, let's get out of here!"

It snowed ten inches, I guess, in no time. We walked about an hour or so, and I said, "Wait a minute, boys. I'm going to do an old Boy Scout trick. Everyone get a blanket and cut it in half."

They didn't want to do it: "We're going to sleep on it."

I said, "Put it on for a sweater. You can freeze to death." I cut mine in two, gave half to my buddy. When they saw that, they cut theirs in half too. We put them over our heads, nothing but our eyes showing. I don't know how long it was before we took them off.

We walked all night in snow up to our knees. We still had one can of food left, and we all had something to eat and struggled on.

Everyone was getting jumpy; wasn't anything there, but we really got scared.

At ten o'clock we took a ten-minute break.

We walked all night and all the next day. From one hill to the next, we didn't see anything but burned-out trucks, jeeps, and railroad cars.

Some guys were sitting on the side of the road saying, "I can't go any further." They just gave up: "I'm through." Those of us who could walk tried to help them get started again: "You've got to go on, the enemy's right behind us." Someone who weighs 200 pounds is hard to get up off the ground.

Next night at five o'clock, we set down to rest. We were without food for two days. Didn't have nothing but what you could find in your pockets.

Everyone got chocolate bars in their rations. If they were going to throw it away, I said, "Don't throw it away, I'll take that." I had two pockets full of candy. Fifteen or sixteen bars, and I divided them up; "Don't eat the whole bar or I won't give you one. I want you to suck it, you haven't had anything to eat for three days." I sucked that bar, and it did me more good than if I ate it. I was a Boy

Scout, and when we went on a hike, the scout masters did the same thing.

That's all we had for two days and a half. "Well, I saved your life for one day, at least." The third day we got some food.

About daylight a tank from the 89th Tank Battalion was stuck on top of the mountain. I said, "Hey, put it in high gear, don't put it in low. When you put it in low, you're spinning; in high gear it will jump ahead."

He said he didn't know that.

"And turn that gun around to put weight on the back instead of the front."

We finally got him out. I said, "We're going to ride you out of this place."

He said, "Ride all you want, I appreciate it."

One man said he could run faster than the tank. He jumped off, and the snow was up to his knees. Sitting on the tank was cold, but it was better than walking. Two-three hours later the tanker said, "Well, I'm going to have to leave you fellows here." When we got down the Americans were burning railroad cars, trucks, jeeps; everything that couldn't run, they were setting a-fire.

Yancey:

I heard the Americans' "Long Tom" firing. It could reach up to 28 miles, had a huge barrel, took three freight cars to carry it. It was big enough for me to get down in the barrel, and I weigh 243 pounds on the hoof. It was enormous. The shells were so big, you could hear them going through the air. Every weapon has its own sound. This had a wobbly sound – *whirr, whirr, whirr.* So we walked in that direction, and that's what led us back. We walked a couple days.

This was our "strategic withdrawal."

The object was to try to stay alive and stay alert. But sometimes you found it so doggone hard to do. You didn't have time to get a good eight hours rest. Everyone can't handle adversity the same way. The longer you stay in the battle area, the more alert you become. You see many of your comrades getting shot, so stay alert. That's war.

I was leading the patrol, and a guy says, "A tank's out front."

"Halt and be recognized."

I said, "Do I look like a damn Chinese?" He must have been losing his mind!

We slept under tanks at night. You'd wake the hell up when the engines cranked up. All of a sudden before dawn this bugle is blowing, tins banging, hollering like Indians.

Even Yancey didn't escape frostbite:

I got 60% of my disability from frostbite. They sent me to battalion headquarters to be intelligence sergeant.

Mathews:

We walked for days. Don't tell me you can't sleep when you're walking, because you can!

Captain **Robert Jones** was sent to take a hill over-looking the highway. He led two platoons almost to the top, then went back down to bring up his reserve. (Didn't he have a walkie-talkie?) There he met Major **Crosby Miller** of Richmond, the battalion executive officer (second in command).

Jones:

Just then I felt I'd been kicked in the chest by a mule. The concussion dropped me to my knees. I was stunned. I knew I'd been hit right in the heart, yet I was still alive. Major Miller helped me rip open my jacket, and there was a .30-calibre machine gun slug sticking out of my chest. It pierced the flesh, but first it had hit the steel button on my left breast pocket and bored a straight through a 70-page notebook.

It was finally stopped by a rib. The major picked the bullet out and handed it to me with a grin. "Here's a souvenir for you, Jones," he said.

Jones patched himself up with tape and gauze from his firstaid pack and went back to the hill. Two days later he reported to an aid station.

He received a Silver Star.

Oliver Hendrix, a medic from Nashville told the Baltimore *African-American:*

Two a.m. on a rainy night the enemy killed one man and wounded some others. Five of them were lying in a gorge, and I had to crawl through a ravine, and across an open field to get them.

Just then the moon came out, while I was lugging one of them out. The Chinese kept on firing, and we kept on crawling until we got to our wounded, and dragged them back to better cover and finally got them to an aid station.

Williams:

They sent me on guard with **Chuck Smith** from Cincinnati. He was a little cocky, but he was a good combat man. Later on he won the Silver Star. Smith went to sleep on me, so I started whipping him in the sleeping bag to wake him up.

He wasn't the only one who went to sleep. After walking all day, even though your life may depend on it, you still want to go to sleep.

I've seen guys have a smoke when lives could have been lost. They'd light cigarettes at night and try to hide them under a poncho, which wasn't possible.

Another night they told me and Smith to go down the road to wait for a truck coming with ammunition. We waited for a few hours, but nothing happened, so we went back up the hill.

I don't know why the Chinese let us back in. In ten minutes that hill was surrounded. All hell broke loose. All night long we battled, laying down fire to try to keep them away. Our ammunition set a fire, and I could see a Chinese guy down there. We thought he was dead, but his body kept moving; I think it was the bullets hitting him.

We got two or three people wounded, but we managed to bring them out with us to another hill. We came to a fork in the road. My brother went to the right with his company, D, and my company, A, went to the left. That's the last I saw of him. He got wounded a couple days later, I don't know how, and got sent home, but they sent him back before the war ended to the 24th Division.

Fields:
The Chinese breached barbed wire with their bodies. They just lay down and made a human bridge, and the others stepped on their bodies across the wire.

Jones:
We walked, I guess, two or three days. We kept on withdrawing - I mean "moving south." I was cold, hungry, my feet freezing, hands freezing. I couldn't take any more.

That's when my mind played out. I blanked out right there for two or three days maybe. My memory went out. When I came to, I was in a truck. "Where are we? How did we get here?"

They said, "You're on your way to Pyongyang. I didn't care.

Pyongyang

December 4. General Walker reached Pyongyang. Why his Army wasn't a collection of walking icicles, is a miracle.

Clyde Jones:
Airplanes were all sitting on the ground. "Oh, man we made it!" We were the last truck coming out. We were the end of the Americans, because the 77th Engineers were laying land mines on the highway behind us. Nothing

behind us but Chinese, two-300 yards behind. You could see 'em.

Kimber:

It was snowing so hard, believe it or not, you could hardly see. About eight of us heard an aircraft engine roar and a C-47 [*transport plane*] taxiing for take-off. Me and a couple friends ran over and hit the side of the plane with our rifle butts. When they opened the door, they hollered, "Friendly troops!" and pulled us in.

Ellis Dean (A Company):

We were occupying a factory in Pyongyang, and we heard shouting and bugles. I said, "I'm so comfortable, I'm not going anywhere." But we had to leave. We were the rear guards. We let the 1st Cavalry through so they could get out. I was separated from my company for a while. I was listed as missing in action.

Fields:

Orders were to destroy the city. It was the capital of North Korea, and we wanted to do a hell of a job on it. And we did. A plane took pictures to show the job we did.

We had to clear Pyongyang by 1800 hours; after that it was open target for the Air Force. But we still had to blow hell out of the railroad.

My target was the rail yard, and I did my best to blow every railroad track in the city. Then I tried to bring down buildings to block the roads. Other engineers were blowing up reservoirs, oil storage tanks, electric transformers, and sewer lines. You name it, we did it.

We checked the inside of each railroad car before we went to work, and some of the cars had brand new GI overcoats, woolen caps, parkas, and new field jackets, all in the rail yard, waiting to be destroyed; the Air Force was going to napalm the cars.

We got all the winter clothing we needed and more. GIs came walking and in vehicles, and we let as many as possible get clothing. There was no color-line, just U.S. soldiers.

LeTellier:

Lieutenant Haezel Peoples, our supply officer, knew the transportation companies in the rail office. One of the loads he came back with was sleeping bags. They made a difference at night! Before that we just had liners that go inside the bags. He got enough for the whole company. Somewhere we got "bunny hats" with ear muffs. We got all the clothing we could possibly wear.

Hubbard:

Someone threw me a jacket, and I don't know who did it. I wound up with a jacket and a hat.

Yancey:

They had these winter coats in crates, but they weren't issued to the troops. We didn't have time to get them out - the Chinese were on our butt. Supplies, jeeps, equipment - we had to throw them in a fire and burn them up.

Fields:

A major told us we were stealing and we had no right to let the GIs take them! We told him we had orders to destroy them.

"By whose authority?"

"Twenty-fifth Division headquarters."

He finally was driven away.

This is just one example of the incompetence that Negro soldiers had to deal with. We lost 10-15 minutes because of that dumb-ass major, so we were six minutes late setting the charges and the fuses.

But the Air Force was on time, and we paid for it. Three planes, each with eight machine guns, made a pass. The first plane didn't drop any flares but opened up on us. You could see guys diving off trucks - me, for one.

261

John B. Holway

We jumped in ditches, but Sergeant **Jackson** of the second platoon was sitting in the front seat of a truck and was killed. He was one of the best in the business. That was a hell of a way to die.

I have questions on the selection of Regular Army senior officers assigned to an all-Negro unit. Someone in headquarters decided to send us the dumbest ones in the Army. How could some of them have been promoted to a senior grade? We'll never know how many Negro troops were killed because of incompetent white officers.

The second plane dropped flares and saw the stars on our vehicles and saved us from further attacks.

The I&R platoon was behind us to maintain contact with the enemy. Their lieutenant was the last one to withdraw.

We set a bridge up for demo when the last ones went through. They were the tail end of the division, and the lieutenant pulled his men over to the side and said he would like to watch us do the demolition. So we wired it up to a jeep battery and said, "Lieutenant, would you like to set it off?" Boy, was he excited! We said, "Now!" and he touched the two wires to the battery, and up it went! It scared the hell out of him, and he jumped like it was an in-coming.

Next we stopped to blow a switch-house to prevent the use of the railroad beyond that point, While we were at it, we decided to take care of a steam engine too.

We lit the fuses and headed out, running as fast as we could with our lights on. The night was colder than a witch's tit.

The Chinese came in to get the clothes, but the Air Force moved in again, and we could see the explosives going off as the sky lit up. Some say it looked like the 4th of July. Air recon checked the damage the next day, and reported many dead Chinese.

December 5. The Chinese and North Koreans marched into Pyongyang amid a celebration.

Fields:

The Chinese came in to get the clothes, but the Air Force moved in again, and we could see the explosives going off as the sky lit up. Some say it looked like the 4th of July. Air recon checked the damage the next day, and reported many dead Chinese.

Jones:

They could have got us at any time they wanted to. They had us in Kunu-ri and at the railroad tracks too. For a reason I'll never know, I'm still alive. If we hadn't been 18 years old, we never would have made it. And if it hadn't been for the snow, they would have killed us all. It stopped them too,

A new recruit, **Curtis Morrow** (G Company), arrived from the States. The book he would write, *What's a Commie Ever Done to Black People?* is one of the most powerful and honest accounts of combat ever written:

I joined the Army from Michigan, a small town, Buchanan, between Benton Harbor and Niles. There were no stop lights, just go right on through. I was there from 12 to 17, and those were good times. I did a lot of fishing. There were seven of us. I was the oldest.

I always dreamed of some day going off to some war, fighting gallantly, and returning as a hero. Yeah! With a chest full of decorations and maybe even a slight limp. All the young girls would be drooling over me, and I'd have my pick, man. A different woman every night.

I took demolition training but dropped out two weeks before the course ended and volunteered for duty in Korea. Why? I wanted to experience how it would be to participate in a real war. I wanted to fight, man. I wanted to know how it would feel to kill.

John B. Holway

Three of us were sent to the 24th at the same time: me, **Albert Simpson** - a tall guy - and **Columbus Mathews**, a BAR man from Little Rock.

The road [*from Inch'on*] was lined on both sides with disabled vehicles... There were hundreds of Korean civilians carrying all they could on their heads and backs, with their small children walking beside them... Bombs and artillery fire turned the skies a crimson red. The cold winter air was heavy with the smell of burning flesh, garlic, and gun powder.

In the distance trucks drew near us. On one of them I noticed what I thought were duffel bags stacked neatly and covered with canvas. Then the wind blew gently and lifted the canvas for us to see that they weren't duffel bags but bodies. It was obvious who we were here to replace.

Morrow joined his new squad just north of Pyongyang, the North Korean capital. Normally 12 men, they were down to four until he arrived. While they shivered around a fire, he watched the others pulling lice from caps or clothing and dropping them into the fire. He was embarrassed in his clean warm clothes and new boots "while the others looked like ragmen."

Then they were called to move out.

It was ten pm, and we hadn't had more than a few minutes of dozing in the last 36 hours on a truck."

My first night of combat was spent evading the CCF [*Chinese*], whom we occasionally glimpsed as they dashed along the ridges of the hills on our flanks, trying to encircle us and set up ambushes.

They picked their way in pitch darkness along the narrow, frozen dike of a rice paddy. Morrow dozed as he walked, until an exploding artillery round startled him awake and he slipped through the paddy ice. "What the hell you trying to do," the sergeant hissed, "get us killed?" They trudged on until Curtis bumped into the man in front of him:

Looking up, I noticed the moon emerging from the dark clouds. Next I heard the explosion of a hand grenade, and everyone began firing their weapons at once. The air was filled with the whining of enemy bullets as they searched the sky above our heads.

I just shot at the muzzle blasts. It was over within seconds. I don't know if I hit anyone or not.

They resumed marching, past enemy bodies and toward a crimson sky lit with the blasts of bombs.

Milton Bailey was my squad leader in the first squad. He was from Milton Pennsylvania, an only child, raised by his grandmother. The library lady there, Mrs Goodrich, told me his grandmother was a historic person, heavy on the woman's issues. The lady was writing something on her.

That guy never got any medals, but he was very protective, like a platoon sergeant. He saved my life at 35 below. They warned us not to lay down and go to sleep, and we watched each other to keep from falling asleep. But it was too tempting, and I dozed off. He had a problem trying to get me up.

Morrow dedicated his book to Bailey.

Leon Warren – "Red" - from Washington DC was the best fox-hole buddy I ever had. He was an interesting dude. You could put him on a desert, and he'd come back with a chicken. He was a good fighter. He had that attitude, he wanted to go out like a soldier.

My platoon leader, Lieutenant **James Hale**, was from Oklahoma. He was always saying, "Let's Go!" We called him, "Lieutenant Let's-go"

Jones:

They could have got us at any time they wanted to. They had us in Kunu-ri and at the railroad tracks too. For a reason I'll never know, I'm still alive. If we hadn't been 18 years old, we never would have made it. And if it hadn't been for the snow, they would have killed us all. It stopped them too,

Man, it was cold - 40 below zero. If you take your blankets off, you freeze to death. We took them off anyway and shook them a little bit. Then we put them back over our clothes and wore them until we got to the other side of the Han River.

Going back toward Seoul we still had to fight the Chinese, but it wasn't hand-to-hand like in North Korea. The Air Force came in and protected us, and the artillery did a lot of shooting.

Meanwhile, where was Nicholson?

I wasn't there for the massacre. I was down in Inch'on, having fun. We had stateside breakfasts, eating eggs sunny-side up, French fries, fried chicken. You didn't get that on the front line. We were living it up. Actually, my friend was having most of the fun - he got drunk. I was drinking apple cider. We went to sleep, soundly, in the truck.

By then the whole Army was moving south. The Chinese were pushing us back fast, and everything was chaos in Inch'on. They were moving everything off the shore, because they didn't know how far the enemy was coming.

The Navy put our truck on a boat, and we woke up in the middle of the morning on the sea, still under our canvas. We told them we had to get back to the front line, so they brought us back to shore, gave us a brand new six-by, two tubes, and a breechblock, and gave us directions to find our battalion.

Captain Franke was pleased. We were gone about two weeks. The 24th got slaughtered, but I wasn't there.

Nicholson numbers this as one of 20 miracles that saved his life.

Walker kept right on going. He decided that saving his army was more important than holding the city. He even doubted that he could hold Seoul. He was already thinking of making another stand at the old Pusan Perimeter, joined by Marines and Almond's GIs, who were escaping on Navy ships on the east coast.

Meanwhile, in the East the Marines were slogging through snow at the Chosin Reservoir, struggling to reach the coast, where navy ships were waiting tp rescue them. Navy F-4 Corsair fighters took off from an aircraft to cover them.

One of the pilots was **Jesse Brown**, the first black pilot in the Navy. He had grown up in poverty in MIssissippi as the son of a sharecropper but won a scholarship to Ohio State, where his hero, Jesse Owens, had starred. The Navy had selected 5,000 men to begin pilot training at colleges around the country. Brown was one of 14 blacks chosen. He won his wings in 1948.

This day Brown caught a bullet from ground gunners and crash-landed in the snow as fire crept close to his fuel tank.

His wingman, Thomas Hudner, from an exclusive New England prep school, deliberately crash-landed next to him and dashed to his aid. He found Brown unconscious with his leg pinned under the plane. Hudner tried to put out the fire with snow, then tried to wrestle the pilot out from under the plane. He called for helicopter support, and both pilots tried to free Brown without success. As darkness fell, the copter had to leave the dying man.

The Navy chastised Hudner for destroying his own plane and putting the copter in danger. Then they awarded him the Medal of Honor.

Melvin "Red" Jackson was a former Red Tail flying a P-51 "Mustang'."

Jackson:

Korea wasn't a very exhilarating war. In Europe there was more of a spirit to get the war done.

Colonel Dean Hess was training South Korean pilots and wanted some volunteers. I should have known better. You know what they say in the Army: "Keep your head up, your other part down, and never volunteer." But I volunteered. We were going up to attack Chinese facing the Second Division. The Americans were in full retreat, the Chinese were chasing them, and we were trying to kill as many of them as we could.

We were doing very close ground attack when I heard my plane get hit. Black smoke from the engine cowling covered my windshield with smoke and oil, and I couldn't see. The P-51 has portholes on each side, and fire was coming out of them.

I was losing altitude fast. I yanked my cord, and the canopy flew off, but I could see trees beside me, and I knew I couldn't bail out. Unfortunately, I had ripped my seatbelt open and had no time to fasten it again.

I said, "I'm going to land on this road." I looked out the side of the windshield, and there in front of me were cars, bikes, jeeps, everything - a stream of vehicles bumper-to-bumper, running as fast as they could. I was going to land on *that*?

So I peeled off to the first little hill I saw, and my wing hit one of the pines and jerked me around. I remember the shock from hitting, then blacked out. An ambulance crew came over and pulled me out before the plane burned me up.

Colonel Hess told the people that Captain Jackson had been killed - burned up. They packed my belongings and sent the word home that I was dead.

December 10.

Bussey:
Thousands of ragtag troops, mostly stragglers, mostly leaderless, trudged down the road, which was choked with vehicles abandoned when they ran out of fuel. A shameful spectacle - "leaderless hordes, hell-bent for Pusan.
The engineers picked up as many as they could. Every pair of hands could fit a D-handled shovel. But after a day the guests were eager to rejoin their infantry units.

December 23. The 24th took up a position on the south bank of the Imjin river and burned all boats on the north shore. The engineers pushed bangalore torpedoes – long pipes filled with explosives to break up the ice and prevent Chinese crossings. But, according to Bussey, Corley made them quit - they were disturbing his sleep.

Williams:
General Walker landed in our division area in a helicopter. I remember him walking around, just before his jeep had an accident and rolled over on him. He died the next day, Christmas Eve.

December 24. In the east the Marines and the rest of X Corps were safely on board their warm Navy ships, along with thousands of refugees. The ROK units and the entire 8th Army in the west were left to battle the winter and the Chinese. It would be two months before they would sleep safely in warm beds.
Meantime in the west clerks in a blacked out Korean hurt broke down mail by units, loaded the bags on blacked-out jeeps, and headed off to the battalions. Corporal **Clarence Jackson** headed up a snowy road into the mountains. He was met by Lieutenant **Ray Harrison**, who told him, "You'll have to hand-carry it the rest of the way." So Jackson slung the bag over his shoulder. The previous mail clerk had been killed, so Jackson

kept a nervous eye peeled, and trudged until he ran into an outpost and handed his bag over.

That night guns rumbled over the mountains and frozen paddies as the GIs read their letters by the light of bursting flares.

December 29.

Bussey:

The Chinese made a bold assault across a sheet of ice that never should have been allowed. About 50,000 stormed across before artillery chopped the rest. Hundreds of civilians were also slaughtered.

Those Chinese who got across charged into the rear and fanned out. "We were forced to leg it for all we were worth. "

December 31. In his year-end report, General Kean couldn't bring himself to say "retreat." Rather, he wrote, he was conducting "a continuance of the southward movement to more advantageous positions."

"I wasn't running," Fields insists with a smile, "but I passed a lot of guys that were."

Walker's replacement was Mathew Ridgway, a paratroop general at Normandy. His symbol was a grenade pinned to his chest. That a three-star general would ever need a grenade is unthinkable, but the symbolism was powerful, and he brought a new fighting spirit to the army.

He also believed that segregation was "un-American and un-Christian."

The New Year

Clyde Jones:

They put us in trucks going south again. We were the last ones, and I was the last man on the truck. We drove about 300 yards - right off the mountain. We took the wrong turn, and the truck turned over seven times, they told me. All I could remember was, every time it turned over, I'd say, "Am I dead? Am I dead? Am I dead?" Some of the men rode all the way to the bottom of the hill.

It threw me out.

I passed out. When I woke up, I had neck injuries, back injuries, and foot injuries. It just crushed me all over. I couldn't walk, couldn't move. I tried to stop the next truck from coming down on top of us, but I couldn't walk.

My helmet was the only thing that saved me, but it was on the side of my head, and I couldn't get it off. One man sat me down and said, "Hey, I'll take your helmet off." But he couldn't get it off either. It hurt. It took two of them to pry it off my head.

They had to go down and get all my buddies to the top of the hill, and they laid us in a truck like fence posts. I couldn't move. Some were hurt pretty bad - "My leg's broken" - or broken backs and necks. We had 15 miles to go to a first-aid station. Those old roads they had, it was rough riding. We said, "Don't drive so fast!"

The aid station turned us down. They gave us another shot of morphine and said, "Keep going." It killed the pain for a while, but some of them guys, it didn't do any good.

Finally they got us all in a building and took all our clothes off to see what was broken. They felt my chest, said, "Here?" But I couldn't talk, because blood had closed my mouth, and I couldn't move, because I was paralyzed. They put us on a train, and that's all I remember.

When I woke up two days later, I was in the Pusan hospital. I had a head injury, my lower back and upper back were crushed, both knees were messed up, my left foot was crushed, and my left arm was knocked out of place. I stayed in the hospital seven days, but they threw me out, because I could walk. I couldn't carry a rifle; but the Chinese were still running over people, and the hospital was full. They put me in rehab. For three days they exercised me and made me walk, then they threw me out of there too.

I was back in the line in about 14 days. And I still couldn't even carry an M-1.

The Americans stumbled back across the 38th parallel.

Bussey:

We had gone north a proud and seemingly invincible army. We had been greeted with hysterical cheers of woman and children. It was sad going back over the 38th parallel. I was ashamed. I had been taught that Americans were invincible. I had come to realize that this was untrue. Americans could be defeated - we *had* been defeated.

We were defeated by the ineptitude of our politicians and generals, who gambled with our lives that the Chinese wouldn't enter the war. There had been no guarantee to the Chinese that we would stop at the Yalu. We moved up without reconnaissance, plan, or coordination, and we were defeated in the same manner. The troops weren't trained in night fighting, guerrilla warfare, arctic combat, and survival.

The gamble had been idiotic, and our losses had been staggering.

The army continued through Seoul, the third time the city had changed hands. By then it was a ghost town, with only a "carcass" remaining.

Jones:

When we came through Seoul, there wasn't anything left. I didn't see a building standing. Everything looked blown down. No people there. The Air Force came in and protected us, and the 159th artillery did a lot of shooting.

John French:

We made it all the way back safely until Yong Dong Po, south of Seoul, when we got strafed by our own damn guys. The pilot went down our ranks firing and came back before someone in the tanks finally radioed to him.

My platoon sergeant got it. A 20-mm cannon shot, right through his cheekbone. I was lucky, because the truck I was on had all the company's gas.

Williams:

The wounded got all the way to the rear. Eventually we ran into a truck, and he took us back. I looked back and saw all this smoke where they had hit a mine. One guy was blown half in two. They didn't move the bodies out. They laid there for about three days until someone came up and got them.

Ralph White of Virginia (I&R Platoon) was ambushed one night, covering a withdrawal from a village.

White:

Lieutenant **[Lee] Beech** of Charleston shouted, "Get out of here if you can, boys." He had blood on his lip, where a bullet creased him.

White ran to a jeep, but it wouldn't start. He tried to hide in a paddy with another man, but the enemy spotted them and started shooting.

I ran until I couldn't run any more, then dropped and crawled until I could find cover to hide again. The other guy kept going and got hit five times in one leg.

White watched civilians strip his dead buddies and hid until morning, when he started down a road until bullets convinced him he "better go the other way."

The army tried to hold on the Han river, south of the capital.

Jones:

We had to pull guard duty on the Han. The Chinese would blow the refugee boats out of the water, but in the night the people would come across anyway. They were on the bank, and we would let them through. Refugees by the hundreds - the roads were just full of them, and the Chinese would be in the middle of them - the Chinese weren't dummies. The soldiers got to dressing in refugee clothes so we couldn't pick them out from the people. When night came, the soldiers would keep walking. Next day here come 500 more refugees, and we would try to pick the Chinese out again.

Many of them infiltrated among civilian refugees hurrying across a railroad bridge. Bussey said the engineers could have erected a barrier, Instead, the army dropped leaflets that it would blow the bridge, but the people ignored them. So did the Chinese.

Hundreds of woman and kids were surely blown to bits. Possibly a significant number of Chinese soldiers too. It was needlessly brutal, but highly effective.

Sanders:

The Division finally caught up with us and said, "We're not going any farther. We're going to regroup and go back." Ridgeway drew a new line south of the Han River, which was to be the point of counter-attack.

It was not the Yanks who stopped the Reds. Rather, they had out-run their supply lines. After driving the Americans back 250 miles, they had few trucks and no planes or trains to bring food and ammunition forward. It gave the Americans a chance to re-group and re-supply.

Jones:

The sun came out! We looked around at different soldiers, but we didn't know anybody. Every officer in our company was gone except Captain Petrosky and

Lieutenant **Blackshear**. They were the only two. Our buddies in the company just didn't show up.

They gave us jackets, and we took off the blankets, and they gave us new ones. They gave us sleeping bags. Oh, boy, we thought we were in paradise. *Warm!*

We got better weapons, and the new M-1 rifles. Before that we had 1903 Enfields and old World War II M-1s. We also got brand new BARs, machine guns, and 4.2" mortars. The old machine guns' barrels got hot after firing. The new ones had handles on them and something to go across your chest and sight down the barrel. We got a carbine [*smaller rifle for officers*] with a telescope you could see at night with. Before that we had to wait until the enemy got close to us.

We got new radios too.

Oh, and a shower. I only had two showers in seven months. Two! Only one haircut. Didn't need one, because it was cold!

Yancey:

The 24th was the only unit to spend 129 days in a row without any shower and change of clothes. The doggone lice and crabs would tear your balls off. You'd be itching all over. They poured gasoline over the old clothes, set a match to it, burned the lice up. Sounded like corn popping. We went through a trailer, got hot showers, and came out the other side, the medics sprayed DDT on your pubic areas, under your arms. You felt like a new person.

I survived, that's the main thing. I'm just grateful. I don't intend to question The Man Upstairs.

Hubbard:

I myself don't believe it: How did I get through that and stay alive? It doesn't sound right to me - and I was there!

They made me a runner. I'd run to different companies with messages. They didn't do me any favors with that damn job. They sent my ass out there by myself. Go over the hills with orders to find another company.

I preferred going in and out during the daytime. But there were times I had to go at night. I was scared as hell. I needed a compass. I didn't know how much to the left or right I was walking. In mountainous terrain, you may be drifting way over. I'd come back on a line I didn't go out on and coming back to areas without an invitation. That wasn't too smart; they wouldn't know who I was. I had to scream or holler.

One night, Friday the 13th, it was getting dark, and I missed my turn, and I ran until I ran into a farmer's stone wall. I was getting ready to urinate when I heard voices in Korean or Chinese getting closer and closer.

All I could do was get down flat by some bushes as they were walking toward me, a few feet away. I rolled myself into a hedge and just lay there. They were talking and joking, and this one guy started pissing on me - on the middle of my back!

I didn't move! Then it got cold, like ten degrees below zero. I stayed right there, from about four o'clock in the evening until the next morning well after daybreak. I crapped on myself. And it was cold as hell

Finally they started leaving the area. I knew that wasn't the direction I wanted to go, so I went the other way.

My lieutenant, who became my brother-in-law, said, "Jesus Christ! You stink like hell!" I told him what happened, and he started laughing like hell. Years later I told my daughters about it, and they cracked up too.

Being a runner was hairy. I was glad when I wasn't anymore. Later they put two guys on it together.

Nathaniel Nicholson:

We got orders to put our jeeps on straw or wood so the axels wouldn't freeze up. I did, but when I went to sleep, somebody rolled my jeep off and burned the wood to keep warm. So they busted me for not taking care of my jeep. I got busted from pfc to private. It was the second time I got busted.

The mail often brought hard news.

Timmons Jones:

I was told to go to battalion and see the chaplain, and he told me my father had died and he had a flight set up for me to San Francisco. I asked when the funeral was. He said, "Eighteen days ago." That really shook me up.

Womack:

The Red Cross notified me that Aiko was dead. She read about the Chinese attack and killed herself. It messed me up. I wanted to see my kids, and I went AWOL for the only time in my career. I went to Pusan and got on a boat going back to Japan, but they caught me and sent me back to Korea. Aiko's father put the kids in an orphanage, and they died there. They were three and four years old.

John B. Holway

The POWs

Robert Fletcher:

We got to Camp 5 on the Yalu River border, where I spent most of my time. It was the biggest camp, I was told, probably 4,000 men in all. They put us in barns or shacks, and we slept on the grass or on floors

The camp was in a factory town, which our bombers had bombed out, and there were still big craters.

The Chinese turned us over to the North Koreans. They didn't have anything. They were beat, and they hated us; they wouldn't do anything for us.

By the time we got there, there were probably 30 or 40 of us alive from C Company. Just about every one of us was sick. We didn't get any winter clothes. The clothes were for guys 4'9 or 5'2. None of it would fit us. That's why we lost so many guys. We were burying about 100 a day.

I was lucky. When I had arrived in Japan, the army had misplaced my shot records, so I had to take tetanus, typhoid, and diphtheria over again. It knocked me for a loop - I thought it was going to kill me. But it probably gave me enough steam to get through that winter.

January 10. More recruits arrived.
Otto Garner (I Company):

I was born in Orangeburg South Carolina October 4 1930, the second of five kids. My father was in the South Pacific in World War II, but I don't remember too much about him. My mother cleaned houses to keep us going.

I didn't complete school, just a young, dumb individual, who wanted to do something and go someplace. There were no jobs, just cleaning houses or working for somebody, and the Service looked exciting to me. I was 17 years old.

I took basic training in Fort Dix New Jersey in an all-black training unit. In 1948 I went to Germany in the black 370th Infantry, mainly pulling guard duty. Luckily, the people I served under required that you learn, obey orders, and do what you're told. I had good sergeants, who were infantry, and they taught me a lot: If you're not a know-all, you learn something - you learn how to survive.

Then back to Fort Bliss Texas in a coast artillery battalion. Fort Bliss was segregated, and it was rough. We had work like watering the grass, even though we lived in the desert. We had segregated theaters and libraries and our own PXs. We rode in the back of the bus on the post, and of course always had separate latrines and drinking fountains.

So in January 1951 I volunteered for Korea. Just for the excitement.

It was cold, and we were issued warm clothing - most of the people who had been with the unit still didn't have warm clothes.

I thought I was going to the coast artillery, but they handed me a gun and made me infantry. I had good infantry training in Europe, but a lot of people we got weren't infantry. When you put people in combat, they've got to know what they're doing. But they were just not trained in that skill - they were field artillery or tankers. It's hard when you're not used to it - even if you *are* used to it.

The company commander was Lieutenant **Kirksey**. He was black - we didn't have many white officers - and he was a good company commander. Lieutenant Blackshear, my platoon leader, had gotten a battlefield commission. A good fighter, wasn't afraid of anything, and used good judgment in his tactics.

I was a corporal BAR-man, but we didn't have a platoon sergeant, so I was performing as platoon sergeant.

John B. Holway

From the time I arrived, we were in the attack. The first day, I don't know exactly where we were, but we rode off to attack a Chinese hill. We cleared it - there wasn't much opposition - and went on to other hills the next da

Nathan Street (E Company):
I joined the army in July when I was 17. As soon as you turned 18, you were drafted, but if you volunteered, you got a choice, and I chose armor. But when I got to Korea in January 1951, there was no black tank outfit. The 24th was losing more men than bullets, so we were all changed to infantry.

The 24th had been pushed all the way back and were about 50% strength and were building back up.

Lieutenant **George Shuffer** [*black and later a major general*] was E company commander, a hell of a nice guy, a good leader.

Fields:
We were just south of the Han river and were setting up defensive belts of barbed wire and mines. I was a demolitions expert and laid a lot of "bouncing betty" mines and booby traps.

We had a new white lieutenant, Lieutenant **Pitts** from Texas, and we were kind of shy of him. I don't think it was a matter of black or white: When you're laying mines, you only work with people you trust, and we hadn't felt Pitts out.

Until he shot a poisonous snake trying to strike us. The snake was behind us, about 20 yards away. We didn't see it, but Pitts did. He popped its head right off with his carbine. He was so good, he didn't even set any of the mines off. Boy, he was a dead eye with a carbine! We believed in him right then! He stayed with us, and that's rare.

Other companies were not so fortunate:

280

Albert Kimber (I Company):

We got a new commander, **Teague,** from Florida, who totally resented black folks. I was assistant platoon sergeant, and when I tried to explain something to him, he'd get red in the face. I come from the South, and I know what prejudice is. We were under tremendous fire, and he told me to make contact with friendly forces. It was so fierce you could feel the bullets passing your face. I said, "Sir, this is an impossible situation."

These were his exact words: "I'll get myself killed if I have to, just to get you killed."

He attempted to provoke me into anger, thinking he'd get me court-martialed. But my training wouldn't allow me to do it. I realized I was fighting for the U.S. Army, not for him. My job was to secure his safety and the safety of my platoon.

Womack:

The ones we enjoyed being with were the Turks. And they enjoyed us. They had a "Gurkha" knife. Whenever they pulled it out, they couldn't put it back unless they had gotten blood on it. The Chinese didn't mess with them.

Clyde Jones:

The Turks were tough.

They could light a fire, but our headquarters wouldn't let us do it: "Put it out!" That lasted about two weeks. Then it got cold, and we said, "Well, we're going to build a fire."

Some lieutenant said, "Blue Tango 6 to Item 3 [*2d Battalion headquarters to Company I*]. Put that fire out."

We said, "You're not our Old Man, you're not our captain. The son of a bitch who puts this fire out, dies. Item 3, Over."

He didn't say anything. Lieutenant Colonel **[*William*] Mouchet**, who replaced Blair, came up next day and chewed Item Company out, said, "I never heard words like that from a soldier!"

Hubbard:

We had a road block set up on the south side of the river, and this guy's barreling down this damn road in a six-by. He jumps out, and I hear this whistle. I stopped. That's a family whistle, we used it to find each other in parking lots, and I see this grin a mile long. It was my brother, Bill! I cried like a baby. We were crying in the middle of the road. People are beeping. A colonel says, "You get the hell ..."

I said, "Colonel, he's my brother; I haven't seen him in three years."

He was in the Air Force, carrying big tractor-trailers of gasoline up to the front. His captain said he could take three of four days off, so we came off the line and went back to hang out. He said, "I've got good news and bad news. The good news is I'm going home. The bad news is you can't come with me."

Another time two privates were supposed to be guarding the OPLR [*Outpost Line of Resistance*] in front of the troops. They fell asleep, both of them. Lieutenant Wilson was creeping around, checking the perimeter, and took their guns and helmets and crept back with two knapsacks filled with rocks and put them in the hole with them. Early morning, still a little dark, the Chinese started shooting. The two guys jumped up and grabbed for their rifles. He came up and told them, "There's your ammunition - throw rocks at them." You should have seen to hell looks on their faces.

We'd do that to each other, fooling around - hit you on the helmet with a rock like a bubble-head doll. It really brought you to attention. Wilson kicked it up a notch. It was part of the war scene to him - to be hit, shivering, cold, and frightened at the same time.

Clyde Jones:

We were coming up back north, below Seoul. They were in this school house, but we didn't know anybody was in there. We were just walking through the town, and they started picking us off like ducks, so we brought a .50-calibre and started shooting in the house, started tearing up everything. When they came out, they were women, had their rifles over their heads. One man shot them. I can't tell you who, because it was "un-Geneva."

January 15. The GIs entered Kunsan in the middle of "a miserable, cold, barren land, a winter desert." But it was a good chance for some quick R&R. Bussey traded a truckload of rice to the mayor to set up a "relief station" of 16 young women. Everyone got a shot of penicillin. Ditto every GI.

The question was asked whether to have a separate station for officers. "But I considered that less than ethical. The officers did.without."

Otherwise "the result was a success: No women molested. No VD." (But we don't know how many bastard babies grew up to face a life-time of discrimination.)

Corley Sacked

February 19. General Ridgway replaced Walker's division commanders with his own men. General Kean was out. General **Slayden Bradley**, a decorated regimental commander in New Guinea, was temporarily in.

It took Corley one day to get into a loud argument with Bradley, and Corley followed Kean out the tent door.

Timmons Jones:

They sent Corley back to the States and gave him a desk at the Pentagon. Corley had no business behind a desk. He died at his desk, but he was a helluva field commander. He fought his best to get recognition for our regiment.

Corley had to wait 14 years to get a star. His Irish temper must have made other enemies in addition to Bradley.

A heavily bundled General MacArthur flew in and pinned on some medals, including a DSC for Sergeant Pugh. *BSWA* printed the picture but did not report how Pugh had won it - saving Colonel Blair at Battle Mountain.

For the winter campaign (September - February), the Deuce-4 again suffered more casualties than either the 27th or the 35th.

	KIA	WIA	Total
24th	258	1,872	2,130
27th	429	1,469	1,908
35th	299	1,125	1,424

Source: 25th Division Command Report, Feb 28 1951.

Surely General Kean knew these numbers; they were published over his signature.

V.

The Bloody Han

With no permanent commander, the Deuce-4 prepared for a modern army's most difficult assignment - a major river crossing under enemy fire.

LaVaughn Fields:

The 25th Division was given the task of an assault crossing to re-capture Seoul. All three regiments were to be on line, with the 24th to the west to make a secondary attack.

Carroll LeTellier:

If there had been a major counter-attack, it would have come from Seoul and would have hit the 24th first.

The River and the Gauntlet

Curtis Morrow (G Company) reconnoitered "the monstrous-looking mountain" looming across the partially-frozen river.

Carroll LeTellier

There was a railroad that ran parallel to the river bank on the north side - the river, then a roadway, and on the other side of the road was the railroad. There was a lot of fire from the Chinese on the north side of the railroad bank. A GI stuck his head up and got hit by a .50-calibre and split his head wide open.

An FO came in and said he'd like to do some registration [*to check the range to the enemy positions*]. But the return fire came in on our position instead. We said, "No - no thanks, we don't need any registration, thanks."

The thing Curtis Morrow hated most were the patrols. They arrived at a small ridge over the Han. "We need a point man," the sergeant said. "Morrow, you just volunteered."

Morrow:

I dropped down to a prone position and crawled to about five yards from the bridge. I picked up a stone and threw it under the bridge and heard a frightened sound.

"*Iri wa!*" I called in broken Korean - "Come here!" I removed a grenade from my bandolier and was preparing to throw it when I heard the frightened cry of a child. I replaced the pin and cautiously made my way beneath the bridge, rifle ready. There was a small boy, holding an ox by its rein. He was bundled up - even his shoes had rags. I came very near killing him. Man, He'll never know how lucky he was.

We arranged for him to become attached to the Korean labor force at battalion headquarters, and I would see him when my company was back there in reserve. He would always smile and salute me. I would return his salute. I still see him sometimes in my dreams.

Behind Enemy Lines

Clyde Jones (I Company):

We had patrols that went across the river. A little lieutenant from the I&R] Platoon liked me, but I never saw him before. I was walking up the road, and he just picked me: "When I go across the Han, I want you to go with me."

I said, "I ain't going across no Han river with you!"

He said, "I'll be looking for you."

"I ain't going."

But when he got ready to go across, he came and got me.

They put us in a big tent, dimmed the lights, and pulled us up to a sand table. They showed you every hill, every creek, every rock, the lieutenant going around the table, showing you what's what. You read maps, and they tell you what your mission is. On the other side of the river the Chinese had a train tunnel and put ammunition in it; that was their supply dump.

There it is! It looks pretty on the table.

There were 22 of us – two lieutenants, some demolitions people, and me - I was the sharpshooter.

We stayed there around three days. Good food - the best of food! Every night you go out on patrols, learn how to walk at night. I had that new carbine with a telescope site so you could see at night. Plastic explosives - they'd put it on something, like around a tree, and it would blow it up. I was scared of that stuff. They equip you with everything you need. You're ready to go.

Two o'clock in the morning. We got down to the river and paddled across. They took the boats back and left us. We didn't have any way back. Damn! We might have to swim back.

We started up the hill and came to a road and saw someone walking down it. "I'm a captain in the Korean army." she was a woman! She was leading the way, and we got up almost to the top, and she stopped. Daylight was still an hour away. She camouflaged us and disappeared. No one moved all day. Chinese patrols walked within 20-30 yards of us - about 30 men, laughing and talking. They were good at tracking someone down. They could turn over a leaf and tell which way you went.

At dark she came back from nowhere, and we moved on. We got to the objective before daylight and stayed there that day.

The tunnel was about 100 yards off. I went up on top, because I was the sharpshooter. The lieutenant said, "Two guards is all they've got." The woman decided to go down and talk to them, and two men from I&R killed them.

The guys with demolitions took the primer cord for the explosive into the tunnel, and they stayed about 20 minutes and came out running. "You've got 15 seconds!"

"To do what?"

"To run like hell!"

We *ran* like hell. Everybody was running for their life. We ran, ran, ran! At night it was kind of hard to run, but didn't any of us fall down. We got about 50 yards away: "Cover up!" It didn't go off.

Then it *blowed!*

Ah! We made it.

We started running north - they would be looking for us to go south. We went two miles and bedded down, and here came a patrol right by us. We hit the woods again, going north. We walked all the rest of the night and set down in a creek bed.

Next morning the sun was shining, and we stayed there two days. That night we decided we were going to start back south. We ran into another patrol, about 28 of them talking Chinese. After that we slowed down a little, because the patrols were getting heavier.

Finally we got to the river-side of the mountain. That was the best side, because the Chinese were setting up on the other side. We got into a trot, the best we could do at night, and ran into this little village, and a woman said, "There's no Chinese on this side."

We stayed there another night, ready to hit the river, but daylight caught us, and we had to wait until night-time. We took off to the river at six o'clock when it was dark and notified the Army that we were getting ready to go back. They started shelling the river, and we started across, and the Chinese put a mortar right side of my boat. It hit the boat beside us and blew the back end of it out. Three men got wounded, two of them pretty bad.

The artillery lighted up the whole area, and that boat's sitting in the water. I said, "We can't stay here," so I jumped out - it wasn't deep - and put all the men we could in one boat. "Wait a minute. I've got ten hand grenades, I'll just throw them behind us." Hand grenades kill more people than shooting does. Then we started pushing the boat out onto the water. The mud was bad, but I ran in the water until I could run no more.

We got them all out.

The River Ran Red

March 7.
Fields:

Tanks of the 25th Division moved out onto a small peninsula, and before dawn each morning they made a feint to cross with tanks and artillery to draw fire, pinpoint the enemy's weapons, and return fire on them.

The 24th had our Engineer Company; the rest of the Division had the white 65th Engineer Battalion. The 65th went out at four o'clock in the morning to build a bridge, but they drew heavy mortar fire and had to get the hell out or take casualties. Our company continued rehearsing the river crossing. Each day the enemy's fire decreased. On the fifth day we received no fire at all. And that was to make all the difference.

It was a ruse to lull the Chinese into ignoring the actual crossing, and it succeeded brilliantly.

Morrow:

We boarded trucks to the river. There was very little talking. Some tried to get some shut-eye, despite the potholes in the road. At 1600 about a quarter mile from the bank we left the trucks for the last time and marched off to get some hot chow and pick up ammunition. There was a strong smell of gasoline, exhaust fumes, gun powder, and garlic. The garlic was from napalm, but it smelled like the garlic my mother used when cooking beans.

In the evening we wrote letters, read Bibles, or cleaned rifles. I slept under a poncho on the hard ground.

March 8.

Morrow:

I woke at 0430. The sergeant was shouting, "All right, men, rise and shine. We got a war to fight!" I pulled on my boots and slid down a hill to make a bowel movement

We moved out at 0530. We each had a pack of 35-45 pounds - C-rations, and water - plus a nine-pound rifle. And I weighed only 112 pounds. I carried at least four hand grenades and 200 rounds of ammunition, the more the better - they'd issue you all you wanted. I prayed a soldier's prayer that we wouldn't run out of ammunition. Thank God we never did, though at times we cut it pretty close.

The 2nd battalion would lead, with E and F companies spear-heading. I could barely make out the hulking mountain and the deadly river. For many of us, it would be the last body of water we would ever see. Three chaplains came up. I remember thinking there was nothing they could do for me now. I didn't need their help to talk to God.

Fields:

Before dawn our Engineer Company attached trailers with assault boats to the rear hitches of the tanks. As the infantry moved up to help put the boats into the river, our tanks, artillery, and mortars began to fire to cover the noise. But the Chinese made no return fire at all, and the boats slipped into the river under the cover of darkness. The enemy were still asleep, and we took full advantage of it.

Womack:

About 4:30 or 5:00 o'clock in the morning, I woke them up by driving a stake in the ground to anchor the pontoons for a bridge.

Street:

The weather was 15 degrees, and the artillery began firing 5,000 rounds on a 125-yard front. It was the largest artillery barrage of the war.

Elements of all three regiments crossed the river 20 minutes before dawn. The 24th had two assault companies, Easy and Fox.

Williams:

Crossing the Han was an amazing event. Hub-to-hub artillery and tanks as far as you could see and as deep as you could see. Early in the morning we opened up with planes and artillery and napalm on the enemy. You'd swear nobody could live through that. But when you got up there, the Chinese would still be resisting. Man, how could a man live under that? It's hard to kill men.

Morrow:

The mist lifted, and three SABR jets made strafing runs with rockets and napalm. But I knew many of the Chinese soldiers would still be there waiting for us.

Then I heard the command I had dreaded: "OK, first platoon, move out!"

"Fuck it!!" I

"Fuck it," said to myself. Then, "Let's go!" I yelled, more to relieve the tension in my stomach. Then the sounds of screaming warriors charging forward toward their landing crafts.

John B. Holway

The river was a hundred yards across. When we were half-way across, enemy mortars began striking so close that water splashed over the side and onto us. I heard a scream of pain from somewhere inside our craft. But we were so packed in, I couldn't see who or how many were hit or how bad.

Finally we reached the other side and charged off like madmen, screaming from the pits of our stomachs. We were met by a hail of rifle fire and exploding mortars.

Timmons Jones:

We got hit in the middle of the river. Some of the guys got out and swam. I was the only one on the boat who couldn't swim, so they took me in near to the beach, and I jumped out up to my waist.

They said we'd meet light resistance. It wasn't light resistance! We lost a lot of people.

My platoon leader had just returned from the hospital in Japan the night before. Just as we hit the beach, he got hit again, so we had him about four hours. Out of the 13 months I was there, for nine months we had no officers.

Womack:

We went over on the first wave, dumped the infantry, and paddled back. We were getting ready to make the second run, but by then the Chinese were awake, and all hell was breaking loose.

Jones:

The 2d Battalion spearheaded it. We watched that! G Company went across first, but the Chinese could shoot down your throat. G Company couldn't get up that hill.

F Company to the right, they hit the hill, too, and almost got wiped out.

Morrow:

We had to cover at least a hundred yards to the base of the mountain. I ran forward among dead bodies of our men. Bullets were whizzing by me, sometimes even glancing off my steel helmet. There was no place to duck.

All along the paths our own dead were strewn with the enemy. Sometimes the fire was so intense, we would have to take cover behind something, even if it was the body of a fallen comrade or enemy soldier.

"Let's go, you men over there! Let's go!"

Up we would go, yelling like madmen.

I noticed a viaduct and dust began kicking up around my feet. I hit the ground, pumping shot after shot into the entrance until my rifle was empty. From the corner of my eye I noticed my buddy, Red, still shooting. I threw a grenade, and it exploded in the mouth of the viaduct. We jumped up and charged toward it even before the smoke had cleared. Two enemy were dead, and one was dying. The last thing he did before we killed him was spit at us.

I'll remember the look of defiance on his face for the rest of my life. When I die, I'd like to die as bravely as he did. I often asked God to spare me. But if I am to die in battle, I prayed, please allow me to die like a soldier, like a warrior, like a brave black man.

Our guys were dropping all around me. I figured any moment would be my last. But when the orders were given to move out, I moved with the others. We charged up the treacherous mountainside.

Womack:

We went over on the first wave, dumped the infantry, and paddled back. We were getting ready to make the second run, but by then the Chinese were awake, and all hell was breaking loose.

Bullets hit my boat and let the water in, and two guys with me couldn't swim. I learned how to swim in elementary school. I was a lifeguard; I still swim now. So I jumped out and pulled them to shore. They put me in for a Bronze Star.

Their mortars from a cemetery on the other side were blowing up the bridge. They shot up a search-light unit and a quad-.50 supporting us.

Bullets hit my boat and let the water in, and two guys with me couldn't swim. I learned how to swim in elementary school. I was a lifeguard; I still swim now. So I jumped out and pulled them to shore. They put me in for a Bronze Star.

Fields:

As the assault battalion broke through the first defense line and began to assault the higher positions, the engineers began their next mission, building a footbridge.

When the fog lifted, there was no cover, and we began to draw fire from a heavy machine gun that could look right down our throats from the hill across the river. Bullets began to kick up sand all around us, and it was one hot son of a bitch! I hollered to my men to keep low. But we couldn't move, and the footbridge was not going up. So I asked one of the tankers I had the bridge site. He did. He also moved another, so now the two of them fired a "V" for protection while we worked.

Sergeant **Monroe** had another idea. He looked at the river and saw so much fire coming in, he knew it would be a while before the infantry could clear the other side. He said he'd take care of it. He turned his 'dozer toward the river, raised the blade as high as it would go, as a shield, and in he went. As I hit the ground and watched, I thought he wasn't going to make it. I could hear the rounds bouncing off the blade. He crept deeper into the river and the engine fan began to throw water, which was now up to the top of his track. Monroe just lifted his feet up and kept going.

I hollered and pointed to the river, and we saw something happen that was not supposed to happen. Monroe reached for his weapon as the front of the dozer rose up on the far bank. Monroe had crossed the Han

297

with a bulldozer under fire. No one had ever done that before.

I was on my feet now, running toward the tanks. I told the commander how high the water would come on his tank and told him to raise his gun as high as it would go so he wouldn't get water down the tube. I took him to the spot I had marked with my foot in the sand and told him not to turn right or left but keep straight ahead, and off he went. When he made it to the other bank, he radioed for the other tanks to follow, and they cleaned the area out real soon. It made a big difference in the enemy fire we were getting. The sites were now cleared to build the rafts for the bridge. Within the hour the job was completed, and the infantry started across, and we took the objective about two days ahead of schedule

Sergeant Monroe's guts made it all happen.

Street:

A lot of histories leave out the fact that the 77th Engineers built a pontoon bridge, but ten or 20 minutes later it was knocked out by three artillery rounds. Each one came a little closer, and the last one hit it. The rest of the men were ferried across in assault boats operated by the 77th.

Kimber:

They let us get about halfway across the bridge and opened fire on the front and then on the back. Everyone else was stalled in the middle. I was shot and fell in the water. It wasn't that deep, but a lot of guys got shot and drowned in that river. It was running with red blood.

I was picked up by 77th Engineer boats. A lot of people got on and got carried across to the other side.

Meanwhile, Morrow was struggling up the mountain:

Hundreds of bullets and fragments of shrapnel were whizzing past my body, yet not one touched me.

Two-thirds of the way up, the Chinese fire became so intense that we had to pull back to the base of the mountain. Our planes and artillery pounded it. From time to time short rounds fell on us, killing and maiming.

"Just ten minutes of rest," I prayed.

"Second squad over here!" yelled our platoon sergeant. I grumbled and scurried backwards on my stomach.

We retraced our steps back up. This time we reached the top, and planes dived into the valley in pursuit of the fleeing enemy. The area in front of our position was covered with dead bodies - how can human beings be so brutal to each other?

Old-timers told of bugging out. Well, I missed all that. By the time I arrived, it was fight or die.

My trigger finger was actually sore.

We, the survivors, looked around to see which of us hadn't made it on a hill none of us wanted.

After seizing our objective, we had to dig in and secure it. Imagine trying to dig a five-by-five-by-four-foot hole through or between rocks, while being shot at by concealed snipers. Then there's the in-coming mail - mortars and artillery. But we had to do it.

By the time we settled down, it was too late to make fires to warm our canned rations. So we ate them half-frozen. I often imagined sitting down to a good hot meal of meat loaf and mashed potatoes covered with gravy, plus candied yams, cornbread, and butter. Man, how I remembered those neck bones my mother used to cook. Thus I fantasized as I opened a can of cold corned beef hash. Some days even C-rations weren't available, and we would seize and eat anything that resembled food.

At 1700 hours we tried to get a little shut-eye while the Chinese fired "harassment" fire.

That night I was awakened by the sharp rattle of rifle and machine gun fire. As the sky lit up from over-head flares, I saw them, shadowy figures, below, a mass of screaming Chinks charging up the mountain slope, less than 50 yards away and closing fast. I saw a blur as an enemy soldier ran past me. The 159th Artillery concentrated their firepower a hundred yards to our front, then slowly drew it back toward our position until shells were exploding less than 40 yards in front of our troops. The mountain began to vibrate. My rifle began cooking the flesh on my hands.

Jones:

The 24th was the only regiment that was counter-attacked, to my knowledge. We pulled back to a secure position for the night, but we were hit at three a.m. by a reinforced battalion.

F Company was forced off its hill down to E company's hill about 100 yards away. But they couldn't withdraw, because the bridge was out and we couldn't swim the river. There was no place to go, so we had to hold at all costs.

American tanks and half-tracks on the south side of the river also opened up on us with quad-50 machine guns. We were lucky that casualties were light. Also luckily, we were in radio contact and told them to cease fire.

March 9.

Morrow:

About an hour before dawn the Chinese broke off the attack, and we began to hear the moaning of the wounded and dying. At daybreak I was surprised to see so many dead enemy soldiers. They covered the ridge in front of our position.

For breakfast we were given C-rations of cold corned beef hash, which I didn't like, plus two chocolate bars and ten cigarettes apiece.

G Company had lost 20 men in the counter-attack.

Our own artillery had killed 13 men of Fox Company. I wonder if the gunners were ever told. We passed their bodies laying side by side, some with no heads, some with large holes in their bodies. Several had been hit in their backs. Some, in one piece, looked like they were just lying there sleeping.

I dug a hole four feet deep. It was OK for fighting but not for sleeping. The engineers laid barbed wire in front of us.

2030. I was informed that patrols would be sent out every hour as listening posts and I had just volunteered for the first one.

After we came back, I went to sleep again but awoke with a jolt. The sky was lit up like a Christmas tree. The Chinks were hitting hard on F Company on our right flank. The clouds parted, and a full moon lit up the whole mountain. F Company was completely overwhelmed and was pulling back fast. We were being outflanked,

"First platoon. Get out of here fast!" I left my position with a hail of bullets ricocheting all about me. I jumped from a ledge and fell some 15 feet, but I held onto my rifle and took off down the ravine. Looking back, I saw blazing muzzle blasts as the Chinese fired at us. I somehow fired three or four shots in their direction, which brought a retaliatory hail of bullets in my direction. I got the hell out of there fast.

March 10.

Morrow:

At daybreak we were told we had lost 34 killed, wounded, or captured.

Carrying the wounded down was hard enough if the enemy wasn't shooting at you. We knew we were going back, and it was one of those times I felt like shooting myself in the arm and taking a chance on getting away with it.

At 1100 hours we were off again to retake the mountain. This time the resistance was light.

Street:

On the second night we got a new artillery forward observer, **Hatton** of the 159th. He used an "artificial moonbeam" - search lights to reflect off clouds and light up enemy positions. But it also lit up our positions. They say that was the first time they used it.

The artillery was supposed to mark the target with white phosphorous, but they fired a defective round, which landed on us.

The second bridge wasn't completed until the next day, when the rest of the regiment crossed.

Jones:

When we crossed the river, we had about half a company and lost part of that. We lost every officer out of the two companies except one - Lieutenant Shuffer commanded the remnants of E and F. Some officers were wounded two or three times - Lieutenant **Trotter** and Lieutenant **Rich.** Lieutenant **[*Walter*] Redd** was wounded for the fifth time.

The two companies accounted for about 44 enemy killed and 71 captured. But we suffered 102 casualties – 17 killed and 85 wounded.

Lieutenant Shuffer received the Silver Star. He retired as a brigadier general and wrote a book, *My Journey to Betterment.*

By daylight we were still in heavy combat, but we pushed to within 150 yards of taking the objective back.

March 11.

Jones:

Item company had to take over from Fox. They were going straight ahead, but they couldn't go over the rock either. I was trying to tell them how to do it, but they didn't listen. They had ropes, going to try to climb up it. I said, "You can't climb it. The Chinese have got a machine gunner sitting on it. He'll kill all of them. I know how you can get around it. You have to wiggle your way around it."

"How do you know?"

"I'll show you what we did."

They said, "You were *in* on that deal [*the raid*]?"

I said, "Yeah, I was." Like a dummy. I was always at the wrong place! I took I Company the way we had gone.

It was the first time we experienced a bunker. The artillery would shoot, but it would glance off to the side - they were no dummies when they built them. We threw a hand grenade in. When it went off, it scared us to death.

The thing that stopped the Chinese were the P-51 fighter planes. They made a wagon wheel, strafing over and over. They dropped white phosphorous "eggs" - napalm - and they would flare and set the enemy on fire. That was wonderful! The Chinese would stop to look at the planes. That would give you two, three, or five minutes. Five minutes is about five years; you didn't need too much time to move, and we took that hill.

Marion Enos was the toughest man our company had - no one knew what he was going to do. His best friend had got killed a day or two before, and they brought five Chinese from across the hill. He lined them up, got armor piercing bullets with a black cap - they would go through a railroad tie - and got down on one knee. "What are you *doing*!?" He looked at me, pulled the trigger, and shot three or four of them. "Oh, mercy! Oh-oh, he's cracked up."

Tough! He was tough.

Street:

We were relieved by K Company, and they took the objective with very little resistance.

We were pulled off the line to bring the company back up to strength.

The new executive officer, **James Ammerman** from Texas, was a hell of a nice guy, later got hit in the arm and neck, hit by a rocket in a friendly fire fiasco.

The First Battalion was the last to go across.

Ellis Dean:

I was a staff sergeant then. The river was red with blood, but we had no protection whatsoever while we paddled across. We had just got to the other side when I was wounded in the hip by shrapnel.

They took me to a MASH and started questioning me about some enemy who were wounded - big guys. They kept saying, "Mongo... Mongo." They meant Mongolians.

I was put on a ship to the Osaka General Hospital.

New recruits began arriving. One was **James Williams** (Able Company):

> We got on one of those old trains and got there in the evening. The 24th had been up there two or three days. Company A was already across the Han. Everyone had just about got shot up.
>
> We got off right behind the lines late in the evening, almost sundown. You could see the flashes of the artillery.
>
> A full colonel was standing on a mound, told us, "Remember when you left home, you were told you were coming to fight for your country. You were all BS'd. You're fighting for your lives. Every SOB who jumps up in front of you, you kill him. Or he'll kill you. Don't try to be a hero, you'll get yourself killed. But you might come out of it alive. I'll leave you guys with that good information."
>
> He jumped in a jeep and took off. Never did see him no more.

The crossing was a success, but the price was high. For the month of March, which included primarily the Han crossing, the Deuce-4 again took the toughest punch the enemy could throw. Although it was supposed to be making a diversionary feint to take the pressure off the other two regiments, the 24th actually lost more men than the 27th and the 35th put together:

	KIA	WIA	Total
24th	65	346	411
35th	104	114	218
27th	24	163	187

25th Division Command Report, March 31 1951.

Was Michaelis' 27th given the weakest sector with easier terrain or a weaker foe? Was the 24th assigned the toughest mission, whether by design or a failure of intelligence? Either the casualty totals were the result of a deliberate decision by the commanding general or a stain on his conduct of the battle.

When I visited the site 60 years later, both banks of the river were dotted with restaurants, where guys took their dates to sip wine and enjoy the view. One young man asked what I was looking for, and I said a great battle had taken place there.

"Oh?" he said. "Who was fighting?"

March 12. The 24th finally got a new commander: **Henry Britt,** a former battalion commander with the black 92d Division in Italy. Unlike Corley, who had led from the front, Britt stuck close to his strongly fortified headquarters tent in the rear. He was not well-respected.

Morrow:

We got R&R for a couple of days. We were deloused,

got a hot shower, a change of clothes, a few hot meals, and a chance to write letters. If only I had listened to my mother and kept my ass in school. But no use writing to her about trying to find ways to get out of the fix I was in.

I couldn't shoot myself in the arm - the whole idea was to get home in one piece. And I couldn't just run away, cry like a baby, and be a coward. Once I realized this, I experienced a strange feeling of release. A heavy load had been lifted.

Then it was back to the front and a hard drive - pursue, defend, pursue again - to the next objective.

March 27.

Morrow:

Sometimes they would be running so fast, they would run between my foxhole and the next one. I would catch only a fleeting glimpse of them as they passed. Usually they were badly wounded and would collapse and die, even falling into a trooper's foxhole. Then the high-pitched sound of a bugle, and the attackers fell back. Moans came from the wounded and dying.

I looked down at my watch. 0300. Softly I said to my fox-hole buddy, Private **Boyd,** "Heh, man, today's my birthday."

He said, "Oh yeah? How old?"

I said, "Eighteen."

Next morning at daybreak we found the whole mountaintop covered with dead bodies, theirs and ours. I heard the count was 90 Chinese and 20 of our men.

Truce talks opened. But the killing went on for two more years.

Back North

Clyde Jones:

We were going back north, walking through a town below Seoul, and the Chinese were in this school house

and they start picking us off like ducks. So we brought a .50-calibre and started shooting in the house, tearing up everything. When they came out, they were women, had their rifles over their heads. One man shot them. I can't tell you who, because it was "un-Geneva."

The Yanks went through Seoul for the third time.

John B. Holway

Richard Sanders:

The Army said, "We've got to be sure the 38th parallel is back in our hands." So we went back and re-took the line. Our outfit went up to straighten out the line.

We got on top of a hill, and I said, "Don't get in your sleeping bag. Put your feet in your bag, but if you get too warm, you'll go to sleep."

Next morning one man had been sleeping in his bag, and he had been shot all to pieces.

We went back to a hill - it was really a mountain - and walked along a ridge for three-400 yards, carrying rifles and ammunition, leaning up against a ledge, the whole platoon behind me. We were struggling to get up this little incline, and I said, "I'm going to take a look and see who's in front of us."

I took two or three steps, and all I heard was a sound – *whoosh* – and it blew me away. The captain came up and pulled me off the mountain. I had passed out.

Anderson, our medic, gave me morphine, and he walked along with me and went to get some help. The aid station gave me a shot and put a temporary splint on my left leg and put me on a truck. I don't know if I was thinking or not. Didn't know if I was alive. I kept going in and out of consciousness.

The driver kept saying, "Sarge, you all right?"

I'd say, "Yes, I'm OK."

I didn't realize until later why he kept asking. If you were still alive, they took you to the field hospital; if you were dead, they took you to graves registration. That's the reason he was calling to me.

I spent two years in the hospital: four transfusions, three operations. I've had shrapnel removed from my foot and my chest. I had a cast down the left leg. Just to walk.

Hubbard:

When we got up to the 38th parallel, hell broke loose. We had an FO from the Air Force, and they dropped bombs on the wrong side of the damn marker on the top of the hill and killed a couple of our guys. We cursed them, but they called it "the fortunes of war."

James Williams:
"A" company had 15-20 old guys from World War II. Sergeant **Malone** was a World War II guy. He had been retired about six months, had 28 years, and they called him back. Was he mad!

I had 16 weeks infantry training, but most guys after me had only eight weeks. We suffered so many casualties, because they just had half the training.

They sent me to M Company [*heavy weapons*] as an ammo bearer. I was a rifleman, didn't know much about the machine gun, but when there was a break in the action, you would break the gun down and put it back, break it down and put it back, until it came naturally. The machine gunner got killed, and I ended up with his job.

The life expectancy of a machine gunner was about ten minutes.

Nathaniel Nicholson had another one of his miraculous experiences:
One dark night we were walking over a stone bridge across some shallow water, when something told me to jump off. Someone lit a cigarette, and the light gave them away. Everyone got shot down except me. I was shaken, but I was alive.

Jones:
Every night "Ol' Putt-Putt Cheese" flew over our lines about 11 o'clock. Just an old, old, light plane, sounded like a lawn mower. He'd drop hand grenades on us, just to let us know they were still there. Finally got himself shot down.

MacArthur Sacked

April 5. General MacArthur and President Truman had been waging their own personal war over the Korean war. Truman was determined that the war must not spread beyond Korea. MacArthur demanded that he be allowed to bomb China and use Nationalist Chinese troops on the ground. The feud flamed when the Republican leader of the House, Joe Martin, read a letter from MacArthur severely criticizing his Commander-in-Chief.

That was it. MacArthur was fired.

General Ridgway replaced him. He received the news while visiting the front line to kick off his next major assault, another difficult river crossing.

The Last River Crossing

Ahead lay perhaps the last river crossing the American army will ever make under fire.

April 11. The fast-flowing Hant'an was relatively narrow, but it had only a few good crossing sites and steep cliffs on the far side, from which Chinese gunners could pour down fire. It would be the last major river crossing the U.S. Army has ever made or perhaps ever will make.

In his first major operation, Colonel Britt studied his maps and chose a crossing site, but after his units had all reconnoitered their sites, he changed his mind at the last minute and picked a different one. This led to hurried changes by every unit down the line to squad. No one was happy.

Clyde Jones:

We were laying on the river, waiting to cross. Colonel Mouchet came up, said, "How you boys doing?"

"All right."

Two enemy had crawled up there during the night, just laying there on the other side of the road, and one jumped up with a knife in his hand. Red shouted, "Watch out! He's got a knife!" Red shot him. Then another one came from nowhere. He had a knife too, and Red shot him too. He shot both of them.

We fogged the river with smoke bombs. Me and Marion Enos were the first ones in our battalion who waded across before the fog lifted. We had to wade up to our chests. They opened up on us as we got on the other side.

We were going up the hill, and Enos asked me, "Is that your buddy down there?" A friend of mine, a short fellow - **Fugate**, from Pittsburgh - was fighting that water: "I can't swim! God, I'll drown!" I had to go get him. Went back down to the river. They shot at us three times, but I pulled him out.

They dropped a mortar barrage behind us. I said, "Let's get over to these rocks. Get out of here!"

The first platoon came behind us. We got half-way up the hill, and there was a big ditch. Some of the Americans had gone through the ditch, and the enemy was sitting up on the top and shooting down with a machine gun as the GIs came out of it. I had to radio and tell them to stop, and we went up and knocked the machine guns out. A guy named **Windham** got the third gun with a BAR, and they gave him a Silver Star.

We got all the way to the top, clearing out foxholes. I told them, "Secure that side, secure this side!" because everyone up there wasn't dead.

Jim Thompson (L Company):
Our company crossed that morning. The Second Battalion went first. The 3d Battalion started laying down fire. Then we crossed, firing as we came across. As we got to the far side, the Chinese were down, they weren't moving.

We had the best artillery in Korea, the 159th. They never lost a gun, and they could load and fire so fast the Chinese asked us, how did we get "automatic artillery?"

Quite a few of us got wounded by enemy artillery. George Bussey [*Note: not Charles*] got hit. I got hit in the right arm. I stayed as long as I could, because I knew the others still had to get to the other side.

They took me to the battalion aid station, then to regiment, then to division. They had us on stretchers - colored over here, white over there. The doctor came out. "Who's' next?"

The aid man says, "This soldier here," pointing to me.

The doctor looked at me. He looked over there, said, "Bring that [*white*] soldier."

Next time same thing: "Who's next?"

The aid man says, "He is," meaning me.

The doctor took another white soldier, said, "You hear what I say, soldier?"

The aid man says to me, "We're taking you down to the Swedish hospital ship," and that's how I got out of there.

That still hurts.

April 12.
Jones:
Six months on the front line. That's too long to stay and not get wounded. Not many stayed for six months and lived: "Old Joe, he's gone, man."

We started out the next day. We had to get up the next mountain. We started out, but we couldn't do it - just couldn't do it. Got half-way up, and that was it. They had a machine gun bunker up on top of the hill. We were losing a lot of men trying get to the gun there. We ran out of ammunition and had Koreans bringing some up.

Over on the side I heard a machine gun on top of a rock ledge about 25-30 feet high. Everyone got down. Our medic stuck his hand up, and they hit him in the palm.

"Get down, man!"

We moved up our machine gun and waited about 10-15 minutes. Captain Petrosky said, "We've got to go over there and take that ledge." We called in the mortars to pop some rounds on it. We kept waiting for a 57 recoilless rifle, so we could shoot at the bunker.

We decided to go around the other side. Just as we got there, a friend named **Boyd** was running down the hill. I saw him go sideways. He's down! He's hit in the rectum:

"I can't move!"

"They got Boyd!" I ran over there, picked up Boyd, got him under the left arm, and pulled. "Come here, help me get him over on his side." They all ran over to him. Someone grabbed one side, I grabbed the other, and we pulled him behind a rock. "Medic! Medic! He's been shot in the ass."

We gave Boyd a morphine shot.

"Watch out! They've got a machine gun!" Two fellows in front of me went down.

I just turned to the right to look and I got "pumped." That was the end of my career, right there. They got me.

I went down, but I didn't know I was hit. I didn't know how it felt when you got shot. The only thing I knew was I was laying on the ground, and one arm was twisted behind my back. I said, "Get that machine gun!"

My buddy jumped beside me, said, "Man, you're hit. Stay down." I couldn't comprehend that I was hit. I didn't know what had happened. I got my M-1 in my other hand, but he said, "Lay down that damn M-1," and he pulled my arm around in front of me - oh my goodness, it hurt !

He took my field jacket off and tore my shirt off. He stopped the blood, because my boot was full of blood - there was blood running down inside it.

He said, "Don't look!"

"Why?"

"You'll panic if you look at it."

I looked. "Oh, my God."

I stood up.

"Can you make it to the river?"

I started off that hill, and two recruits said, "Can we give you a hand?"

"I can make it, you all go on up."

The enemy dropped a mortar, and the two men ran in a house. I yelled, "Get out of the house!" Before I could say it again, they dropped another mortar on that house and killed both of them.

I got back down across a rice paddy, saw a woman building a fire under a house. We were fighting like dogs, and she was building a fire!

The enemy was still dropping mortars. They tried to drop one on me too, but they dropped it over to my right. I said, "Boys, you almost got me," and just kept walking on the dike.

I was almost ready to go in the river, and the company executive officer came out to meet me and called me by name. I told him, "The first hill, we got, but the second hill was where we were hit. The other side of this hill - that's where our artillery ought to be."

Two men carried me down the river bed, both from Tennessee; I played football against them in high school, and we were in Fort Knox together. But they didn't have any boats to get the wounded across. They took a tarpaulin and made a boat with some blankets on the bottom and stitched it together and pulled me across the river by rope.

On the other side was my best friend, **Bobby Joe Bennett** - we graduated from high school together; he was in M Company. I left him that night. They gave me a morphine shot, and I was in paradise. I can't remember much more after that.

By five o'clock there wasn't any more Item Company. In October we had 310 men in the company. When I left there were 40.

The next day they got the 57 recoilless rifle.

When I got home, my mother said, "Son, you know the reason you made it back? I've been praying for you."

I said, "Mom, I didn't even know how to pray."

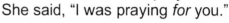

She said, "I was praying *for* you."

April 13.

Curtis Morrow (G Company):

We fought our way across the river after being beaten back three times. Company G, with the first squad in the lead, had advanced about two-thirds of the way up a very high, tree-covered mountain. A lone enemy soldier manned an automatic weapon. He was dug in close to a giant boulder and had a clear view of the entire area we had to pass. Three of our people had already been hit. One, I understood, was still lying there wounded or maybe even dead.

Red Warren and I devised a simple plan. He would crawl along the side of the mountain trail while I proceeded along the trail. When I drew an enemy's fire, he would be able to get him with a hand grenade.

I was carefully advancing up the trail in a crouched position with rifle ready, and the next minute I was face-to-face with a soldier. Our eyes locked onto each other at the same instant, and at the same instant we both fired. I felt hot air as bullets from his machine gun passed through my trouser legs.

Red yelled, "Get down, Morrow!" I hit the ground hard and fast. Seconds later a member of my squad was kneeling beside me, asking if I was all right. After a few seconds I got to my feet and hurried to catch up with my squad. I noticed the body of the soldier I had just slain. If I live to be 100, I'll never forget the look on his face.

He missed. I didn't.

As a cold rain fell, we fired round after round at the hundreds of enemy coming up the hill at us. Our targets were their muzzle blasts flickering on and off like a thousand hopped-up lightning bugs. The charging Chinese were yelling, "Eeaaaa!" the death screams of men being torn apart by hot shells and grenades.

They took the hill.

Red and I went to fetch water. I heard a muffled voice from a cave and yelled inside. No answer. The second platoon was returning from a patrol, and the lieutenant took charge. Red and I hadn't gone 20 yards when we heard a grenade and the scream of a woman. It froze us in our tracks. We turned and saw her and seven kids emerge, splattered with blood.

Morrow blamed himself for calling attention to the noise. Red consoled him: "All they had to do was come out."

"Yeah, but it's too bad the woman's baby was killed." What kind of God would allow such things to happen? he asked himself.

Rain, Mud, Mountains

Rainy season, April and May, we'd get drizzling, all-day rain. It would keep us bailing water from our fox holes with our helmets. We used our helmets to boil eggs, if we had some, to wash in, and to make toilet in. They protected us. But in combat they can also slide forward and interfere with your vision. The seconds it takes to adjust it can be fatal.

The most physically demanding aspects of war for the infantrymen are hiking, walking, running, jumping, crawling, falling, dunking, carrying supplies to and from, up and down hills and mountains. And also digging, digging, always digging. Hole after hole.

I was always hungry. There was never enough food or water. On top of this there was the killing, again and again.

April 15.
Street:

The day before Easter they sent us up a hill that Intelligence said was poorly defended and we should be able to take without any problem.

Intelligence was wrong.

There were a lot of Chinese troops up there, more than we thought. We couldn't take the hill, and we had to tear the door off a village house to carry the wounded out.

, Latin Americans received eight Medals of Honor in Korea.

The next morning we re-grouped and took the hill under a "walking" artillery barrage. We found most of the enemy had bugged out. There were tunnels all over the hill. The Chinese left during the night in such haste, they left cases of ammunition behind and enough equipment to supply a company. We took two or three prisoners and killed a dozen or so.

The weather had been overcast and cloudy for about two or three days, then it cleared up, not a cloud to be seen, and the Air Force put up every plane they could and hit hills way out, 1,000 yards in front of us. Then for some reason they hit the hill I was on. I was hit by the first plane. It fractured my pelvis, urethra, and colon. We got 35 replacements that day. They were coming up the hill as they were carrying me down the hill. Somebody joked that it took 35 men to replace me.

MacArthur returned to America and a ticker tape parade down Broadway. That was followed by a speech to Congress as only the operatic showman, MacArthur, could deliver it. The nation watched with quivering chins as he closed with the words of an old barracks-room ballad, which within hours bloomed into a hit played on every radio station in the country - "Old Soldiers Never Die (they just faaaade away")".

Senator Joe McCarthy talked of impeaching Truman and running MacArthur for president. But before long, MacArthur also faded away.

The POWs' Suffering

Fletcher:
In four months, December to April, 2,000 men died. I was down from 180 pounds to 90.

Sergeant **Aurelius Porter** of Mississippi told BAA:
You'd see a man sitting in a corner, and he'd fall over and never wake up. Every morning the Chinese would come and put the dead and dying in a "death box." I was on the burying detail, and we got from ten to 35 a day.

Corporal **Tommy McCree** of Chicago spent 36 hours tied up in a trench for stealing an onion.
I got sick and stayed sick for three months. My leg swelled up, and it's still no good.

Curtis Bolton:
The death rates went down as we started getting more food - not really enough, but more than we had been getting.

Fletcher:

The North Koreans had no food themselves and turned us back to the Chinese. I think the Chinese realized if we went home in that condition, they'd be the laughingstock of the world, so the diet slowly, slowly increased, and in the fall of '51 they brought in fresher food. But they said we couldn't cook it. We got some pork that had turned green, and we scrubbed it down and sliced it up - no one got a big piece. Later that fall they gave us some rice.

In the winter of '51 they made us uniforms out of cotton - coats, pants, cloth shoes, and hats with ear muffs.

At first I saw no discrimination. The majority of the troops were southern-born and said I was welcome in their homes when we got back - but they soon changed when they got home. The Chinese set up segregation: Blacks in one company, whites in another, Greeks in another, British, Hispanics. We called ourselves the United Nations.

They also separated us by rank. We had to go out in the mountains to get wood, but the officers said, "No, we're officers." The Chinese didn't care about the Geneva Convention, because they had never signed it. So they shipped the officers off to another camp. The sergeants shook their heads too. *Woof!* They were gone to another camp. The rest of us wouldn't get wood either. The guards said that was fine: "No fire, no food. You can fix your own food." So in about three or four days, we caved in.

If you went to town to get some food at night, all Korean farmers kept dogs, and they would bark and alert the guards. At least you hoped the guards would spot you, because the people would really beat you. If they didn't, they'd probably get shot for fraternizing with the enemy.

There was a lot of cool water at the foot of the mountain, but that was what was killing so many. The guards would point to the stream and say, *"buhao"* [*no good*]. We didn't know what they were talking about. It was contaminated, that's what. Human waste would run down into the water. When we understood, it was too late. We were all sick as dogs, and we started boiling the water.

And lice! We couldn't do anything but pick them off each other. But the eggs had already been laid, and *bam*, there's a new batch!

Curtis Bolton:

We had body lice by the thousands. They'd really stick to your army sweater and suck your blood. Every day you had to pick them with your fingernails.

Our daily life was study, study, and study. A Chinese commander would give us the lecture in Chinese. One of them would translate and that would take three times as long. They told us the U.S. was the biggest aggressors, warmongers, and instigators: "Are Americans justified in bombing reservoirs?"

We were supposed to have an opinion on each topic. They expected some explanation from each person. That went on and on and on: Get a lecture and back to the shack.

Fletcher:

They started indoctrinations that communism would be better for us in America, because we were just helping the rich get richer, and in the communist countries there's no segregation. They were really pushing it hard.

Some of our guys believed it. **Clarence Adams** and I slept in the same building, and we'd talk at night. He said, "I have to get off the sidewalk for white people. It's the same all over the world." He'd go up to headquarters. I don't know what happened there, but he enjoyed talking to them. He said they talked about home, school, stuff like that.

Sergeant **Nathan Andrews** organized "an anti-Communist gang" in camp. He was thrown into a six-by-six-foot hole without food or light. His only meal came when a buddy tossed him a potato.

Fletcher:

I was also giving the Chinese hell. I was 18 years old, and at that age you're cocky, nothing can stop you, so I told them, "I can't go for this. In America you could get ahead if you worked and if you set goals. My father had a good job, he was paid well. We weren't paupers. You didn't have to stay a poor man." They didn't like that. They wanted you to be more of a yes man, but I was sticking to my guns. And I was quite vocal. They didn't like that at all.

One day Clarence came back and said, "Keep your damn mouth shut, because they're thinking of getting rid of you."

"What do you mean?"

"Exactly what I said. You leave the camp with guards, and you don't come back. Shut it up now, or you won't be around."

Chinese Hit Back

April 22-30. The Chinese had another major punch left. They poured across the front in massive numbers and drove all the way back to the gates of Seoul.

Yancey:

Ridgway said he wasn't going to give up Seoul. Replacements started coming in, we put automatic weapons [*machine guns and BARs*] every 100 yards and started fortifying our position. When the Chinese hit us, we just stacked them up. We killed so many, they had to bring the engineers in to dig trenches and bury the dead. It was a slaughter.

Morrow:

We heard all the bullshit about fighting the spread of communism to protect our land of liberty. What the hell did we know about communism? What had the Commies ever done to us black people? Have they ever enslaved our people? Have they ever raped our women? Have they ever castrated and hanged our fathers or grandfathers? Any of our officers could be the very one that puts a rope around one of our necks next year.

Those were the questions we asked each other when out of hearing of our white officers. They wonder why we didn't trust them. Would they trust us if they were in our place?

But Morrow also wrote:

I'm proud to recall that all officers I served under, white or black, were damn good officers.

Also platoon sergeants. They are in a way like mothers and fathers to the men under their command. They died fast, maybe not as fast as officers, but pretty fast.

Lieutenant **Harry Davis**, a black West Pointer, was our platoon leader. He was there about two-three months and he got killed. I had captured a prisoner who jumped up in front of me with his hands up. The lieutenant and Sergeant **Little** had just sent me to take him to battalion headquarters. Two minutes later they were huddled around a map when an enemy mortar exploded in their midst. It threw me to the ground. When I regained my footing, there was just a hole where we had huddled.

Home

Hubbard:

Shrapnel from mortars hit me in the back, from the shoulder to the knee on the right side, in the butt, and the big fleshy part of the shoulder. I tell my daughters I got shot in the back facing the enemy.

I was evacuated to the hospital in Pusan, then Osaka General for two months. Then I came home.

The Deuce-4 had been on line since July, more than nine months.

Nicholson:

In April I was number-one on the list to go home, when they called me to the command post to take a battlefield commission and wanted me to sign papers for 18 more months in Korea. I refused it.

Soon after that, "It's time to go back," they said, "you're being relieved." A jeep was sent to pick me up. Just as I was about to enter, a report reached me that another jeep had just blown up, because the road was mined. I refused the ride  and instead ran five miles back on foot. Somehow I avoided the mines and the enemy.

I arrived with a temperature of 106. It was malaria. The doctor said, "I have to send you to the hospital, but if you go, you'll have to go to the bottom of the list to go home, so I'll put you in an ice-making machine." He cooled my body down until my temperature read 98.6, then he signed my papers and let me go.

A triple blessing - prayer answered, mines avoided, and fever broken. Hallelujah! I got on a ship April 16 1951.

USO Show
Burnett:

After Nick left, I said, "I feel lonely here." But I couldn't run away, because I couldn't swim.

They said, "Promotions are coming up."

I said, "I've got a bronze star and three battle stars. I'll give them all to you if you let me go home now."

Joe Fredericks of t Heavy Mortar Company was offered a choice: Go home or a promotion to master sergeant. He chose the former. "I was going home at last!" (Above a USO Show).

Womack:

I almost got killed when I was rotated. The North Koreans were on another hill across from us, shooting down at us. C Company was being annihilated. The enemy had cut loose on my damn hill time and zeroed in on my foxhole.

The GIs kept calling my name to come down to the Command Post. I thought they were going on a patrol, so I told them, "I ain't going," and got back in my hole.

I didn't know I had 1400 points, more than anyone else. The guys hollered, "If you don't want to go, let *me* go!" I jumped out of that hole and rolled down the hill. I left all my shit up there. I left money that I owed people, left my camera, even my pictures of Aiko.

Yancey and the Kongo Maru

Yancey:

When I left Japan, I missed my flight, and the flight went down, and everybody on board were killed.

I came home in October 1951 on the *Kongo Maru* with about 800 on the ship. It was like a banana boat, and we ran into a storm. They said it was the worst storm they had for several years, and one ship sank off the coast of Japan.

It had swinging doors that were made of plywood. The wind blew them off, and when the boat listed, thousands of gallons of water were rushing in. The Japanese crew went over the side - they got the hell out of there. A chaplain was having church services, and when I left the services, two decks were under water. We were standing on the third deck.

I had been in the Navy, so the troop commander, a lieutenant colonel, told me to take charge and told everyone to follow my instructions.

We put the doors back. Men were in their bunks, and I took the mattresses out from under them - they were bitching! I jammed the mattresses against the doors and jammed furniture against them to block the boat from taking on thousands of more gallons of water. I organized a bucket brigade, but we had to use helmets, because we didn't have buckets.

We fought for 72 hours while the storm lasted. There was no loss of life. Only one man was injured when he fell down the Jacob's ladder [*rope ladder*] and hurt his hand.

At that time a black didn't get recognition, no matter what you did. Some officers said, "We're going to put you in for an award" for saving the ship, but they never did. The only paperwork was the chaplain wrote a letter.

I've been trying to find out who the troop commander was. All the troops were from the 25th division. I wrote several letters and had three or four guys put in letters to no avail.

But, hell, anyway, I'm still here, still kicking. The Man Upstairs still loves me. He's still taking care of me.

Davis:

I knew two guys from Chicago were on that ship, but they're both dead now. The Army never even said thank you to Yancey.

John B. Holway

The Iron Triangle

The Deuce-4 had fought back to the "Iron Triangle," three towns north of the 38th parallel in the center of Korea. Once more the Allies were back to where the war had started almost a year before. For the second time they had knocked the Communists out of South Korea. They had made their point - the Communists could not come into the South. And the Chinese had made theirs - we couldn't go very far into the North.

Pork Chop Hill was the scene of some of the most murderous fighting of the Korean, or any other war. The heights were described by Colonel S.L.A. (Slam) Marshall, the most respected historian of the Korean war:

Its cratered slopes will not soon bloom again. They are too well planted with rusty shards and empty tin cans. Never at Verdun [*the bloodiest battle in World War I*] were guns worked at such a rate. The operation deserves a place in history. It set the all-time mark for artillery effort.

The war was a stalemate. But the fighting would grind on for two more years at the cost of tens of thousands more American lives and we don't know how many Chinese and Korean lives. The Allies would fight for a hill, get driven off, and re-take it, but the line wouldn't change much. Every death after this was pointless.

June 3-5.
Morrow:

Rainy season, April and May, we'd get drizzling, all-day rain. It would keep us bailing water from our fox holes with our helmets. We used our helmets to boil eggs, if we had some, to wash in, and to make toilet in. They protected us. But in combat they can also slide forward and interfere with your vision. The seconds it takes to adjust it can be fatal.

The most physically demanding aspects of war for the infantrymen are hiking, walking, running, jumping, crawling, falling, dunking, carrying supplies to and from, up and down hills and mountains. And also digging, digging, always digging. Hole after hole.

I was always hungry. There was never enough food or water.

On top of this there was the killing, again and again.

Some of our heaviest fighting took place on Old Baldy

or Pork Chop Hill.

Those damn mountains. We would have to walk eight to ten miles before we even reached the base. The most physically demanding aspects for the infantryman are hiking, walking, running, jumping, crawling, falling, dunking, carrying supplies to and from, up and down hills and mountains. And also digging, digging, always digging hole after hole.

I was always hungry. There was never enough food or water. Many a day I would have given a month's pay for a canteen of water.

On top of this there was the killing, again and again.

Usually when we reached the half-way point on a hill, we would be exhausted. And no matter how much artillery and air support we got, the Chinese would still be up there waiting for us.

We killed each other by the thousands.

John B. Holway

The paths up the mountains were strewn with bodies - ours and theirs. Joe Chink was a tough cookie. Often a dying soldier would pull the pin from a hand grenade and put it beneath his body. Or a retreating soldier would place an armed grenade beneath a dead comrade.

One day, as a rain fell, we fired round after round at hundreds of advancing soldiers coming up the hill. Our targets were their muzzle blasts flickering on and off like a thousand hopped-up lightning bugs. If I had a dollar for every bullet I'd shot at an enemy soldier charging toward me with a blazing weapon, I'd be a wealthy man. They were yelling, "Eeaaa!" and it seemed to come from their very bowels - the terrible death screams of men being torn apart by hot steel bullets.

Sometimes snipers would keep us pinned down all day, and we would just have to live with the ripening corpses. In winter frozen bodies could be used as a barricade against incoming rounds. But hot weather was worse - sickening smells, plus insects in a feeding frenzy, feasting on the dead as well as the living.

A soldier's death, a warrior's death, is preferable to a slow agonizing death in great pain. I prayed that if I were mortally wounded, they would put me out of my misery with a bullet to the brain. This was wishful thinking, because the Chinks usually used their bayonets for "cleaning up," because bullets were more precious to them.

We, the infantrymen, had no idea of the damage we were inflicting on the enemy or on innocent civilians who got trapped in the middle. I, for one, couldn't even start to guess how many times I had killed. We hardly discussed the killing we might have done. I don't recall anyone declaring hatred for the enemy.

Connie Charlton and Otto Garner

June 21. Sergeant **Connie Charlton**, one of 17 children of a West Virginia miner, arrived in Korea in May with a service unit but volunteered for combat with the 24th. ("I don't feel right sitting here while others are fighting.") He was assigned to C Company as an assistant platoon sergeant, and his CO put him in for a battlefield commission.

Before it arrived the company was attacking a fortified hilltop when his platoon leader was killed and Charlton took command. With six men he attacked a machine gun position but was knocked flat by a grenade that hit him in the chest. He got to his feet and hurled his own grenade, killing the gunner. Then he led his platoon on an attack but was driven back by heavy rifle fire and grenades.

Despite his wound, he led a third charge, against a bunker, before he fell from the shot that killed him.

His platoon took the hill.

June 24. Three days later Sergeant Otto Garner probably should have received a Medal of Honor too:

The company got pinned down in a narrow draw. Around the middle of the day, I led my platoon up the hill. It was pretty steep, I was crawling up through shrubs and couldn't see the rest of the platoon back behind me, and they couldn't see me. I thought they were right behind me, I didn't realize I was so far in front, so I just kept going.

I tried to outflank the enemy from the right, but those Joe's with the machine guns changed my mind about that. A fly couldn't have gotten through. I had to reverse my strategy and go around the other side and try to get them. There was a little place I could hide over there, and I crawled around the mountain

329

and came up from behind. The machine guns were still firing up on the top.

When I got a little below the crest, I was all alone. I didn't expect to run into anything like I did.

There were Chinese all over, resting in their foxholes. I don't know how many - quite a few. They must have thought they were secure, and I guess I surprised them. The first guy saw me, and I saw him. I had to protect myself, so I fired and killed him.

They all started coming out of their holes shooting at me. I ducked behind a rock to reload, then fired again. Some of them could see me, ducking in and out, trying to get cover.

L Company was on another hill about 50 or 75 yards to my right. They could see what was going on, and they fired to draw

the Chinese fire away from me. That gave me a chance to leave my position and fire some more. I killed two or three more. They didn't know what to do, and I had a field day. I was lucky I didn't get hit. Most of the firing was by me; they were busy trying to run for cover.

I don't know how long before my platoon got there - between ten, maybe 20 minutes - I don't know, things were moving so fast. It was steep, maybe that's why they were so slow catching up. By the time they got there, everything was over.

They counted 11 Chinese bodies around me and four more a few yards away. And I was smoking a cigarette! I guess I was trying to chill out. I was in shock - all those people dead.

Some of my men put me in for an award. They witnessed an affidavit, and my new company commander, Captain **Noah Armstrong**, wrote it up and sent it to battalion. They claimed it was lost between battalion and regiment.

I had a chance to get a copy of the citation, but when the unit faded out, I goofed and didn't get it.

Garner has been trying ever since to find witnesses who can testify on his behalf:

There were several people I could think of who were with us on the hill. One was Felix - I don't know his last name, he was Creole. The other one was **Joule "Drumgooga"** - that's how he pronounced it. And there was a witness from L Company on the next hill, they saw the firing. They got killed or were rotated, and I lost contact with them.

But it's in the 25th Division history. The Los Angeles *Sentinel* wrote it up, and it was in the 24th Regiment book. (Garner on left.)

I don't expect to get anything out of it. It was so long ago. But I was told the 24th Infantry did not give awards that much. The commanding general said we didn't deserve them.

July 17.
Curtis Morrow:

It was hot as hell. Private **Davis** from Florida was my foxhole buddy. I broke him in. He might have stayed for a month,

We had just stormed an enemy position, and I saw him walking toward me carrying his left arm in his right hand. I don't think he knew it had been completely severed and was being held only by his own blood-soaked jacket.

One time I was point man on patrol. Before advancing up this hill, we asked a *papa san* if any Chinese were up there. He waved his hand: "Oh no, oh no. oh no."

I made contact - sometimes you can sense them - and popped off a couple shots and hit the ground. We received incoming machine gun fire, and I rolled off the ridge line and looked back and saw Christopher Mathews standing there on the ridge, firing his carbine.

A couple guys didn't make it back. Milton Bailey was one of them. One of the guys saw him go down, but we never did recover his body.

When we reorganized at the base of the hill, we had to re-cross a rice paddy, and I noticed the same *papa san* again. I laid down and took careful aim and got off a shot. I thought I hit him, but it was time to return to our position before darkness. The following day a patrol discovered the dead Korean. He had a radio strapped to his back.

G Company went on the defensive.

My entire area was lit up by tracer bullets that criss-crossed the night air around us. Every few minutes dirt was in my eyes from bullets that struck within inches of my face.

In the heat of the fight, I could smell the fuckin' Chinese' breath. Some of them looked like they were drunk the way they staggered around, firing their weapons. I would see one of them charge right into a murderous hail of fire, waving his men on. Every so often, one would charge right into our position, falling dead within feet of our bunker.

They just kept coming at us. When they ceased coming at us, we would go after them, and they'd keep killing us.

Later we were going through a minefield that had been cleared and marked by the engineers. But one of our guys accidentally got his rifle tangled in the barbed wire, setting off a mine. We removed the splinter-shrapnel with our fingers, but one piece imbedded in my left eye. It could have cost me my eye, but it didn't... .

There was a little girl sitting by the side of the road and eating grasshoppers that she roasted in a tin can over a fire that had once been her home. There were dead, burned, and decapitated bodies all around her.

My squad members appeared to be indifferent, like they saw but didn't see. Occasionally a sniper would aim a shot in our direction, or there would be a long burst from a concealed machine gun.

We dived for cover among the bodies. The little girl was still sitting there, eating the grasshoppers, seemingly undisturbed.

"Let's go, soldier!"

I ran to catch up with my squad and noticed that the legs of my trousers were covered with blood and human guts from bloated bodies that would burst when I stepped on one.

"On the double!"

We took off on a run, shells exploding all around us. One-two... Then one-two-three. Adjusting to our range, I thought. I saw a hole and dived into it, landing in the lap of a dead Chinese soldier. I twisted my body to see his eyes. They were still open. The barrel of my rifle had penetrated his bloated stomach. I jumped from the hole, yanked my rifle out, and quickly cleaned it on the body of another dead soldier.

Once, we had a hard time taking a hill in a drizzling rain. Joe Chink was throwing everything they had at us, and we were advancing up a muddied, slippery hill, ducking and dodging while firing a weapon. At the very moment when I thought we might have to un-ass, on the left of my platoon, I heard someone singing church songs. He was well in front of his platoon, and they had to double-time to keep up with him. In fact, I found myself quickening my pace to keep up and even pass him in a race to reach the top.

Another time we were sitting hunched over in our muddied bunker, which we had partially covered over with our ponchos, I asked my fox-hole buddy, Boyd: "Heh, man, did I imagine it, or did I really hear somebody singing a church song, "Didn't It Rain, Children?"

"Nah, you didn't imagine it. It was that *gung ho* second lieutenant in E company."

It turned out to be Lieutenant **[Louis] Daniels**. He had fought in Europe with the famous 761 Tank Battalion. He got a battlefield commission after C Company got wiped out, then he went to E Company. He was 32, he was "the old man" to us teen-agers.

Boyd said, "If it hadn't been for him, I think today's action might have had a different ending."

I said, "Maybe you're right, my man, maybe you're right."

We had a hell of a lot of respect for him. After each battle, we would ask if he survived.

I also hummed classics - Chopin, Tchaikowski, Wagner - as I clawed my way up a mountain. My favorite was a Russian song, "the Volga Boatmen" ["*yo-ho, heave ho*"]. I'd force myself to keep pace with the music, barely able to put one foot ahead of the other.

In August an artillery FO with Company , Lieutenant Gaston Bergeron, reported that the 24th moved up to replace a white unit coming off the line. As the two passed each other on the trail, the whites unleashed a barrage of racial insults while their officer did nothing to stop them. It was "ten hours of crap," Bergeron said, and it wasn't the first time he had witnessed it.

One wonders if the white GIs hated their Chinese enemies as much as they apparently hated their black comrades. One also assumes that they didn't know that the blacks had given many gallons of blood more than they themselves had.

As Al Smith, who ran for president in 1928 said, "It's not what you don't know that gets you into trouble - it's what you know for sure that isn't so."

September 1.
Morrow:

I joined Boyd in our five-foot-deep hole.

I checked the hand grenades on a shelf we had made, unsnapped the flaps of my cartridge belt, and sat back to wait.

In the far distance I heard a bugle. Then a blinding flash. Then nothing. Only the feeling of being hurled through space. Then a terrible pain engulfed my whole body.

Then darkness, like being in a dark tunnel, at the end of which I saw a bright light. Strange feelings entered my body, forcing the spirit from my body. I saw myself floating above a beautiful green valley. It was very peaceful. Everything was clear, no pains. Then out of nowhere appeared a ghost, its hair snow-white, and it had cold steel-gray eyes. From head to foot it was covered by a white linen. Through a heavy mist that surrounded it, I noticed that it was a woman. Her month was moving but made no sounds. I got the feeling she was trying to reassure me.

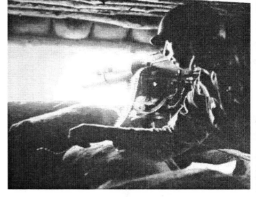

I saw Private Davis carrying his left arm. Then I heard horrible sounds. God, oh God! it sounded like six .50-calibre machine guns blasting away. "Damn," I screamed, "we're under attack!" Then I identified the noise; it was the fading sound of a helicopter.

Suddenly there was light, men were rushing around, some had uniforms, some had pajamas. Then I noticed I wore pajamas. I was in a hospital in Pusan.

It was the first bed I had slept in in ten months.

They told me I was on the verge of a nervous breakdown. I had been blown around by a concussion, and I was in the psychiatric ward. That night I thought about the other guys who were still up in front, and after burying my face in a pillow, I cried.

Just about every night I would re-live some horrible front-line experience: the little girl eating grass hoppers... Davis carrying his arm in his hand.

I screamed and catapulted to a sitting position. I was drenched with perspiration.

Years later Morrow learned that Columbus Mathews (abve) lost his leg below the knee the same day. They came to Korea together, and they left together.

As soon as he could, Morrow went AWOL to a whore house:

I heard a buddy, Red, and a woman in the next room screwing. I quietly put on my boots, took a deep breath, slid open the door, and yelled at the top of my voice: 'BANZAI!"

The last I saw of Red, he was suspended in the air.

I ran out, laughing like a madman. A few hours later, I was found by two MPs in a ditch, sleeping it off. They took my drunk ass back to the hospital.

September 29. Meantime the war in Korea ground on. Private **Robert Gipson** of Burlington Iowa:

My younger brother, **George,** and I were with the Seventh Cavalry [*Custer's old outfit*], but we never saw a horse.

We were trudging along together, approaching our object and talking about how we were going to celebrate his birthday. He was lugging a BAR, and I had an M-1 [*rifle*], lighter than his, so when the enemy opened up, I dashed about ten feet ahead of him. A bullet whizzed by my head and hit George in the neck. I turned to help him, but the squad leader yelled to keep moving.

It wasn't until two days later I learned what had happened to him. I got first aid, but he was sent to Tokyo to the hospital. He'll be paralyzed for life.

Meanwhile, Ellis Dean was enjoying life in Japan:

When I got out if the hospital, they gave me limited service, because it was my second wound, and I was sent to a black MP outfit, patrolling Yokohama harbor. Then I was sent down to Kokura, trucking equipment to ship to Korea.

I wanted to get married, but my company commander, Captain Collier - I'll never forget that name - didn't want to approve it. He tried to court martial me and trumped up something that I was insubordinate. I even went to the stockade. But I had a good rapport with the base commander, who knew my overall record was good, and I was acquitted of the charges. The C.O. was shipped to Korea.

Then, even though her grandfather was in parliament, it took seven days before everything was approved.

We were married in September, and our first child was born in Itazuke air base.

I was manager of the Kokura army baseball team. We played against the Japanese professional teams - the Orions, the Swallows, the Dragons. I remember Kaneda [who won 400 games in his career]. I had offers to play with the Dragons, but I had my heart set on the States. The Phils were interested, but I didn't want to sign with them because of the way their manager, Bench Chapman, treated Jackie Robinson. I was approached by a Red Sox scout, and I signed with them.

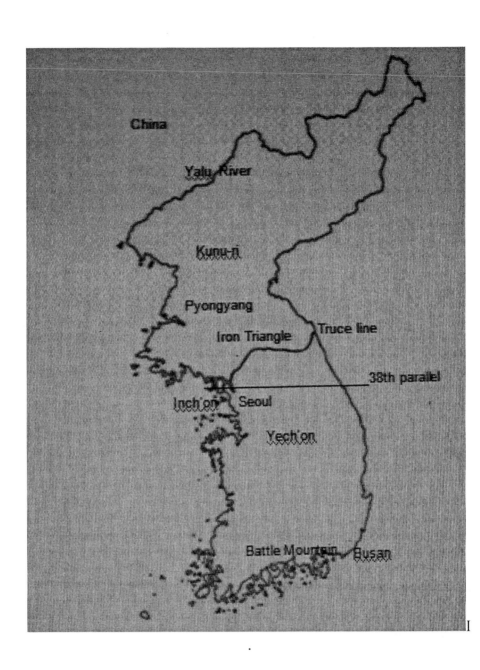

I

VI.

The End of Deuce-4

October 1951. Three years after President Truman had ordered an end to segregation in the armed forces, the US Army decided to obey its Commander-in-Chief. It disbanded the Deuce-4 and distributed its members among white units. The old Blockbusters of el Caney were no more.

Ellis Dean: "We won more medals than any unit in the 25th Division, July 1950 to October '51." The Army's Office of Military History says it has no totals, because some were conferred by Division, some by Corps. However, 24th Infantry historians made their own study and believe the following are the best available for the 25th Division:

	24th	27th	35th
Medals of Honor	2	4	2
Distinguished Service Crosses	24	28	18
Silver Stars	240	309	258

The totals for the 24th cover 15 months, through September 1951. The totals for the 27th and 35th include 36 months - more than twice as many - through July 1953. Pro-rated on a 36-month basis, the totals would be:

	24th	27th	35th
Medals of Honor	5	4	2
DSC	57	28	18
Silver Stars	576	309	258

The 24th was also first in gallons of blood spilled. Through September 1951, their last month on the line, the division's official figures show:

	KIA	WIA	MIA	Total	Avg
24th Infantry	550	3,737	564	4,887	44%
27th Infantry	631	2,343	205	3,179	29%
35th Infantry	532	1,895	551	2,978	27%

Source: 25th Division Command Report, September 30 1951

That's 50% more casualties than either of the two white regiments. The numbers support the suspicion that Division

343

commanders gave the 24th the most dangerous and most thankless assignments while protecting the two white units.

The figures were available to the authors of BSWA, who regularly quoted the daily war diaries in the Command Reports. If they had quoted these totals, their book would probably not have been published. And this one would not have been needed.

The Army signal corps left a record in the Archives of photos of 25th Division personnel receiving Silver Stars. Pictures of whites being honored exceeded blacks by a ratio of 8-to1. The actual ratio of whites to blacks in the Division was 2-1. Photos of blacks being honored totaled only 11.

William Ball   Harry Boone   Willie Bryant

James Harris   Edgar Johnson   Harrison Dillard

Wyman Lee   Willie Ponder   William Roberts

Most black recipients that day were not photographed.

Fields:

We'd do things and get no credit. When you see the History Channel, the blacks are left out. We have to pass this history on to our children.

Integration

Otto Garner:

They broke up our regiment, and I joined the 35th Infantry. It was brief, because I had enough points to come back to the States. The company CO wanted me to work for a buck sergeant. I told him I was *not* working for a sergeant as long as I was a sergeant first-class. So he called me a few names and said, "Get out of the orderly room!"

I was never given any assignment. I was told to stay in the tent until they decided what they wanted to do with me. I stayed there a month and found out that people with less points were going back to the States. It was a matter of stepping up and demanding that I be sent back.

Jim Thompson:

I went to the Dixie Division! [*laughs.*] They didn't keep me long!

John B. Holway

Albert Kimber:

To my surprise, after we arrived back in Fort Lewis Washington, we received a welcome home. Going to Fort Jackson South Carolina everything was fine, we could sit anywhere on the train and use the dining car. Oh my, we were all glad to get home. I thought segregation was over. I said, "Oh, man, this was worth it."

Until Cincinnati. Then the dream came to an abrupt stop. The conductor said, "Blacks, move to your cars." I was shocked back into reality. "This is where I left."

We reported to Fort Jackson. I was a staff sergeant. Me and a sergeant first class and a master sergeant, all black, were assigned to KP. I'm not the one to disobey orders, so here we are, three o'clock in the morning, we reported, and a white pfc said, "Sergeant, you want to be inside man or outside man?"

I said, "I want you to bring me a cup of coffee. I'm an infantry man, I'm not pulling KP." Can you believe it was so segregated back then? What an insult! Under a pfc!

Captain Stone came in, and I explained to him, "Sir, we're combat NCO's, just came out of Korea. We don't pull KP."

He said, "OK, I'll transfer you."

Five o'clock that afternoon we were all shipped out. Guess where they sent us. To an army base way up north, in Fort Sheridan Illinois, to cooks and bakers school. Would you believe that? Personnel there laughed. I was sent down to Indiana as first sergeant with a quartermaster bath company. That's where I was discharged in 1952.

I made up my mind I had enough of the Army. I joined the Air Force. It was already integrated - thank God for President Truman - and I continued my career in an administrative personnel position and retired in 1970.

Curtis Morrow went to Fort Leonard Wood Missouri.

I discovered I had been awarded the Bronze Star.

But the fort was racist. The only way to get out of there was to f-up. So I made up my mind I wouldn't do KP. I just decided I was going to disobey. So the company commander preferred court martial charges. Investigators urged him to reconsider, but he stuck to his guns. The court martial reduced my time to six months, and with good conduct I got out in three months and went back overseas. I chose Japan, and they sent me to the 187 Airborne, kicking cargo out of planes. Most of our air drops were in Korea.

Vietnam? No. Korea was enough for me. A lot of guys got killed there for nothing.

Robert Yancey:

They sent me to Fort Benning Georgia to an MP outfit. They still hadn't implemented the order outlawing segregation. The company commander was white, and the first sergeant was white. The major told me, "You ain't got no business with all them stripes, and I'm gonna get them."

I said, "Major, I got them fighting, and that's the way I'm gonna lose them."

He sent me on patrol in Columbus Georgia: "But you don't stop a white soldier for anything. Your duties don't start until you get to the black district."

I'm thinking, "Where in the world am I?"

I see two black guys and two black soldiers mixing it up, so I was shaking them down when a white police sergeant said, "Give me them boys."

I told the two civilians to go with him. He said, "I want them all."

I pulled my gun. I said, "You don't get nothing now."

My major said, "I got you now!" He put me in for a court martial and restricted me to my room for about 30 days. Then I went to see a legal officer, and he called the major in, and they dropped all charges against me.

Next they gave me a corporal's job, showing prisoners how to paint stripes down the middle of the

347

road. A colonel saw me, said, "Sarge, that's a disgrace." He chewed the major out. He said, "The Army's changing, and if you can't change, you should get out."

In a few days the major wanted to see me. I knocked on the door and went in. The first sergeant says, "Who told you to come in?"

I said, "You get mixed up with me, I'll whip your butt. I'm tired of this. I respected you and gave you courtesy. You return it."

The major said, "Don't talk to the first sergeant like that."

I said, "Sir, I'll talk to you the same way if you disrespect me."

I went to the colonel, said, "Sir, I'm tired of this. You can send me back to the battlefield."

He said, "Sarge, we need more men like you." They sent me to Fort Sam Houston Texas, and I became a medic.

Joe Davis:

I went to the Philadelphia anti-aircraft defense in Swedesboro New Jersey. That was the worst assignment I ever had in the Army. I had never been in the artillery in my life. They put me in charge of a missile pit. Everything was by computer, and I just couldn't cope with it.

The commanding officer, Rudolph Smith, a white officer, was a general's aide instead of going to the Korean war, and he couldn't be trusted. Had a white first sergeant name of Hutter, a captain at one time. Hutter was a rat. He ran the whole clique. The captain was doing what the first sergeant told him to do. They would smile in your face, then stab you in the back.

There was a lot of stuff stolen out of the Navy Yard - paint and stuff. Captain Smith had a house downtown, used a sergeant to put in the electrical stuff. He kept everything covered up.

And Hutter was in on it. He stuck it right to me: "I'll 'section-eight' you out" [*as psychologically unfit*]. They put a lot of stress on me, trying to break me down inch-by-inch. But I wouldn't bite. They gave me a summary court martial. It was a set-up. I didn't have any witnesses. They fined me and busted me from sergeant down to corporal. He said, "Well, I got Davis' stripe.' It was racial, as far as I'm concerned.

Later Smith went to the Pentagon and made colonel.

The battalion commander was a pretty good guy and sent me to Valley Forge hospital in ration breakdown [*allocating rations to each unit*].

But I couldn't get my rank back. I didn't have any money to pay my debts and feed my wife and my baby. I had to take my family to my mother's. My wife ended up going to an insane asylum. That was a hard bullet to bite.

In 1961 the first sergeant got me transferred to Korea, the First Cavalry. Then my troubles were over. Within 42 days I made my stripes back.

POWs Look Up

Fletcher:

By the fall of '51 we weren't losing any more weight. Guys got stronger. Everyone was exercising until we were feeling pretty good about ourselves.

We could do sports for propaganda. The second winter we could play basketball, and they let us go on a tour playing the other companies.

Curtis Bolton:

We leveled off two soccer fields; we also played basketball.

Fletcher:

In 1952 we had a huge olympics with a big parade, and we got points for track and field - we were integrated, by the way, black and white.

Then we tried to figure out how to get softballs. The Filipinos unwound a sweater and wrapped the yarn around a rock. They cut up leather combat books and fitted them together for a cover. That was pretty neat. We had stone-age gloves. But we played and had a little fun.

An Associated Press reporter got captured, and they let him keep his camera. He took all kinds of pictures, but they had to develop the film and gave him back the pictures they approved, and he sent them out through Czechoslovakia.

We didn't get mail until 1952. You were allowed to write as many letters as you wanted to, but that didn't mean they were going to go out. My mother received about six letters. You always had to say something nice about the Chinese – "they treat us great" – or it didn't go out.

Summer of '52 the Americans bombed the town. Every day at one o'clock we watched the American planes fight the MIGs [*Russian jets*]. That was our entertainment.

Robert Fletcher:

They brought in winter clothes for us. We got caps with earflaps. The smaller Americans, 5'6 or-7, got clothes that would fit them, because a lot of Chinese were that short. They were cotton quilt uniforms, and if you kept your arms inside the sleeves, you could keep warm.

In '53 they stopped pushing Communism at us, because they figured it wasn't going to work for the average POW.

Some of the guys were trying to escape. But number one, you didn't know exactly where you were. Two, in Korea, there were no African Americans; they wouldn't let white POW's shave - they had "bushy beavers," so the people could tell them. Three, you were weak, because you weren't getting enough food.

Most of us had made up our minds we were going to be there forever. I spent 33 months, almost three years, there.

In March 1952 this author reported to King Company, 17th Infantry, Seventh Division near the Iron Triangle. He was a "Buffalo Soldier" (!) because the 17th was called "the Buffalo Regiment" and officers wore a buffalo crest on their epaulettes. The colonel, Bill Quinn, called himself "Buffalo Bill" and wore a large Buffalo Bill mustache and demanded that his officers did too.

Integration was just percolating down, and my platoon had several specks of pepper in the previously all-white salt shaker. If there were any problems, I was not aware of them. However, I never saw a black officer in my battalion.

Doug Wilder

August 1952. Four months after I left, 22-year old Douglas Wilder reported to A Company.

He was from Richmond's Church Hill, the poorest black ghetto in the city. He grew up in "gentle poverty." His mother made him learn a new word from the car-word puzzle every day. He shined shoes and washed windows, then waited tables to put himself through college, studying chemistry.

Wilder was a "militant" black, who thought Martin Luther

King's non-violence would never work. His hero was Jomo Kenyatta, leader of Kenya's "Mau Mau" independence movement, and he signed his letters as Kenyatta did - "the Burning Spear."

When he was drafted, "I had some very mixed feelings," he wrote, "fighting in another country for freedoms I didn't enjoy in my own."

Wilder could have been assigned to a chemical warfare outfit, or even to special services, entertaining the troops - he had a fine singing voice. But if he went to a rear area job, it would take him 18 months to get home. The Infantry would be nine months. He decided to "get it over with." Plus, he got $45 a month combat pay.

Wilder:

Korea was my first interaction with members of the Caucasian race - sleeping together and eating together. And some of the officers were black. That made a difference, seeing people of color being in position of authority that heretofore I had not seen.

They lived in trenches in "hootches," covered with sandbags and rocks - the latter to detonate any enemy shells before they reached the sandbags. The two armies took turns knocking each other off the same hills. "They didn't want our hill; they just didn't want us to have it."

He told biographer Donald P Baker, he was often sent out on a listening post half a mile in front of the main line. A squad went out each night from dusk to dawn.

Wilder:

One man named **Skinner** was hit "*Zzzwham!* Have you ever seen a chicken with his head cut off? He's still running. Well, that's what happened to him... After that the front got very quiet. Then all hell broke loose over the entire front. My platoon was literally wiped out, more wounded than killed. So they pulled us off the front.

Next day I went to the company commander: "Sir, I've been thinking about that chemical warfare job, and ... ."

He laughed and said, "Wilder, you're stuck here."

Doug's unit spent one month at Cheju Island, guarding POWs, while the truce talks stalled over the issue of what to do with those who didn't want to go home.

When you come off the line, you're mean, you slap the prisoners around. One said in perfect English: "Why are you angry with me? What have I done to you? Is this what your Mr Jefferson and Mr Lincoln taught you?"

"Shut up!" I slapped him again.

A South Korean soldier told him, "It's not nice what you're doing."

'Whattaya mean, not nice? These guys have been trying to kill us."

But after a few days, you start to become more humane.

Wilder had problems with his platoon sergeant, Quiros, a Mexican-American, who sent him on patrol too often. He told Quiros, "You know, I've been out here a lot."

"Well, you know the terrain."

Doug found a nice safe cave and memorized everything he could see. "We had hills named "the three sisters" for [*buxom movie stars*] Marilyn Monroe, Jane Russell, and I forget the other one"

When Quiros called and asked, "What do you see?" Wilder, safe in his cave, answered, "The three sisters."

Quiros told him to choose the men to go on patrol with him. "I didn't like that, because then they started hating me."

A friend, Jim Cunningham, "a big white guy," asked Doug to go out with him to repair wires that had been cut.

Wilder:

On the way back mortar rounds started coming in: *Hoo-ee-rumf!. Hoo-ee-rumf!* With mortars, if you can hear them, you're already in trouble.

"Come on," Cunningham yelled, "let's move!" He pushed Doug through the door of a hootch, then fell on top of him. Wilder lay there a minute until the firing was over. "I think we can go now," he said.

But Cunningham was dead.

I couldn't get over it. if Jim hadn't pushed me, it would have been me. So many of those things happened that you couldn't explain. Other people, better soldiers, were killed or wounded. So you're lucky. You came to understand that it didn't matter what color a soldier was who had drunk out of your canteen or eaten with your fork.

Another day a Sergeant Bette told Wilder to help carry wounded down the hill. "We'll have to go through that small-arms [*rifle*] fire," Doug protested.

"You just have to do it," Bette said.

Wilder thought of how he could get rid of Bette:

People were doing that. You'd be surprised how many. If they didn't like some guy, they'd slip into his hootch, open a grenade in there, and blame it on the Chinese.

A short while later Bette came running by; he had been hit "between the legs. "

Wilder went to visit a friend in another company. He returned to find his hootch gone:

It looked as though it had never been there. Blown up. A direct hit. Three of us had shared it. I wondered where the other two were.

April 18 1953. Wilder's platoon leader, Lieutenant Alves, sent him up Pork Chop Hill to bring wounded down:

There were four of us – me and Wyatt, from New Jersey, plus two Koreans. We thought the hill was ours, but as it turned out, we had half of it, and the Chinese still had half. But how could you know? One of the little Koreans, who were ahead of us, got taken down [*killed*]. The second little fellow got wounded.

Wyatt called back that the fire was coming from a hootch I asked him to go around to the back. We had thermite and white phosphorous grenades and thermite grenades. I told Wyatt, "Take your bayonet and dig through the sandbags and put the thermite grenade in there, I'll cover the door.

He did. He exposed himself, pulled the pin, and shoved it in the hootch. The North Koreans started hollerin', and we shouted

354

the Korean equivalent of "Don't move or I'll shoot" - "*hee-ay-yan-do!*" There's two of us, but they thought we were a whole bunch of people. They paraded out, and I yelled, "Drop your weapons, hands up!"

That's when it's important to have an automatic rifle, but Wyatt had the BAR. I was carrying an M-1, so if one of those guys had fired at me, I would have gotten off one shot, and then it would have been over for me.

We ended up with 20 prisoners.

They faced a 30-minute walk back under mortar fire. "I told Wyatt, "I'll lead, to be certain we aren't ambushed from the front." The prisoners followed with their hands behind their heads, and Wyatt in the rear.

On the way down, I heard a shot. I counted the prisoners again. There were only 19. I could tell by the look on Wyatt's face: One had probably said something smart to him, and he got a little excited. Wyatt had developed a real hatred for the Chinese and North Koreans, It happens in war.

Lieutenant Alves said, "There's only 19 here."

I said, "I guess I counted wrong, Lieutenant."

Doug wrote Wyatt up for an award but didn't hear anything.

Meantime, blacks complained that they had been passed over for promotion by whites, even new arrivals, who didn't have enough experience and thus put others' lives in danger. Wilder, still a private but acting sergeant, took their case to a black sergeant, who didn't want to pass their gripes on.

Wilder decided to go to the battalion commander, Major Earl Acuff, with about 100 black soldiers, but "about half of them ducked out, saying they wanted to take a shower or some other lame excuse." Acuff, a paratrooper and amateur boxer from idaho, welcomed them warmly. But when he asked for examples, the GIs were silent. So Wilder led off, and the others followed. Acuff listened for two hours, then called in his officers and told them:

The Army was founded on citizenship, and you can't have second-class citizens in it. The battalion lost a lot of men taking Pork Chop. They were fine soldiers, many of them black. They were fighting just as hard as anyone else.

Within days promotions started coming, including one for Wilder to corporal.

Wilder:

It helped me realize that not all white guys were against us, and you could rely on their word. It had a very early profound effect on me; it said the system might work.

However, on the ship coming home, you started seeing the camaraderie and the closeness slowly dissipate as you got closer to Callifornia. The whites stayed on one end of the ship, and blacks on the other.

Back in the States, awaiting discharge, Wilder, now a sergeant, was told he couldn't go off base Saturday, because he would have to attend a division parade. "You're getting a medal, the Bronze Star, for Pork Chop."

Lieutenant Alves also got a medal - the Silver Star, one step higher than the Bronze. Wilder thinks the lieutenant wrote himself into the report. "He wasn't even *there*, wasn't anywhere *around!*"

Wyatt got nothing.

Peace

July 1953. Fletcher:
There were no jets overhead. We knew something was going on. The Chinese didn't tell us that the war had ended. We found out about the third or fourth of August. Then they told us we were going home "if we wanted to." Twenty-one at first said they were going to stay. Three of them I personally knew.

The war was finally over, about 60,000 American deaths after it began.

Out of C Company's 240 men, there were about 17 of us left.

We left the camp on the seventh of August for the DMZ [*Demilitarized Zone between North and South*]. When we saw Freedom Village, we started pulling those Chinese clothes off and throwing them away until we just had pants. They made us put our shirts back on.

A U.S. colonel sounded off with your last name, and you sounded off your serial number, and you stepped across the "Bridge of No Return," a little narrow bridge. I looked up and there was Old Glory, flying in the breeze. A colonel said, "Welcome home," and shook my hand. Tears ran down my cheeks. I guess I thought I was never going to see the flag again.

Wilder:
On the ship coming home, you started seeing the camaraderie and the closeness slowly dissipate as you got closer to Callifornia. The whites stayed on one end of the ship, and blacks on the other.

Fletcher also boarded a ship home:
There we got interrogated, and this captain says, "How was POW camp?"

That pissed me off. Did he think we were on vacation? "It's like going away to college for four years. How the f- do you think it was?"

He looked at me funny and said the weirdest thing. "What is eight times eight?"

I looked at him. "What the hell does that have to do with anything? In my school it was 61." I got up and walked to the door.

"You can't go out."

"Fuck you." I opened the door and walked out.

Later I saw on my record: "This is a young colored man who doesn't understand what he is going through. If he stays in the Army, we need to interrogate him much more closely, because he is a security risk."

When we landed in California, there was no hooplah, nothing like the Vietnam veterans from the Hanoi Hilton got. A little band was playing. None of our parents met us. We were told we couldn't go off base - they didn't want us to get VD. I flew home and asked my mother why she didn't meet me. She told me they said, "If you want to go meet him, you have to pay for it." Back in the '50s no one had a lot of money to throw around.

VII.

The Home of the Brave

Experiences in the civilian world were mixed.

Donald Womack:

When I got back home, they gave me 10% disability for shell shock and 10% for frostbite. I couldn't go to sleep at night without my fatigue hat, like Linus' security blanket. A psychiatrist in the VA hospital told me I needed to get married and put it behind me.

I took the GI bill and took a three-year course in electrical engineering in Philadelphia. Forty people started the course, and I was in the top 20. I could make a radio or a TV from scratch. There were several white guys I helped to graduate. When we finished, I went over to the Philco [radio] company with several white guys in my class, and they got jobs. They had never even been in the military.

But the company didn't have anything to offer me. I was speechless, Then I created a disturbance: "What do you mean?" They asked me to calm down and offered me a job putting tubes into TVs on a conveyor belt. That's all they offered me! I raised hell. "Everyone else got a job in the office. I've been in school for three years, and you're offering me a job a janitor can do!"

Wilfred Mathews: had a similar experience:

I finished high school. Then I went to Michigan State university and studied engineering and went to work for the telephone company as a repair technician.

However, Richard Sanders had a much happier experience:

If it wasn't for the Army, I would not have gone to college and would never have met my wife. t Department of the Army said, "We're going to make sure you go to college."

"Why are you sending me to college?" (I'm the only black in the outfit - did they want to get rid of me?)

"Well, we're looking out for your future."

They sent me to the Presidio in San Francisco to personnel school. I met my wife there teaching school.

Next: "We're sending you to Arizona university to get an engineering degree." I did R&D on infra-red and lasers.

Then they asked me if I wanted to go to Panama. When we got there, they said, "We want your wife to teach school here as well."

Ellis Dean:

I signed with the Red Sox and went to Sarasota for a tryout. Guess who my coach was? Bobby Doerr *[who went on the Hall of Fame]*. They sent me to Class A ball, the other guys were going to AA ball, but they couldn't carry my glove or my bat. I said, "How come I'm not going?

The manager said, "Oh, you're the nucleus of the team."

So I reenlisted.

I reported to Fort Carson Colorado to the 11th Armored Cavalry Division. A clerk at headquarters looked at me and said, "Where'd you get these orders?" He said, "Just a minute."

In a few minutes the adjutant, a major, said, "Send Sergeant Dean in." I saluted. He says, "What's wrong?"

A captain says, "Well, sir, we don't have no niggers in the unit."

"Well, you have one now."

So I was the first black in the 11th Armored Cavalry. When I see guys with that patch, I give them that story.

Floyd Williams:

I got out of the Army in '53. I was a pretty young sergeant first class, but my wife was pregnant, and I decided to enlist for three more years. I ended up with 22 years in the Army.

LaVaughn Fields:

In Fort Belvoir I was first sergeant for Captain Bussey. I couldn't hide. He'd yell, "Fields, come here!" I also served with Lieutenant Lenon; he retired as a colonel.

Otto Garner:

After my first enlistment, I kind of liked the Army. I went back to Korea in 1954 as a company first sergeant. In all, I pulled four tours in Korea, two on Taiwan advising the Chinese army in administration, and one in Okinawa.

David Carlisle left the Army as a lieutenant. He spent the next half-century working to get Bussey a Medal of Honor.

John French:

I was sent to Germany, then France. I had another officer from the Citadel, and he was one fine officer too, like Lieutenant LeTellier. The Citadel must produce good officers.

I was still hitting my books and passed the GED [*high school*] test with a score of 98. I finished a year and a half of college at American University.

I applied for OCS. Six of us - five blacks and one Jewish guy - were paneled out for "lack of leadership ability." How you going to argue with that?

I told my wife I was going to transfer to the reserves, but I had two kids and had never been on my own out in the civilian world working.

I was scared of heights, and I said, "I'm going to give myself a challenge. If successful, I'm going to leave active duty." Monday morning I applied for transfer to the 101st Airborne Division. We had to make five jumps to graduate. It rained four days the last week, and we had to make four jumps on Friday. We were scared as hell, but we graduated that afternoon.

I left active duty in 1960, got admitted to seven colleges and universities, and graduated from American University in '62. I went to law school at Howard University for a year, then ran out of money and did social work in Cleveland and Kentucky.

Nathaniel Nicholson:

When I got home, I was doing everything bad. I wasn't a good boy any more - I was a bad man.

My best friend, James Burnett, bought a 1951 blue Oldsmobile, and that was all I needed to round out my party life. I didn't go to church. I danced. I partied - I was a very good dancer. My brother, Delmer - "Big Nick" - was a professional dancer, one of the "Lindy Hoppers of 1952." You ever hear of the Harvest Moon contest at the Savoy Ballroom in Harlem? They won a prize, and the promoters put them on a tour around the world.

I went to business college to become an accountant until I learned that blacks weren't hired as accountants.

When I moved in with my mother, she cautioned me about girls who were, as she called them, "fresh-tailed." I met Dolores, a girl in my typing class, and we went to New York to see a play and have a spaghetti dinner. I decided she was the one. I got some disability pay from  the Army and bought a Pontiac for $800 and met her at the bus. But she had already paid her 20 cents fare and refused to get off.

So I did what any man in love would do - I picked her up and carried her off.

On Christmas day I asked her to marry me. We bought a house in Scotch Plains for $1,000 down and a VA loan.

However, Delores said:

When Nick went for a job interview, they made him sit there all day long. He went back the next day and didn't get anywhere. He was very mad - "I'm not going there any more!" But then things got better, thank the Lord.

Three years later this box came to my door. It was from a service club hostess in Japan. Inside were all my personal belongings from Japan. My pictures, everything were erased or frayed away so you couldn't read them. All I could read was the psalm on the chapel program June 25 1950: "Yea, though I walk through the valley of the shadow of death... ."

Something came to my ear again, and the Spirit of the Lord said: "Now that I've saved your life, what are you going to do with it?" I went to church that day, and something moved in me and told me to go to the altar. I was banging on the altar table and saying, "You can't preach the Gospel unless you're filled with the Holy Ghost!" The pastor of the church was the bishop of New Jersey. He gave me a minister's license right there and said, "The Lord called you to preach."

I went to the North Eastern Bible Institute and became an ordained minister in the Church of God in Christ. I was a pastor for 30 years in Elizabeth New Jersey and also state superintendent of Sunday schools, supervising 60 or 70 churches.

Donald Womack:

In 1962 I went back into the Army, because I was asked, based on my background. I was in Fort Belvoir, the Engineer school, and had my own swimming pool and a 50-foot boat, big enough to sleep six people. Cost me $500.

I had a dog, a German shepherd named PJ I raised from a puppy. You didn't want to mess with him. You didn't want to put ashes in the ash tray with PJ watching you! He'd stand up, his ears would go up, and his tail would go out straight, and he would growl - *aaargh*! I'd say, "Watch it, PJ," and he would sit.

He'd go get my shoes. "No, PJ, go get the other shoes," and he would go back and get them.

I'd go swimming with him. We used to go down to the beach and swim out.

I was assigned to the Green Berets in the first group of 100 men; 16 of us were black. I was like a fly in a cup of milk. I was in demolitions, medics, intelligence, operations. I went to Germany to learn to ski. The women there were told we grew tails after eight o'clock at night, so they'd feel back there to see if it was true. Even in Sweden!

In Special Forces school, they told us, if an alligator chases you, don't run straight, you've got to zigzag, because he can run faster than a motorcycle. And don't go to sleep under a tree; there might be a coral snake, as big as your middle finger. If he bites you, you're not going to live but 15-20 minutes. The other one you don't want to mess with is the cottonmouth water moccasin. They don't run away fom you; you'd be sitting in a boat, he would stand up on his tail and pull himself right in there.

Womack learned to make HALO jumps - high altitude, low opening, or free-fall:

We could get 11 people out of the plane in nine seconds - "Go! Go! Go! Go!"

You keep your arms of your side, your body is straight, like a pencil. You carry a bottle of oxygen and wear an oxygen mask over your face and mouth. You can't hear any noise at all, you can't even hear the plane. And you can't see the ground, because you're above the clouds, and at night you can't see anything. You have an altimeter on your arm with a red face so you know when to open your chute.

When you get around 600-700 feet, that's when you open it. If you're not careful, and you don't have your arms at your sides, your body starts spinning like a top. But the chute doesn't spin, so you put your hands up on both sides of your neck and stretch the risers [lines] apart so your head doesn't get caught in them and pedal like a bicycle to unscrew yourself and stop your body from spinning.

Vietnam

"Vietnam was a Sunday school picnic compared to Korea," Floyd Williams said. Jim Thompson agreed.

And, Otto Garner added, "It was quite a change in racial makeup."

It was America's first integrated war.

All the complaining about black soldiers in the past century and a half abruptly stopped! I know of no instance when white leaders, from lieutenant to general, bad-mouthed their black troops. Could there have been a miraculous genetic change in ten short years?

Incidentally, blacks served and died out of all proportion to their number in the population, while middle class whites like George W Bush and Dick Cheney bugged out to grad school or the National Guard.

Blacks finally won a healthy number of Medals of Honor - 20. That compares to aero in World War I, zero in World War II, and two in Korea. The country retroactively recognized one black hero in the First World War, six in the second, but none in Korea. It's high time to re-open the books and give long overdue credit to Charlie Bussey, Otto Garner, Curtis Pugh, Earl Phoenix, Levi Jackson, Wayman Ransom, and others.

LaVaughn Fields:
During the Tet offensive in 1968, I was first sergeant in the 4th Infantry Combat Engineer Battalion, which was hit pretty heavily. I was in charge of communications and rations for all the units and shipped their wounded out. I was running a jump-off point for the whole battalion, and they put me in for a

Bronze Star.
Robert Yancey:

I was getting close to retirement, and they told me promotions are in Vietnam, so I said, "Heh, that's where I'm going."

I was first sergeant in a medical unit for 26 months, 1966-68 and ran a dispensary for 30-50,000 troops. The Vietnamese had one doctor for 65,000 people, so after the military sick calls, the civilians would come in - 2-300 a day. Snake bites, malaria, everything. If they had an infection, they'd put maggots in there to eat the infection. We'd take a syringe and flush the maggots out, so it would heal from the inside.

Sometimes I went out to supervise mass casualties, like when an ammunition dump blew up with 65 civilians killed and wounded. They told me not to leave the compound without a military escort. But the escort didn't come, because there was a lot of fighting. I was needed, so we left without them.

When I got there, they told me to sit in a hut, but I said no. A half-hour later the hut blew sky-high. All the wounded were screaming, and I was shooting them with morphine and putting tourniquets on, and we got them onto trucks. Didn't lose a single patient. They gave me a Bronze Star, but my greatest reward was I saved a lot of lives. I guess that's why the Good Man Upstairs has saved mine.

The battalion commander didn't have an officer qualified to be company commander, because the doctors were all "90-day wonders" without much military experience, so he sent me back down, and I had to be first sergeant, acting as commander. The doctors had a choice - go back to battalion or stay with me - and they chose to stay. I knew my position and they knew theirs, and I didn't have any trouble.

When the enlisted men goofed up, I had

them filling sandbags: "You got a choice: I can send you to battalion, where they'll take some of your pay away from you, or you can fill sand bags. The choice is yours." I never had any problems.

I stayed there over a year. The colonel said, "Sergeant, I'd like you to stay another six months." I ended up 22 months in Vietnam.

Another three-to timer was Red Tail **Charlie McGee**.

When the Tet Offensive broke out, six or seven of our planes were hit on the ground. Most of the pilots were at our walled compound off base. There were only six of us on base, and for three days we flew all the squadron's missions. The Viet Cong started mortaring the place; we had foxholes, but I'd just put my helmet over my head and stay in bed. Who knew where a round would land?

I flew 143 combat missions in Europe and Korea, and 176 in Southeast Asia; that's 419 missions and 1100 combat hours.

Floyd Williams:

I went to Vietnam in 1968, right after the Tet Offensive. The first day I got there, I met Chuck Smith! We had been in the same squad in the 24th. He was going out on a long-range patrol - they would drop him out there and come back and pick him up. I thought he had paid his dues, but he was in great spirits. He seemed to like combat! He always was cocky.

They gave me a nice cushy job, but then they saw I had been in the infantry and changed the orders to the First Division.

They sent me to a night defensive position [NDP], about 30 miles west of Saigon, not far from Cambodia. It was a little place with sandbags, bunkers and wire around it. A few hundred yards away was a village - there was a lot of hate there. It was used by the Viet Cong to re-supply, and they shelled us two or three times a day. But their mortars didn't seem to be as effective as the

Koreans'. We got a lot of people wounded, but not a lot killed.

To get in or out you had to fly, you couldn't go down the road. In the day-time we'd go out patrolling, search and destroy, or go in a village and look for any contraband. One day my company ambushed the VC. A guy was wounded, a few killed. A Vietnamese *papa san* was yelling for his son. Someone said, "Put him out of his misery." So someone did.

We shouldn't have done that.

I had people's lives in my hands, and I took it very seriously. I volunteered to go out on patrol or ambush. I'm not a hero - it's not that. If you're going to be in charge, you can't send men out unless you set some kind of example.

The days belonged to us, but the nights belonged to Charlie. At night our job was to keep the Vietnamese from infiltrating into Saigon. We would send platoons out on the trail to ambush the North Vietnamese as they were trying to bring supplies. They never learned: You might ambush them one night, but the next night they'd come down the same trail again.

Some of the young guys didn't want to go outside the wire; they'd say they were sick. But every man counted; you were already under-strength. We had 17-18 men in a platoon; it should have been at least 30. I'm hard-headed. I insisted on them going out, even if they had 11 months in Vietnam. I sent them out, with the chance they would they get killed.

One night it rained mortar rounds every minute or two. You could hear the rounds splatter everywhere. They also put out claymore mines [*which explode when tripped*]. I went from hole to hole, talking to people. Next morning we discovered the

VC had their claymores up against our fence, but they didn't make it any farther. It was no big thing. I was just doing my job.

[*Williams received the Bronze Star for valor.*]

I ran into a friend: "Let me take you around and show you Saigon." We went around to those houses filled with AWOL soldiers and pretty girls. He took me to a hotel with a swimming pool on top and a lot of beautiful girls. Thirty miles away we could hear the artillery fire, and I'm out after dark without a weapon with this guy, living the good life.

Joe Davis:

I went to Vietnam as a mess sergeant. A rocket came and hit behind the mess hall. That was my third wound. I said it was time to get out of the Army.

Bob Jones, Jim Thompson, and Donald Womack went to Vietnam as Green Berets.

Jones became an instructor to a South Vietnamese unit in the Mekong delta. Jumping from planes aggravated his back injury, and Agent Orange, a poison dropped to destroy the jungle cover, would give both him and Womack serious medical problems in later years.hes

Thompson is not allowed to talk about his duty there, which is still classified.

Womack:

PJ went over with me on a military plane. Animals were supposed to ride in the cargo area below. PJ wouldn't go for that. He sat between my legs.

We lived in hootches with sand bags all around. PJ wouldn't let anyone in that room where I was. I had a boa constrictor in the ceiling that big! Swallowed rats and everything else. I fed him. Hell, yes! But if we were being shelled, I was afraid the snake would drop down on us.

Special Forces are like the Engineers. Everyone depends on everyone else, regardless of your background. Like Rangers or pilots.

I have five Purple Hearts, a couple of them in Vietnam. In Vietnam who in hell is the enemy? Everyone looks the same. I can't remember the first person I shot in Vietnam. Do you remember the first woman you had sex with? But who was number-five?

I got pissed off at Donald Rumsfeld, the Secretary of Defense. He came over, and we asked him, "How come we don't have flak jackets or Humvees [*military vehicles*] - all the right things?"

He said, "Well, you know, when you go to war, you go with what you got."

And what dumb-ass determined we had to wear a beret? That's like putting a target on us.

I was on a helicopter that had 12 people on it. We used to turn our helmets upside down and sit on them so a bullet wouldn't come up through the floor and go up our ass. One bullet came up and hit the pilot. He started bleeding profusely, blood was on his seat, and he didn't have any muscle strength in his arms and legs. People started hollering, "We're gonna die! We're gonna die!" By my being a medic, I put a tourniquet on and stopped the bleeding, and his strength came back. I was put in for an Air Medal [*for non-combat heroism*].

Remember the name, "Phoenix?" That was the assignment I had, on the Ho Chih-minh Trail [*a Communist supply route that went through Cambodia*).. It was "body odor" - black operations. You've heard of "no bodies left behind?" We'd have to take them out with us, because we weren't supposed to be there.

Delta teams are made up of Navy SEALs and Green Berets. Get in and out. We didn't have dog tags, no pictures of the family. We called it "sanitized." We went in on four-man patrols. Planes would drop listening devices, and ground troops would parachute in and make sure the devices were straight up in the ground. Then, if they heard any movement, five B-52s came in, bombing.

We would also parachute in and assess the effects. No one sees you, you're dangling and swinging in the air. We had to come out by foot; we'd walk out to a site where a copter could land, or they'd drop a skyhook and snatch us up. That's called "extraction."

Or we flew up the Mekong river [*on the border*] by helicopter, PJ jumped from copters with me, like a papoose in front of me. The other men didn't object. They knew PJ wouldn't bark, only growl if he sensed danger. He'd protect me, and they were with me, weren't they? When it was time to be extracted, PJ got in his sling, and the 'copter snatched us both off the ground.

In Cambodia or Laos we flew up the Mekong river to get inserted. That's when I was eating monkey brains shishkabob.

I was on a five-man patrol and gave some candy to one of the kids. There was a bridge up the road, and the kid called me back, kept pulling on my sleeve, didn't want me to go. The others moved on, and I said I'd catch up with them. The next thing I knew was a loud explosion. They were all dead. That's another thing that sends me to PTS classes. I still have that guilt: I should have died with them. I had to take some of those "calm-down" pills.

Womack had to say good-bye bye to an old friend:

PJ got arthritis, couldn't walk two steps. He had a stroke, and you had to pick him up and take him outside to pee. He knew he was dying, and it made me cry when I had to put him down.

The nation finally changed policy. For 60 years and three wars it had awarded only two Medals of Honor to blacks. Now, with integration, it awarded 21. They included the first black officers and the first black Marines ever honored.

James Oscar Rodney Lawrence
Anderson Austin Davis Roberts

Wiley Ralph Milton Charles
Pitts Johnson Olive Roberts

Clarence John Dwight Robert
Sasser Warren Johnson Jenkins

Webster Eugene Clifford Melvin
Anderson Ashley Sims Morris

Garfield Donald Rupert
Langhorn Long Sargent

Blacks went from two Medals of Honor in Korea to 21 in Vietnam. Either they underwent a miraculous genetic change in ten short years, or the Army did. The latter is more likely. The time is long over-due for it to recognize the many brave black men, whose heroism in Korea deserves the nation's highest award.

After the Army

Donald Womack:

When I came back home, my wife got an abortion; that's when I found out she had violated our marriage. I wanted to kill her. It's the second time I went to Alcoholics Anonymous.

In Virginia, going to Fort Lee, I was three rows behind the bus driver. "Either get in the back of the bus or get off." I didn't know he was talking to me - I'm from Connecticut.

In Phenix City Alabama, across the river from Fort Benning, the sheriff's got a gun down to his knee. "This your car, boy?" What you doin' down here?"

"I want to get some gas. I gotta go to airborne pathfinders' school, coming back from Vietnam."

"Get your gas, and don't come here no more." The Army put Phenix City off limits to soldiers. I was scared to jump out of the plane over Alabama.

John French's experience was more positive:

I decided to give law school another shot, saved my money, came back to law school in '66, and ran out of money again. I just couldn't get a job. One day I was going down the street and saw a "Help Wanted" sign in the window of a McDonald's. I went in and had one question: "How far can I go in this company?"

The guy told me, "You can go as far as your ability will take you."

I started out as a hamburger flipper at the minimum wage of $1.30 an hour. Because of my years in college, he raised me to $1.50. What he said was true. McDonald's made the American dream come true for me. I went to management training my second year and became regional vice-president of Washington DC.

One thing I learned in Korea was: Whatever your mission is, do it! Do it to the best of your ability. And I learned from Lieutenant Lenon that you can kick ass and get the job done - as long as you're standing there. It's better to make people happy so they're into what you want to do.

In 1976 I went to Hamburger university in Washington as an instructor and that same year became vice-president of the company. Ray Kroc, the president, was

one of the finest gentlemen I ever met. My wife and I traveled all over the world. I never had my black ass kissed so much.

I retired and bought four McDonald's stores. I promised my daughter if she got a degree in business, I would go into business with her. She went to work for a bank and was calling me every day: "When are we going to go into business together?"

One morning the mailman came with a letter from Mr Kroc's lawyers: He had died and left me $50,000 worth of McDonald's stock. I sold my stores back to the company and bought two buildings in Washington near Howard University for $80,000, then I sat on them until property values improved enough so I could go into a bank and borrow enough to open two restaurants.

Charlie Rangel went to law school and then into politics in Harlem. In 1970 he unseated the powerful and controversial Adam Clayton Powell for a seat in Congress. He rose to become chairman of the Ways and Means committee, one of the most influential posts in Congress and by 2013 was serving his 43rd year in the House.

After his discharge Doug Wilder went on a spree of partying.

That partying almost ruined me. You could go to a party almost every night if you've got the time, and I found the time. I just started off on the wrong foot.

Then he settled down and entered law school. That led to politics, and in 1983 he became the first black governor of Virginia.

Richard Sanders:

In 1976 IBM said, "If you come with us; we'll hire your

wife too." They even paid for my grad school in business administration and production planning. I got an MBA. I had worldwide responsibility for 8,000 distributors of communications equipment.

I'm very grateful. The Army paid for me to go to college - or the tax-payers did - so I want to pay it back. You want to leave the world better than when you came. in.

I became a financial counselor for a company and vice-chairman for a senior citizens advisory group. I'm assertive. I know how to get through the minefields that other people don't know how. I find it very rewarding. I was talking to a lady with six kids; she was unemployed, and I helped her. It does me good to see a smile on a person's face and hear her say, "I didn't know I could do that."

Virginia Senator Chuck Robb put me on a selection committee for the Naval Academy, the Air Force Academy, and West Point. Collin Powell named me to a board for assignment of personnel. I was the only one who had business planning training. I got the 24th re-activated through General Powell. If I had sat on my butt, I wouldn't have accomplished what I did.

My son graduated from Princeton with honors in clinical psychology. My other son graduated from the University of Texas in engineering.

When I'm walking down a hall sometimes, I see someone looking at the ceiling or down at the floor rather than say hi. They should be grateful for what I did for my country and say, "Thank you very much for your sacrifice."

I've been fighting with the Army to get my wound up near the Yalu recorded. I didn't know it was unrecorded, because the 24th was de-activated. The doctors at Bethesda Hospital just didn't correct it. I tried to tell them what happened, but they said, "We don't have records, they were destroyed in a fire in '73."

"You've got to be kidding me."

Ellis Dean:

I went to a black VFW club in York Pennsylvania and looked up Leon Gilbert, the officer of who had disobeyed an order back at the beginning of the war. When I mentioned his name, believe me, you could hear a pin drop.

He said, "Dean, I don't know what you've heard, but it's not true. After all these years, they just don't know, they just don't know," and he started crying.

Curtis Morrow, the soldier/author, worked several years on the book about his Korean experiences. He called it "good therapy." It is perhaps the best book ever written on the Korean war,

In 1965 he decided to search for his roots and answered a call from President Kwame Nkrumah of Ghana to help train the nation's army and develop the economy. With $300 in his pocket, he caught a plane to the land his Ashanti great-great-grandfather had left. Re-named "Kojo" [*Monday's Son*], he tells the story with his usual skill and honesty in *Return of the African-American*:

As we approached the west coast of Africa... I wore around my neck a symbol of Shango, the god of thunder and lightening. I remember having a strange feeling, wondering how my great-great-grandfather had felt when he left Africa, knowing he would never return.

The immigration official who stamped my passport asked, "Are you an American?"

"I'm an African-American," I replied.

He smiled and shook my hand. "Welcome, brother."

"Thank you, my brother, "I replied.

Morrow stayed several years, supporting himself making jewelry from gold and ivory, which he sold throughout West Africa and the States. He also met Maya Angelou, the black American author, but considered her "kind of stuck on herself."

He wrote of the experience in *Return of the African American*.

Next he took a cruise around South America, stopping for two days in Rio to make a photo shoot – he is also a fine photographer. The ship went through the wild Straits of Magellan, which very few men have ever seen, then turned back up the West coast and home. That was followed by a book of Ghanaian children's stories, illustrated by his own boldly-colored paintings, which he does with jazz playing in the background - "it's very relaxing."

He wants to go back to Japan. "That's on my drawing board, trying to re-capture some of my youth."

Correcting the Record

One final war awaited the veterans, a war to win recognition for what they had done.

Floyd Williams:

At Fort Dix I took my kids to the library and checked out Roy Appleman's book, *From the Naktong to the Yalu*. He branded our whole unit cowards! He was writing about people who believe that being a coward was worse than death. Every unit gave way in Korea at one time or another. Why he chose to write only about us, I don't know. It made my blood boil. I lost too many friends who weren't cowards. I almost threw the book out the window.

Black Soldier, White Army? I didn't see any of the stuff they wrote about either. Not in my platoon in A Company. There were some pretty cool guys in my platoon.

The reason I joined the 25th Association was because I wanted to see them modify the record. I'm very proud of my platoon. If I had a choice between the 24th Infantry and my platoon in Vietnam, I'd just as soon be with the unit in Korea. I saw some good men in Korea who did their jobs, a lot of *courageous* men, who got killed too young.

Now I see people waving the flag. Poor people fight wars in most cases. I'm aware of the guys who went in the National Guard, like George W Bush. I knew what they were: "legalized draft dodgers." I've got a lot of admiration for those who stayed in the infantry and did their jobs.

Otto Garner:
I read in some of the books that we weren't considered fighting soldiers. But it was mainly the officers who didn't support us; they didn't want to be in the unit. Consequently they said, "You weren't good fighters, you'd run off."

But the unit I was with, we took every assignment that was sent to us. We had our problems, and sure, we had a couple people who weren't good fighters, but over all, they were good troops, they followed orders and did what they were told.

Ralph Hubbard:
The 25th Division history lied on us like crazy: "The black soldiers ran all the time" - that was a hell of a lot of running! They said we abandoned our position and our guns. They said we lost our colors. Our colors stand today in West Point. Let me tell you: We didn't run any place when everyone else wasn't running too. The Marines said they "attacked to the rear." Hog piss.

There was nothing else about us - we weren't mentioned at all. [*This has since been corrected.*]

We had a lot of brave and honorable men in our outfit, dedicated men who did their jobs and died for it. The first Medal of Honor winner in the 25th came from our regiment. I know damn well we fought, but there's nothing about it in the history.

We have to go through the white officers; they have control, and they use it.

Jim Thompson:
The 25th Division invited us to their reunion. I said, "Go to hell, I'm not going." I never heard of anyone running."

Ellis Dean:
At first our guys didn't want to join the 25th Division Association. But now there are people in the division going over the record of the 24th. The 24th did do the job.

We had some damn good officers and some bad officers. There were a lot of beautiful Caucasian officers, and the men respected them. Lieutenant Komp was one. He later made colonel, and we still keep in touch. Once the men have confidence in their officers, they'll follow them.

Robert Fletcher:
I've got a book written by the 25th Division: "The blacks ran, so we had to get rid of the 24th." That wasn't the reason. Truman didn't want any more black regiments. The Army wouldn't integrate, but they were under pressure.

One Marine had a book showing men coming over a wall. One guy was black. He said, "Oh, I thought it was a Korean."

A British historian - I don't remember the name - never went to the 24th or interviewed any person there. He went to the 27th and the 35th, because they were white, and they said, "Oh, those guys are no good. They're lazy. They dropped their rifles and ran."

He and I got into it. I said, "Were you there? Then what you talking about? Back away." He went to the 24th Infantry banquet, and they booed him out of the place. He apologized later - many, many years later. He admitted he got all his information from other writers. You slit someone's throat with a knife, and then you apologize. What good is that? I'll never forgive him.

Even our government covered everything up.

A Colonel Muelbauer [*of BSWA*] came to interview me. He never recognized anything we did. When we took Yech'on, he said, "You guys didn't do a good job of holding the enemy."

I said, "Man, what the hell you talking about?"

He said, "Watch your language."

I told him, "At one point the 24th was the most decorated unit in the 25th Division. There were white officers who were proud to serve with us. If it hadn't been for the 24th, we'd have lost Korea. They don't know how we hung on by our fingernails.

He said, "I've read one book, and I thought he was too good to you guys."

. . I looked at him and said, "Were you in Korea at the time?"

He said, no.

"Well, how in the hell are you going to tell me what occurred?" He turned red as a beet. I told him I was getting damned upset: "You get the hell out of here!"

He started to say that he had to do the interview.

I said, "It's over."

An African-American colonel, who was working on *Black Soldiers, White Army*, asked me to meet him at the airport in Washington for a drink. He said, "I don't want anyone quoting me, because I can get in trouble, but they're going to blame the black troops and have no blame for the officers. They're really fighting Yech'on, Fletch."

He committed suicide later.

For a long time I wouldn't talk to people writing books.

Ellis Dean:

At first our guys didn't want to join the 25th Division Association. But now there are people in the division going over the record of the 24th. The 24th did do the job.

We had some damn good officers and some bad officers. There were a lot of beautiful Caucasian officers, and the men respected them. Lieutenant Komp was one. He later made colonel, and we still keep in touch. Once the men have confidence in their officers, they'll follow them.

Captain Lou Millet of the "elite" 27th Wolfhounds is the only surviving Medal of Honor winner in the Division. Retired as a colonel, and he didn't like what they were saying about us. "You got a lot of bad ink. They gave you guys a 'bug-out' label. It wasn't you guys, it was the 24th *Division*. They say you ran? We all ran at times."

The 24th Division got slaughtered; they left their weapons and got captured. Artillery units left their damn guns and ran. Yeah, but the 24th Regiment was black, so we got that static.

Timmons Jones:

I was interviewed by a reporter in San Francisco. But he turned it around and wrote it like he wanted to.

At the Korean War memorial ceremony in Washington in 1994, I talked to some of the officers. They said, "You got a bad press. Don't let that bother you. You were just as good as any people over there."

The years since I retired I've met a lot of good white officers, who knew we were treated bad, but they couldn't do anything about it, because they were regular Army career officers. We don't blame them, we blame the racist officers.

Ralph Hubbard:

Jim Thompson (left) and Colonel **John Komp** went out to Hawaii to confront the 25th Division at their reunion and put up a storm. I went to their reunion in 2003 and got a lot of the people together. Believe it or not, there were guys that didn't know of the deep-shit times and how we were treated.

The re-written edition of the 25th Division history is much more positive toward the Deuce 4. There is no longer any report of bugging out. And it includes Garner's story in detail.

But *BSWA* still refuses to make changes.

Otto Garner:

I tried to re-open my award but was told I would have to get witnesses. But it's in the 25th Division history the 24th Regiment book. I don't expect to get anything out of it. It was so long ago.

The author and others asked the Army to re-open Charles Bussey's Medal of Honor case. President and Mrs Clinton and the Congressional Black Caucus took an interest, but no one pushed hard. The result was no change.

Bussey::

I stayed in the Army, which I loved so much. I was put back on flying status, and logged many hours.

But I couldn't sleep well. I had terrible dreams. I perspired by the gallon and sometimes screamed. I went back to the killing floor, and it was ugly, very ugly. When I lay

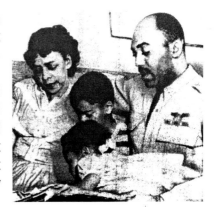

on my back, ten thousand Chinese soldiers trampled over my grave. I sweated and yelled out. Most nights I slept three to four hours.

Doctors had no idea how to treat my problems. I felt sorry for my wife. I needed badly to unload it all, but she couldn't deal with it. Who could blame her? So I carried it in my chest for 12 or 15 years. Nothing was left except divorce.

Retirement

Otto Garner:

I wanted to go to college in the Army, but I was handling Top Secret, and the captain said, "We need you. I can't spare you," When I got out of Service, I went to Cal State university three nights a week for a degree in public administrtion. It was hard, but it was something I wanted.

I'm 82 now. I have aches and pains from when I hurt my back in Korea, and every now and then my knees give me trouble. Some days I can walk, some days I can't. And if I bend over, I can't get up. But I'm not complaining. I just did my duty. I put in 28 years; they were good service times. The Lord was good to me.

My children, I'm proud of them.

My oldest son, David, is in the export/Import business.

My other son, Kenneth (*left*) was in the Los Angeles

Police Department. After Rodney King [*when a TV camera filmed police beating a black motorist*], they made him deputy chief and put him in command of the station where the problem was, where police beat up quite a few people. He met with the gangs, the Cripps and the Bloods, and of them, and got with people in the area and smoothed things over and really influenced the people who had some power. When he died 3,000 people came to his funeral.

Some people say the country is going to the dogs. I think there needs to be a few changes, but we've got some proud and fighting people who believe in the country. We still have to hold the flag up and wave it and keep the faith.

Bob Jones retired after 27 years. He told his son:
I did all that for you, so you won't have to do it. I wanted you to have the opportunities I didn't.

Ernest Collier:
For 25-30 years I've been working for the big Olympic

training center in San Diego. They have a huge center for archery, tennis, rowing. I work in timing and judging for track and field.

My son-in-law made captain in the Navy. I told him, "Keep it up; we need an admiral in the family."

LaVaughn Fields:
I spent ten years in the Post Office. Then my son talked me into going to Silicon Valley as a security guard with Apple. If I keep working, I might stay around a little longer. I just got a new knee. After the Airborne and Korea, I needed a new one. They wanted to give me another one too, but it was too painful. I finally had it done, should have done it years ago.

I have 18 grand kids and 12 great-grand kids. Ten are boys. We have almost enough for a football team. They say, "Grampa, you gotta get some more of that good medicine. Go get another spoonful."

Robert Fletcher:

I never wanted to be rich, but I wanted to have a decent home for my children, I wanted some money in the bank, I wanted to retire before 65 and have my debts pretty well paid off. The wife and I agreed that those were the goals we wanted, and we were able to succeed in them.

We've been married 60 years [*in 2013*]. My wife went on to get her master's and PhD in nursing. She's doing research on Alzeimers and whether there is a link to combat injuries.

We raised five children, and I retired at 62. I started working at ten and figured I'd put in enough years. I told my son, "You've got to pay your dues like everyone else. Nothing comes easy."

I've had a very interesting life, raised four kids, adopted one. Now we've got ten grandchildren and one great grandson. We had them all over last night for dinner. I said, "Did you really think one day we'd have this many kids?" I love them all.

Now I'm doing pretty good. I've had three knee replacements, but my wife says, "You're a tough old s.o.b."

Bloody Ground

Donald Womack was in Panama when the U.S. captured President Manuel Noriega in 1989, but he won't discuss the details, because it's classified.

In 1991, they called me back in Desert Storm. I was command sergeant major for a two-star general in Walter Reed. He used me as inter-face between the active and reserves from the East coast to Mississippi. I was the eyes and ears of the commander.

Things still weren't right for blacks.

I went to Iraq. One general wanted to have a star on his jump wings [*for 50 jumps*]. He refused to listen to me. In a combat zone we were jumping at 600 feet or less. You fall 120 feet per second, so that's five seconds. You're supposed to wait three seconds before you pull your reserve ripcord, so you only have two seconds left. The chute didn't open, and he hit the ground. But you didn't argue with a general.

On one of my last jumps, my parachute collapsed. Another jumper came underneath me and "stole" my air. I yelled, "Slip! Slip!" [*Move away!*] I landed on top of his chute and walked off it. That's when I hit the ground.

I had 800 jumps in - I don't know what the record is. And I don't remember how old I was on the last one, but I wasn't no kid - I was old enough for Social Security.

I still swim. I was scuba diving until eight or nine years ago, but I'm not cleared to dive any more; my lungs won't take the pressure.

This damn Agent Orange shit: I've got prostate problems and colon problems. I had a bleeding ulcer twice. That came from 'Nam. I'm 100% disabled, unemployable, but I can't get the money. The bill is tied up in the Senate and House of Representatives.

I'm a teacher for AARP, for the "55-Alive" drivers' safety program.

In 2006, a year after Katrina, I donated two days to Habitat, building homes in New Orleans. It was worse than a war zone. There were still bodies being found in some of those houses - one year later. The bodies swell up, and the smells are outrageous.

Joe Davis:

After the Army I went into food service in a prison for 26 years and became a top-grade supervisor.

But I didn't heal right. I still have only 80% circulation in my right arm. One bullet is still in it. It took me 40 years to get 40% disability.

Robert Yancey:

I retired from the Army and got my GED, then I went to college and got my teacher's certificate, then my master's in education. A friend knew the director of education at the prison. The director said, "Send me a resume." I mailed it on Monday. He called me for an interview on Friday, asked me: "Can you start Monday?"

I said, "Wow!"

I ended as school principal in prison for 17 years.

When I first got the job in 1976, they said, "Mr Yancey, because of your military experience, we're going to give you our most difficult inmates. You think you're going to have any problems?"

I said, "Oh, no. I weigh 240 pounds. But if I 'get in his collar,' I weigh about 600 pounds."

The students said, "Mr Yancey, you're a veteran of three wars. We know you killed someone. You're no different than we are."

I said, "Don't ever compare yourselves with me. I was a soldier. The warrior has to kill or be killed. You gonna fool around here, you'll make me do the same thing." I never had any problems.

My object is to instill in them that no society can exist without law and order. "You've got to get yourself together and accept responsibility."

About 75% of those incarcerated are African Americans and need someone to look up to. I tell them, "You can make it if you have the determination.

Each one is responsible for what we make of ourselves. The key is education. Do your time, don't let the time do you. Pick up vocational skills or you're going to be working at minimum wage. I can't change you. Change comes from within.

"I got kicked out of school, and I got a GED. So you don't have to stay here. If you had a bad beginning, say, 'Heh, let me get my act together and make something out of myself.' Everyone isn't born to success and luxury. The only reason I'm here is because I took advantage of the GI bill. Once I got a taste for it, I got hungry for it. I hope you do too."

I have about 250 waiting to get into my class. We call that, "giving back." Life's been good. I'm grateful, so I want to use it to turn these kids around.

I retired in 1993. Now I'm 88 [*in 2013*] and I still do volunteer service Monday and Friday, teaching behavior modification. The Man Upstairs is good to me, I try to give back.

I'm New Jersey state commander of Disabled American Veterans, and in 2001 I went to Korea with Governor Christine Todd Whitman, my first visit in 50 years. I thought the plane landed in the wrong place! When I left Korea, there was devastation. Now I saw skyscrapers and dual highways. I said, "I don't believe this!"

When I stepped off the bus, a colonel said, "Who's Yancey?"

"Here he is, right here."

He said, "My father was your platoon leader in 1950, and he told me to take good care of you." His father was a second lieutenant and retired as a full colonel. His son was also a full bird colonel. I reached for my bag, he said, "I'll get that." Wouldn't let me spend any money. They just wined me and dined me.

Later I met the president of Korea at the United Nations.

John B. Holway

A war correspondent gave me 53 pictures of Korea, and I take them with me when I go to high schools with the Tuskegee Airmen and talk to the kids.

I have three girls and two boys, and they all turned out beautifully. My oldest son won a $35,000 scholarship in high school. He was grabbed by General Motors, but he left, because they wanted to give him a job as a foreman. He went to BF Goodrich, who sent him to get a master's. Now he's president of Goodrich Turbine Fuel Technical Unit. I told him he has his mother's looks and his father's brains, but my wife didn't agree with that.

One of the guys in my old platoon named Parker was in a prison camp for three-four years. He lived five miles from me in New Jersey. He died five or six years ago, and the 24th Infantry Association sent me over to see his wife and see what we could do to help her. She pulled out his letters and read them. He wrote about the inhuman conditions and treatment, and we both sat there and cried together.

In 2012 Yancey finally found four eye-witnesses who wrote letters verifying what he had done to save the *Kongo Maru*. He is awaiting approval for a Soldier's Medal, the country's highest non-combat award for bravery.

I have six great grandchildren and six great-great grandchildren. I say they're my wife's, because I'm not that old.

Age is just a number. I'm like Jack Benny, I celebrate my 39th birthday 48 times. I still use my treadmill and do my curls [*weight-llifting*]. The secret is: Don't feed into negativity.

Yancey still talks to student groups. At one, the moderator asked the class, "How old do you think Mr Yancey is?" No one came close. One student said 60.

"I should take that student to lunch!"

John French:

Forty-four years after I left Korea, I was in my office, and someone said, "A white guy, a general, wants to see you." There was LeTellier! Who in the hell ever heard of a goddam major general going to see a corporal? There he was. Standing there! Surprised the hell out of me.

He said, "Bussey told me where you were. I just came to thank you. I didn't know a damn thing about the engineers when I got to Korea." Imagine a major general telling that to a corporal! He said, "Let me give you my card. You come see me."

I said, "I'm so proud of you!" I thanked him for taking the time. A major general!

Albert Kimber:

All the money spent by the U.S. government maintaining and operating segregated bases was a total waste.

I'm not sorry for one minute for the contributions I've made to make this country a better place.

One of my sisters is a retired professor at the University of Arkansas. My baby brother is owner of the biggest black newspaper on the west coast, the *California Advocate*.

I knew General Ridgway in Korea, had seen him a lot of times. I used to go to Fox Chapel, a suburb of Pittsburgh, to see him. He welcomed me with open arms.

Combat soldiers today should be recognized for their efforts. Also the soldiers who fought for years in the military and didn't receive thanks from the United States or Congress or anything. All we want is our fair credit for our contributions. We didn't do it just for black people, we did it for all Americans, because Americans come in all shades.

All I want in this life - and I don't have many days left - is to live in peace and be treated like I treat other people. We should consider the welfare of each soldier, I don't care whether black, white, red, or yellow. I haven't done anything that a good American wouldn't have done for this county.

John B. Holway

Nathaniel Nicholson:

Let me tell you this story:

I've had Parkinson's Disease since 1989 - I'm talking about a lot of pain in my leg. I couldn't put myself in bed, couldn't get out of bed. I couldn't walk, couldn't do anything. The Mayo Clinic in Minnesota said I had a bad case of arthritis. But there was no improvement.

In 1995 I said, I can't stand it anymore. I opened the yellow pages under "Doctor" and said, "Eeny, meeny, miny, mo, Lord, help me," and put my finger on one.

As soon as I walked in, he said, "I can help you." He never examined me, he reached into his desk drawer, gave me some pills and said, "Take these."

In seven days I was bowling.

It's going on 14 years now [2009], and I'm still taking the same pills - Premox.

Then the Holy Spirit started working. It only happens in church, but when the church gets into high spirits, I can run and jump. Oh yeah, *run*! Down the aisles, around the church. Some people don't believe it. It sounds unbelievable. But it gets into my mind, and my mind says I can run, and I *can* run.

Then after church I go back to my old self, and I can hardly shuffle. I bought a scooter - a mobile wheelchair - to get around when I'm not preaching.

I can tolerate it.

I took my wife back to Japan. Camp Gifu had been turned into a deer park, where the deer could be fed by hand. We went to Seoul and Panmunjom and looked into North Korea and looked at the holes in those mountains still left from our artillery shells. It made my heart palpitate.

Thirty-three years a pastor. We never give up the church - we die in the saddle. The Lord's been good to me.

And I still hear the Voice.

James Burnett:

Nick tracked Captain Franke down and called him on the phone. He had Alzheimer's.

I miss Nick a lot!

At his funeral service his wife asked me to speak. Everyone had two minutes. I told them, "He ministered to people long before he thought about being a minister. I spoke for ten minutes, they had to come get me. [*Dolores Nicholson said, "His daughter had to get up and pull on his coat tail."*]

I just couldn't stop.

When I got out of the Service, I was in the police department and didn't like it. I didn't like to carry a gun. I had enough of that! I didn't want to *see* a gun. Then the fire department called me, and I liked that! This is great.

I'm a proud reitiree from the New York Fire Department. I lost eight men from my company in the World Trade Center. Maybe because of my age, that affected me more than Korea did.

I used to walk about five miles. I've slowed down a bit. I'm down to maybe four miles, maybe three days a week. That pleases my doctor. She said, "You don't look 80."

I said, "I'm eighty-*three*."

"Are you really 83?"

I said, "Yep, unless my mother lied to me."

Clyde Jones:

Five years after I got out of the Army, I pulled a piece of metal the size of an eraser out of my back. It was that blamed mortar shrapnel coming out.

I became a pipe fitter, worked all over the South, Chicago, New Jersey. I worked 39 years, and they laid me off. I was 62. I've been a pastor since 1972.

At first, Korea never bothered me. Then, *bam*, I had nightmares, jumped out of bed, threw hand grenades, hit my wife in the back. They said it was stress; medicine can't cure it, it just takes time. I've seen some things that are unbelievable, but my three girls don't like me to talk about it.

Wilfred Mathews:

My feet have been bothering me since Korea and getting worse. The doctor? Hell, he didn't know what it was. They gave me all kinds of medicines, but they aren't doing any good. If it wasn't for the aches and pains, I'd be doing good. The good Lord takes care of his children. Oh, yes!

Ralph Hubbard:

After the war I went to jail - I *took* people there, I didn't *stay* there: I joined the police. So I had people shooting at me both in Korea and in the police; I got it from both sides. But I couldn't let them know I almost got a medical discharge, because back in those days they wouldn't hire you if you did. I was driving heavy equipment. I had a great time. I wasn't working for the police department, the police department was working for *me*.

When New York dedicated a Korean war memorial, that's about when I started doing anything about Korea. I hooked up with the guys in a reunion in and jumped in with both feet.

We started telling all these damn war stories and started believing them ourselves, and we started laughing. I just started talking to my daughters about it four or five years ago. I was embarrassed telling them I was shitting myself in a firefight. I'm laughing while I'm talking.

"How can you be laughing about it?"

"If I don't laugh about it, I can't talk about it." I said. Some of the greatest, most laughable things come from tragedy.

Even now I get little fragments of metal 60-some years later. I itch around my butt, and that's what comes up under my fingernail. Jeez, that stuff doesn't go away.

Hub took a course in writing at the age of 60, and he and his wife enjoy cruises. He's proud of his grandson, who went to West Point.

I had a nephew in Iraq. He wrote to me, "Uncle Ralph, I'm scared as hell."

I told him, "That's good, Frank. If you weren't scared, I couldn't trust you. I wanted no one in my platoon who wasn't frightened. You do what you have to do. I don't want that *macho* standing on top a hill: "Come and get me." I was no fool, and I didn't want any fools on my team. "Get away from me. I want people who are frightened. I can *trust* them."

Hub received the gold shield of a detective before most of his peers, which caused some resentment. His bailiwick was Bay Ridge, at the end of the Verrazano Bridge from Staten Island. It was a neighborhood of Irish, Swedes, and Norwegians - "all Archie Bunkers" - referring to the popular TV show about a prejudiced but funny New Yorker. "I was the Jackie Robinson of the precinct."

Before retiring, Ralph had one last assignment:

One day when I walked into the station house, everybody was walking out, because there was a guy going to jump off the Bridge. They told me, "Mother, we have a new bathroom just finished, Captain Hannegan is going to inspect it."

He was a pain in the ass, made work for people and wrote guys up for bullshit. I said, "I'll fix him." I went and got some peanut butter and put it on the toilet seat and closed the lid.

Ten minutes later I opened the door. There's the deputy mayor, a commissioner, two captains, and two chiefs. I said to myself, "Oh, shit."

They looked at the equipment, the area, all that. I kept urging them all to hurry up and edging them out the door. Just as I'm opening the front door, they see the new bathroom: "Oh, wow! We didn't see this." They go in the squatter, Hannegan lifts up the seat and jumps back. Then they all jumped in and looked. Now I'm trapped. I've gotta explain this.

I reached down with my finger and swiped it across the peanut butter and stuck it in my mouth:

"Um-hm, that's shit all right."

They all took off running like a bat out of hell.

My captain is standing at the door with his arms crossed, looking at me with steel gray eyes. He shook his head and walked out. Twenty minutes later the phone rings. It was the captain.

"Oh, God!" I'm thinking.

He said, "Hannegan went running into headquarters, telling everyone - you had to see this man going crazy. The police commissioner sent him to the emergency ward. It went all through the department."

He roared.

"You did it again, huh, Hub?"

Floyd Williams:

I'm going on 84 my next birthday [2014] and I'm still on the right side of the grass. I have four children, all of them got degrees, one is a PhD in chemical engineering. One played in the Philadelphia symphony orchestra. That wasn't supposed to happen to guys like me with no formal education. My son used to teach at the university of Florida. When he was born, I couldn't walk across that campus without having trouble.

I used to go to Europe every year on space available [military transport planes] - Egypt, Portugal, Italy, Morocco, Haiti, Venice, the Acropolis in Greece, the Berlin Wall, Australia, Thailand When I was in school I remember the Sphinx. Never did I think that I would be on a camel with the pyramids in the background.

I used to be a snow skier. Until two years ago, I'd ride my bike 20-30 miles without stopping. Now I'm kind of slowing down. I only ride 7-12 miles, three or four times a week. I exercise, I don't have a big belly.

And I still check the girls out.

The Army is a hell of a lot better now than what we had. I'm thankful that I was a little part of that.

Ellis Dean:

We had three children, and I'm proud to say all three are college-educated. Two got their masters.

I called Curtis Pugh up, and he was so glad to hear from me, He and his wife took a plane to my town and met my family.

I'm a member of the Negro Golfers' association. I have an 11-handicap, which is not too bad. I had an opportunity to play with Barry Bonds and Joe Morgan. Bonds was not a hell of a golfer, but Morgan was. Tiger Woods' father was in my foursome; Tiger was 13 years of age then.

I played hardball up into my 70s in pretty good semipro leagues. Then I started playing softball.

I was chosen to represent the 24th Korean veterans and pass the colors from Korean veterans to the Vietnam vets. In 2003 I was selected to go to Korea for the 50th anniversary of the Korean truce. I met Henry Kissinger, and the Koreans rolled the red carpet out for us.

My niece, **Emily Perez**, went to West Point. Her grandfather, **Bill Gunger**, and I served together, and he was a Silver Star recipient. She graduated in 2005 and was the highest-ranking black female, a brigade sergeant major.

She was killed by a road-side bomb, the first West Point graduate to be killed in Iraq. I went to her funeral, and she was buried at West Point.

Kazuko was killed in 2010 in a fall at home. Later that year Dean suffered a stroke and died.

John B. Holway

Robert Fletcher:

In 2007 I was inducted as commander of the American Ex-POWs and went to the Korean POWs National Convention. They never introduced me as national commander. They never had my wife and me at the head table. Never asked me to speak. It was just as if I wasn't there. Cold shoulder.

But that never broke my spirit. I thought I could accomplish my goals I set when I went into the Army. I didn't think anything was going to stop me but death.

I love history. History told me where I came from and helped to tell me where I was going. I wouldn't want to do it again. They couldn't pay me to do it again! But this is my country. I love it. I'm an American, and I'll die an American.

Richard Sanders:

I had three major surgeries in 3½ months. Here's the left leg, I got a big cut in the thigh, left an ugly scar. Eight to nine pieces of shrapnel in that leg, six to eight pieces in the right leg. I said, "I think the shrapnel has moved, it really hurts."

They said, "You're getting old, it's probably arthritis."

I decided to go ahead and live with it. Can't do anything about it. Now I'm pretty well patched up. I was very fortunate. At airports they tell me: "Take off your belt, take off your watch, take the money out of your pocket."

I say, "All right, but the metal detector is going to go off anyway." Now I'm getting a slip from the VA, so I can walk up there and say, "Here's my slip."

Donald Womack:

I'm 86 now [in 2013]. I'm a 33rd degree Mason. I have 28 grandchildren, 16 great grandchildren, and five wives. But Aiko is still my first love.

I put in 37 years in the Army, 18 of them as a Sergeant Major. I really miss the military. But I still hear Cunningham calling to me and see Sergeant Witt running with his head hanging back.

John French:

America is the most wonderful place in the world. So many people helped me on my way up. America is going to change, and I'm just glad I've lived long enough to see it change.

Another thing I took away from Korea was simply this:

I paid my dues as an American; my ancestors, all my people, paid their dues for us to be here. Whatever it took to get through the door, I was going to do that. Education

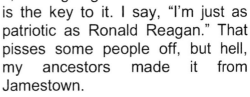

is the key to it. I say, "I'm just as patriotic as Ronald Reagan." That pisses some people off, but hell, my ancestors made it from Jamestown.

Charles Bussey:

If we [*blacks*] did so poorly in Korea, why did black soldiers get such high marks in the Vietnam War, only a few years after Korea?

I have some ideas. When the Army began to respect its black soldiers and give them responsibilities, perhaps the Army in return received respect and responsible soldiers.

More important, in both World War II and Korea, black men had formed the mold for the high-quality performance of black soldiers in Vietnam and today's Army.

Through it all, I think I have remained a very religious person. I learned to pray without an intermediary who knew less of life and death than I did. All my prayers are utterances of thanks. I am happy to be a child of God and a brother of all men.

John B. Holway

I still deeply love the U.S. Army. When I hear the national anthem, goose bumps cover my arm. I will some day die an American soldier – eager, confident, and prepared.

Clyde Jones:

I buried Bobby Joe Bennett in 2004. Peepsight Wilkerson, I buried him about 2008. There were ten of us, we were just kids. I'm the only one left. I always put flags on their graves every time I'm home:

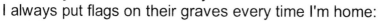

"Well, boys, I'm still a pfc." I was supposed to be a tech sergeant-platoon leader, but I didn't have papers. I didn't get any stripes at all.

But I did what I was supposed to do.

MISSING BLACK HEROES

In March 2014 President Obama presented Medals of Honor to 24 heroes who had been overlooked in past wars because of their color or religion.

Once more no black from the Korean war was among them.

This continued a pattern that lasted from 1898 to 1965, when only two black men were honored from World War I, World War II, and Korea:

By contrast Latin-American heroes received 15 Medals of Honor in Korea.

In Vietnam, the number of black Medals of Honor rose sharply. Had black GIs undergone a miraculous genetic change? Or had the army changed?

I think the latter. After a long succession of southern commanders, American went into the conflict under two northern chiefs of staff - Earle Wheeler of Washington DC and Creighton Abrams of Massachusetts

Today the Army is one of the leading institutions where blacks can rise proportional to whites. But the Army still refuses to honor more than two black heroes of Korea.

John B. Holway

24th Infantry cemetery, Korea

"Fiddler's Green"

Half-way down the road to hell,
In a shady meadow green,
Are souls of all dead troopers camped
Near a good old-time canteen.
And this eternal resting place
Is known as Fiddlers' Green.

Though some keep riding down the trail
To reach a warmer scene,
No trooper ever gets to hell
Till he's emptied his canteen
And so rides back to drink again
 With friends at Fiddlers' Green.

John B Holway

served in the infantry in Korea where he was wounded in 1952. After studying Chinese at Georgetown University, Holway joined the U.S. Information Agency. His books:

Voices From the Great Black Baseball Leagues
Rube Foster, Father of Black Baseball
Smoky Joe and the Cannonball
Japan Is Big League in Thrills*
Bullet Joe and the Monarchs
Blackball Tales***
Black Diamonds
Josh and Satch
Josh Gibson
Man Mircle
Sumo!*
Kick, Mule
The Sluggers
Blackball Stars**
The Last 400 Hitter
Red Tails, Black Wings****
Brave Bessie's Flying Circus
The Pitcher (with John Thorn)
The Amazing World of Baseball Author in 1952
Complete Book of the Negro Leagues
* First books ever done in English
** Winner, SABR's Bob Peterson Award 2008
*** Winner, Casey Award, as best baseball book of 1989
**** Basis of the major motion picture by George Lucas

He has appeared in
The New York Times CNN
Washington Post ABC-TV
USA Today History Channel
Sports Illustrated MLB-TV

John B. Holway

LA Times
Chicago Tribune
and other leading newspapers from Boston to San Diego, Miami to Seattle, Tokyo to London, and Moscow to New Delhi. He speaks four and a half languages, has visited 33 countries and gotten lost in all of them.

Bibliography

Appleman, Roy, *South to the Naktong, Nnorth to the Yalu,* Government Printing Office, Washington DC

Baker, David P, *Wilder: Hold Fast to Dreams*, 1989, Seven Locks Press, Cabin John MD

Bussey, Charles M, *Firefight at Yechon*, 1991. Brassey's Inc, Washington DC , 1991

Bowers, William T, Hammond, William H, McGarrigle, George *Black Soldier White Army*, 1996, Government Printing Office, Washington DC

Blair, Clay, *The Forgotten War*, 1987, Crown Books

Hoyt, Edwin, *The Day the Chinese Attacked*, 1993

Morrow, Curtis, *What's a Commie Ever Done to a Black Person?* 1997, MacFarland Publishers, Jefferson NC

Rangel, Charles B, *And I haven't Had a Bad Day Since,* 2007, St Martin's Press, New York

Ryshell, Lyle. *With a Black Platoon in Korea,* 1993, Texas A&M.

John B. Holway

Photo credits:

Photos of individual soldiers in are courtesy of the men pictured. Photos on page 181 are courtesy of the U.S. Military Academy. All others are courtesy of the U.S. Army archives.

Miniver Press publishes lively and informative non-fiction e-books and print books about history and culture. For more information, see http://www.miniverpress.com